The Situated Organization

The Situated Organization explores recent research in organizational communication, emphasizing the organization as constructed in and emerging out of communication practices. Working from the tradition of the Montreal School in its approach, it focuses not only on how an organization's members understand the purposes of the organization through communication, but also on how they realize and recognize the organization itself as they work within it.

The text breaks through with an alternative viewpoint to the currently popular idea of "organization-as-network," viewing organization instead as a configuration of agencies and their fields of practice. It serves as an original, comprehensive, and well-written text, elaborated by case studies that make the theory come to life. The substantial ideas and insights are presented in a deep and meaningful way while remaining comprehensible for student readers.

This text has been developed for students at all levels of study in organizational communication, who need a systematic introduction to conducting empirical field research. It will serve as an invaluable sourcebook in planning and conducting research.

James R. Taylor is Professor Emeritus and founder of the Department of Communication at the University of Montreal. He is the author, co-author or editor of six books, including the widely cited *The Emergent Organization* (2000), as well of some ninety scientific articles. He is recognized as the originator of the Montreal School of organizational communication research, a unique perspective on organization and the role that communication plays in its constitution.

Elizabeth J. Van Every is an historian and sociologist by training and has worked in both the public and private sectors. She has been the co-author with Jim Taylor of two previous books, *The Vulnerable Fortress* (1993) and *The Emergent Organization* (2000) as well as co-editor of *The Computerization of Work* (2001) and *Communication as Organizing* (2006). She lives in Montreal and is an active member of the LOG (Language, Organization and Governance) research group at the Université de Montréal.

Routledge Communication Series
Jennings Bryant and Dolf Zillman, General Editors

The Situated Organization

Case Studies in the Pragmatics of Communication Research

James R. Taylor
Elizabeth J. Van Every

With the collaboration of:

Andy Blundell
Bertrand Fauré
Senem Güney
Consuelo Vasquez
Sandrine Virgili

For Goffman, the situation is pre-eminent and
his concern is with moments and their men [*sic*],
not men and their moments . . . It is through and by interaction
that all orders, small groups, formal organizations,
institutions, and societies, are created and sustained.

Manning, 2008 (on the legacy of Erving Goffman)

First published 2011
by Routledge
270 Madison Avenue, New York, NY 10016

Simultaneously published in the UK
by Routledge
2 Park Square, Milton Park, Abingdon, Oxon OX14 4RN

Routledge is an imprint of the Taylor & Francis Group, an informa business

© 2011 Taylor & Francis

Typeset in Gill Sans and Sabon by
Florence Production Ltd, Stoodleigh, Devon
Printed and bound in the United States of America on acid-free
paper by Edwards Brothers, Inc.

Library of Congress Cataloging in Publication Data
Taylor, James R., 1928–
   The situated organization: case studies in the pragmatics of
      communication research/James R. Taylor, Elizabeth J. Van Every.
      p. cm.
      Communication in organizations. I. Every, Elizabeth J. Van. II. Title.
   HD30.3.T394 2010
   658.4'5—dc22   2010000911

ISBN13: 978–0–415–88167–8 (hbk)
ISBN13: 978–0–415–88168–5 (pbk)
ISBN13: 978–0–203–84807–4 (ebk)

Brief Contents

Contents

Prologue
The Puzzle of Organization

Organizations occupy a huge part of our environment. We can, if we like, go shopping at Walmart, drive there in our Toyota, have lunch at McDonald's or coffee at Starbucks. We can watch the TV news on BBC World, Al Jazeera, or CNN, fly to Paris on Air France, or Tokyo on JAL, google vacation sites in Costa Rica or Crete or Dubai, and e-mail our friends everywhere on our Macintosh computer. We take for granted the existence of all the behemoths that make those products, and deliver the services we need. Organizations are as much a feature of our daily lives as the birds at the window, or the bus we board to go to work in the morning. We pay attention to them when something goes wrong, of course, as for instance when the ATM shuts down just as we need to withdraw cash, or when the transport workers go on strike, or when there is a power outage. And we are aware that, when an organization such as Shell Oil or the World Bank or Al Qaeda makes a decision, it can affect the lives of millions of people: in the price of gas, in our standard of living, in our very security. If we needed a prod to our memory of how dramatically organizations can impinge on our daily lives, the financial crisis of 2008–9 was enough to remind us. And yet we may not find it easy to answer the simple question, "What is an organization?" We might describe organization as a way to get something done by more than one person, or mention a government or a large corporation by name, or use the example of the place where we work. We could even simply admit, "I can't say exactly what it is, but I certainly know it's an organization when I have to deal with it!"

This introductory chapter is about why, as much for the organizational analyst as for the layperson, the essence of organization (its *ontology*, to use a ten-dollar word) is so hard to pin down, so puzzling. In the chapters that follow, we explore a new way of addressing this question, not just theoretically, but as both researchers and practitioners. We do so from a special perspective: not sociological, psychological, or managerial, but communicational.

For communication scholars, organization is, in one sense of the word, a generic concept: "getting organized" or "organizing" (Weick 1979). When organization is thought of as no more than organizing, however, it is present everywhere, in small groups as much as in large. Whenever we communicate, we organize: who's going to do the shopping, who will take Junior to the ball game, which dress to buy for the prom. In this book, however, we will be concentrating our attention on processes of organizing that are not so easy to conceptualize because they are manifested in, and realized by, the huge corporations and governmental agencies, extended in time and space, that dominate our contemporary landscape. Seen in this light, organization cannot be reduced to the practices of any single conversation, delimited to, and located in, a here and a now: just a few people talking to each other. Organization in the sense we shall use the word becomes that which stitches the conversations together—many heres and theres, nows and thens—to produce a constellation of people, technologies, and practices that stretches over, and links, a diversity of conversations. Organizing is still very much going on, but on a different scale: no longer strictly local.

The mystery is in the personification that occurs with this shift of level: the word "organization" now ceases to be merely a synonym for getting organized (Nicotera forthcoming). The *organization* has taken on a personality. It has become an entity to which we give a name, and to which we freely ascribe features of human intentionality. We say about the organization that it "feels" this and that, or that it "intends" to do such and such. It assumes an identity for us—an identity that is sanctified legally as a corporate person, with a name. It becomes Shell Oil, or Microsoft, or Honda, or the Senate. It embodies a special kind of authority: it becomes a powerful actor, to which we must adapt, singly and collectively, even as it, in turn, must accommodate itself to our tastes and preferences.

What happened? Where was the sleight of hand that can explain an emergence in the ordinary, everyday activities of people, as they go about their daily business, of these strange giants that we call *organizations*? They are powerful actors, clearly, but how did they become recognized as such? We know, on the one hand, that they cannot sit down at the table with us for a meal. When we go to work, whatever the field of activity we are in, they are not going to be beside us, doing laboratory tests, or delivering supplies, or getting in touch with our clients by telephone, or e-mail. When we look around us to see who *is* with us, in *our* world, all we see are others like ourselves, flesh and blood, surrounded by all the material artifacts we have constructed as tools to deal with the "real" world in which we live, and that now reflexively shape our experience of that same world.

And yet? And yet? Those mysterious beings, those "organizations," *are* present, in their way. What *they* "choose" to "do" has immense effects on us. If *they* "decide" to fire us, we have lost our job. If *they* "invest" in a new enterprise, whole communities will discover new opportunities opening up where there were none before. If *they* go bankrupt, we suffer. If *they* "elect" to go to war, our family and friends may well be directly affected.

Although they are indeed powerful actors, organizations somehow manage to act without any specific materialization of their own: like the wizard of Oz, they remain invisible, always hidden behind the screen. They resemble the once famous television ventriloquist Edgar Bergen who animated a dummy called "Charlie McCarthy." We the viewers concentrated all our attention on Charlie, even though we knew, logically, it was Bergen who was supplying the voice and words. But this is still misleading: the "ventriloquist" we usually have in mind is an actual person, an Edgar Bergen. The organization is not like Bergen—not corporeal *in that way*. Unlike a person, an organization has no wired-in physical boundary or limits that are strictly its own. People present themselves in a here and a now. The organization does not. It is everywhere, and yet no single "where"; it is present in the past, "then," but also in the present, "now," and in the plans it makes that project it into the future. When we try to capture it, pin it down, it seems to be no more than a name, an imaginary presence, always offstage, forever out of sight. And yet, somehow, it is this elusive organization that manipulates and dominates the scenery and the actors that we do see. We all dance to *its* tune. It's quite a trick!

"Organization as Machine": Celebrate or Condemn?

The mode of organizing in the large that is so characteristic of today's world is of recent vintage, historically speaking. The notion of a company that we now take for granted took shape over time, no more than about a hundred and fifty years ago, in the second half of the nineteenth century (although there were of course earlier precedents) (Chandler 1990 [1962]). Its status as a legal person was confirmed in the United States only in 1886, when the Supreme Court recognized, in a controversial judgment ("controversial" because it is not entirely clear to historians what the judges' decision *was*), that the Southern Pacific Railroad Company was entitled to the same civil rights, and enjoyed the same legal protections, as an individual. Similar ideas took root in Europe and elsewhere in more or less the same time frame, formalized in various ways, depending on the context. The idea of an "artificial person" is of much more ancient provenance than the conception now being adopted

(Thomas Hobbes, for example, used the expression in his seventeenth-century book *The Leviathan*). Recognizing the company as a legal person ("moral person," in French), however, was new.

The even more sophisticated concept of a corporation composed of many divisions was innovated only in the twentieth century by Dupont, Ford, General Motors, and others (Coase 1937; Chandler 1990 [1962], 1977; Williamson 1975). It is all quite new, viewed from the broad sweep of history. Not surprisingly, theorists of society, sociologists, and others soon began to speculate about the nature of these odd "legal/moral" persons. As Morgan (2006 [1986]) has pointed out, mostly when they tried to characterize this extraordinary new immanence and its rapidly expanding economic presence they resorted to metaphors—images drawn from their experience with other objects.

The first organizational metaphor that seemed persuasive (and the most obvious) was that of *organization-as-machine*. This image dates from the beginning of the twentieth century. It was Frederic Taylor (1911) who seems to be the first to have proposed what he considered to be a rational solution to the question of how to organize the new type of workforce required by the industrial transformations of the time. The organization, he noted, assembles many trades, many skills. Since all these activities involve the performance of a task, then the logical way to proceed is to analyze each scientifically in order to arrive at what would now be described as its "best practice": the most efficient sequence of operations necessary to carry the work out. The overall result, Taylor was certain, would be a smoothly running machine where the humans behaved as "rationally" as the tools they were delegated to manipulate.

In France, Henri Fayol (1925) chose a different image but to much the same effect. He took as his point of reference (and image) the chain of command of a well-disciplined army corps: orders flowed down from the top, carried out to the letter by those at the bottom who then reported back on their accomplishment to their superiors.

Different image, same logic: people as cogs in a machine (the topic of Charlie Chaplin's famous 1936 film *Modern Times*).

The great German jurist, historian, sociologist, and economist Max Weber (1922) developed another rationale for the modern organization: its basis in law. Every official in a bureaucracy, he speculated, works to rule. The writing of the rules is the responsibility of the senior bureaucrats and their masters. In his "ideal type" or model of bureaucratic organization, the question of how to assure reliable administration is resolved since, once the functionaries have been trained in their tasks, the rules, set out from the top, suffice to shape and steer the organization. Bureaucratic organization should thus result in a guaranteed machine-like reliability of performance (Weber also explicitly drew on the image of the machine, at one point, as the inspiration for modern forms of organizing).

In the United States, members of the so-called "classical school" of administration such as Mooney and Riley (1931) were fleshing out the machine model by exploring dimensions such as the best distribution of tasks and the optimal limits of the span of control of supervisors. Schools of efficiency experts began to form, spreading the new gospel to "managers" everywhere (the concept of management was itself a novelty; see Jacques 1996). Throughout the twentieth century, indeed, the idea of organization as a machine repeatedly found expression among both theorists and practitioners: in the "Total Quality" movement of the second half of the century (Giroux & Taylor 2002), and in the even more recent management vogue known as "reengineering" (Hammer 1996; Hammer & Champy 1993). Rational division of labor is an idea that seems to have found its first expression in the work of Adam Smith in the eighteenth century. It is perpetuated today in management schools everywhere: intelligent strategy and design, coupled with effective admin-istration, are the key to organizational effectiveness (Hammer (1996), for example, explicitly evokes the ideas of Smith in explaining the rationale of reengineering).

The machine model, to be sure, is appealing in its way. It *does* seem to explain some otherwise mysterious phenomena: the extraordinary growth of centrally controlled organizations, extended in space and time, that we have witnessed over the past century. It *does* appear to account for features of organization, notably by visualizing it as a mechanism that coordinates a diversity of activities.

The problem with metaphor in its various guises, as Morgan himself emphasized, is that, in explaining some things, it also distorts, and omits, others. What does the machine metaphor most evidently leave out when we apply it to organization? For one, the rationalist/idealist assumption that a large organization represents the forefront of technological achieve-ment ignores its counterpart, the flipside of the coin, if you like, that has found its expression in critical theory and its exploration of the organizational practices of societal domination. Interpreted critically, the new machine is not a better way to organize enterprise, but an increasingly refined instrument of oppression and perpetuation of class distinction: the managers on one side, workers on the other. The current academic literature on organization and management thus exhibits an odd schism between rationalist interpretations (predominantly North American), and the critical analyses (predominantly of British and continental European origin).

For us, however, the most glaring omission in the machine analogy, whether interpretations be rationalist or critical, is to have overlooked—dismissed, even—the reliance of all organization on human communi-cation. Yet, for the rationalist machine model to work, for example, it must be assumed that communication is no more complicated than a simple transmission of information and commands: transparent, uncontaminated by human motive, innocent of any attributions of authority other than those assumed a priori by the theory. From a critical standpoint, communication would also be reduced: relegated to being a tool of the mechanisms of control and power. Yet anyone with anything like a sophisticated understanding of the communication process understands that such reductions are insufficient to explain organization.

It's just not that simple. One reason—the *big* reason, in fact—is that the components of the new "machine" are those ornery critters called "people."

Human Relations as the Key?

Not everyone, of course, had ever agreed that the rational machine image was the solution to the problem of organizing, or, alternatively, the root of all the ills of civilization, not even from the beginning. As early as the 1920s, when the famous Hawthorne studies were launched (Roethlisberger & Dickson 1939), empirically oriented researchers encountered convincing evidence in their field research in a manufacturing enterprise that flatly contradicted the rationalistic predictions of the omnipresent time-and-motion consultants of the time. The interventions of the "experts" led to behavioral consequences that were inconsistent with what had blithely been assumed in the theory. The "machine," it turned out, did not work as had been predicted. The only way to explain the discrepancy between theory and practice, Roethlisberger and his associates concluded, was to posit the existence of local modes of organizing that intervened to mediate, and frustrate, the managerial interventions.

Other contrary voices were soon added. Mary Parker Follett (1941) reminded managers that they left the human dimension untended at their own risk. The Harvard scholar and successful New Jersey entrepreneur Chester Barnard (1938) could see the task of managing through the eyes of an actual company executive head. He knew from experience how difficult it is to exert, in practice, the authority that the theory postulated as residing in the person of the head honcho. It was Barnard, as well as Follett, who first emphasized the role that communication plays in organizational process. At Columbia University, the distinguished sociologist Robert Merton (1957) and his students Selznick (1949), Gouldner (1954), and Blau (1956) were documenting the limitations of the bureaucratic model as elaborated by Weber. Blau, for example, recorded some of the clandestine strategies that employees were using to circumvent the prohibition of conversation at work. People, to employ a term later popularized by Harold Garfinkel, are not quite the "judgmental dopes" that Taylor and his successors had imagined. They compensate for the errors of management; they invent ways to detour around imposed constraints so that the work gets done: "workarounds," Sachs calls them (Sachs 1995).

"Human Relations": But is it Communication?

In the face of this accumulating evidence, Elton Mayo (1933), whose initiative had led to launching the Hawthorne studies in the first place, was one of those who pleaded for a more holistic theory of management (he is sometimes credited with fathering what would become known as the Human Relations School of management). An emphasis on the human quality of the organizational experience was to become a significant influence in the management literature, especially in the period immediately following the end of World War II. It has continued to flourish in the decades that followed, the 1950s, 1960s, and beyond. Its special contribution has been to focus on interpersonal and group process, to study such questions as what leadership practices are most effective; how individuals enter a group culture and become socialized there; how individual attitudes and group norms are reconciled in theory and practice; and what kind of balance works best between a concentration on task performance and a concern for group morale. The study of communication, however, as conceived by human relations scholars, restricted itself to an examination of the interpersonal and the local. What it did not address was the issue of the constitution of the organization itself: how it occurs *in* and *through* communication (Dewey 1944 [1916]).

The human relations literature was humanistic in philosophy and empirical in approach. It could be critical of management practice (in the general sense of that word "critical"), but it was also dominated by a managerial concern for the integration of effective administrative practices in the post-World War II context, whose growing layers of complexity made managerial evolution a necessity. F. W. Taylor's time had long since passed. By the 1950s, the era of the "man in the grey flannel suit" had arrived, and management was being transformed into a corps composed of "organization men" (the two expressions date from this epoch, popularized by books published in that decade, very much male oriented).

As was the case in theories inspired by the machine metaphor, what was still lacking was any real theory of communication as the key to understanding organization: how it supplies the indispensable basis, in both organizational practice and in theory.

A Thumbnail History of the Origins of Organizational Communication as a Field

The field of organizational communication did not even exist as such until the decade of the 1960s (it grew out of a hybrid school of managerial practice known as "business and industrial communication"). When it did emerge in the US, somewhat tentatively at first, it inherited the assumptions of these earlier traditions, in sociology, management science, and social psychology. It also risked perpetuating, according to one of its founders (Redding 1985), an implicit managerial bias—one, by the way, from which Redding and his colleagues were distancing themselves by the mere act of asserting independence as a new field. That organizational communication came to exist at all, as a nascent discipline, was a recognition by its pioneers, Redding, Thayer, Tompkins, Monge, and others, that there was a missing component in the existing literature— to be specific, an adequate theory of *communication*. There had all along been, of course, endless mentions of "communication" and "communications," but in their totality they did not add up to a coherent theory of what communication is, much less how it works to constitute organization (for excellent reviews of the origins of the field see Redding 1985, and Tompkins & Redding 1988; Thayer (1986) outlined his approach to the study of organizational communication in launching a new series whose subtitle was also an injunction, "Emerging Perspectives"). That people communicate had previously been a taken-for-granted, unreflective assumption in the earlier "business and industrial" communicational literature on organization, much as it had been elsewhere in organization studies (Redding 1985). Nobody disagreed that members enable their organization by communicating. The pioneers, Thayer, Redding, and Tompkins, took it as their challenge to go further, to explore the *how* of organizing, as an effect of communication. They brought to the task new insights, drawn from their formations in rhetoric, language, and expression. They set the stage. In this book, we mean to once again pick up the gauntlet they threw down.

Although the new organizational communication literature focused explicitly on communication, it remained for some time, in many respects, a prisoner of its interdisciplinary heritage, and especially that of social psychology. The emphasis was predominantly on the micro-processes of interpersonal interaction, and group process—human relations, in other words. In 1975, the publisher Sage launched a new series comprising an annual review of explicitly organizational communication studies that had been published in the previous year. An inspection of the content of the reviews over the first decade or so confirms that by far and away the dominant stream of research was social-psychological, functionalist, and positivist. There was still no real theory of *organizational* communication. It stayed, with few exceptions, communication *in* organization.

Early on in the decade of the 1980s, however, communication researchers assembled to take stock: to question the conceptual foundations of their new science (see Putnam & Pacanowsky 1983; McPhee

& Tompkins 1985; and for a comprehensive overview of key contributions dating from that era see Putnam & Krone 2006). In doing so, they introduced two new ideas: first, that communication is constructed by those involved in and through their sensemaking practices, and second, that the consequence of such a collective construction of meaning is often an unequal (and indeed inequitable) distribution of power and influence. The emphasis is on sensemaking as ideology and the exercise of power. New ideas were infiltrating the field, but the result was still far from being a comprehensive, generally shared theory of how communication and organization relate to each other (Corman & Poole 2000; Taylor, Flanagin, Cheney, & Seibold 2001).

The decade of the 1990s witnessed a number of efforts to take the next step: to conceptualize the organization as constructed in and emerging out of communication practices. Our earlier book, *The Emergent Organization* (Taylor & Van Every 2000), was one step in that direction, but only one of several, as researchers absorbed and reinterpreted earlier insights developed by theorists such as Giddens, Weick, Latour, Engeström, Bourdieu, Foucault, and others, none of whom were officially identified with communication studies but who all expressed dissatisfaction with the then conventional views of organization.

How this Book Fits into the Current Development of the Field

Our book was written in the conviction that, whatever their virtues, positivist methods can never satisfactorily explain organization. We believe a return to the historical pragmatist roots of the discipline is long overdue. In this respect, what we manage to accomplish in this book needs to be seen in context, as one more contribution to a community of people who study organization, reflecting a diversity of disciplines that range from information science to management theory to sociology to anthropology (Robichaud & Cooren forthcoming). There is now, for example, a rich body of publications addressed to an understanding of discourse in human affairs (Alvesson & Kärreman 2000; Grant, Hardy, Oswick, & Putnam 2004; Grant, Keenoy, & Oswick 1998; Hardy, Palmer, & Phillips 2000; Putnam & Fairhurst 2001; Fairhurst & Putnam 2004; van Dijk 2007; see Jian, Schmisseur, & Fairhurst 2008 for a critique of this literature from a communicational perspective). Interpretively inspired research has become a major influence on the field.

Phillips, Lawrence, & Hardy (2004) have explored another fruitful connection, this time with links to the well-established sociological field of study of institutions. Phillips et al. argue, in particular, for "a relationship between discourse and social action through the production and consumption of texts" (p. 635), a position that is very much in line, as far as it goes, with that which we defend in this book. We too subscribe to the view that "socially produced ideas and objects that comprise organizations, institutions, and the social world in general are created and maintained through the relationships among discourse, text, and action" (p. 637). It is, in fact, those "socially produced ideas" that we call thirdness. Where we differ from Phillips et al. is in our emphasis on the conversational dynamic: the *locus* for this "creation" and "maintenance." The discourse literature has tended to abstract from the conversational embedding of institutions in practice, with the result that the word "communication" (much less "conversation") is rarely, if ever, evoked (Jian, Schmisseur, & Fairhurst 2008; Taylor 2008). As Alvesson & Kärreman (2000: 1145) have observed, for example, in a much cited article, "inclinations to 'jump over' language use in a social context and make broader statements about discourse at an aggregate level . . . may reproduce the somewhat careless attitude to language that the very idea of discourse studies . . . should counter." As they further write, "the move from discourse to Discourse includes a shift in perspective . . . the problem of going from the specific empirical materials to address Discourses is not frequently dealt with in the literature" (p. 1146; by capital *D* Discourse, as opposed to lower-case *d* discourse, they mean "Grand Discourse," such as that analyzed by Foucault and his successors, applicable to society as a whole. Ordinary, or lower-case, discourse, our emphasis, is tied to specific situations).

The nature of the "shift" that Alvesson and Karreman identify is the theme we address in this book: how to conceive it, how to research it, and what its organizational implications are—how, for example, accounting distorts the reality of a situated practice (Chapter 5), or how the grandiose, big-*D* "Discourse" of technology becomes a good deal less persuasive when it is translated into the nitty-gritty little-*d* conversations of normal work (Chapter 7).

Our approach also shares affinities to another "turn": the "practice turn" (Suchman 1996; Lave & Wenger 1991; Engeström & Middleton 1996; Wenger 1998; Schatzki, Knorr Cetina, & von Savigny 2001; Gherardi 2006). Gheradi (2010), for example, reports on a fine-grained analysis of medical practice in Italy exemplified in conversations between general practitioners and consultant specialists, mediated by telephony and distance transmission of images. As later chapters in our own book also illustrate, just beneath the informal and casual conversations of working professionals lurk the for-the-most-part-unstated distinctions of status and authority that nevertheless bubble to the surface in urgent situations requiring immediate action. What emerges from Gherardi's analysis is a perspective on conversation that sees it as a configuration of organizational positions that, as members enact them, enable people to assume an identity, and claim the precedence and authority that accompany such an identity: medical specialist as opposed to general practitioner, for example. The mostly unstated but tacit configuring of roles and statuses that underpins organization is dependent on a mutual recognition by members of its legitimization. This is an effect of what we call thirdness: who people are, what their role is, and what their domain of authority is.

Recognition of the crucial role of interaction in the establishing of organizational reality now informs the thinking of others whose primary affiliation is information systems. Levina and Orlikowski (2009), for example, address an issue that is a theme in each of the empirical chapters of this book: how the presence of incompatible agendas in the agencies composing a single organization leads to sequences of interaction, face-to-face and mediated, where the hierarchy of statuses and purposes must be renegotiated and resolved. The concept of thirdness we introduce in Chapter 1 incorporates both people's understandings of their own practices, their enacting of a world, as well as how they frame the set of human relationships that is the indispensable condition for coordinated cooperative work.

Finally, Czarniawska (forthcoming) supplies a broader historical context that is useful in situating the approach we adopt. As she observes, the field to which she belongs, management science, predicates a theory of organization. Somewhere near the middle of the twentieth century, concurrent with the increasing influence of cybernetics and general systems theory, organization began to be conceived as an organism: ultimately as one with the ability to adapt by responding proactively to its environment, much like other organisms. Not that there was much consensus about the modalities of such adaptation, far from it: there were as many theories as theoreticians, it sometimes seemed. The one thing they all had in common was what Czarniawska terms the "reification" of organization. She, however, proposes an alternative vision as an "action net," where by "action" she means an event to which it is possible to attribute purpose or intention. She further clarifies her idea of action by observing that, "certain connections between actions are legitimate while others are not—or not yet." Czarniawska goes on to argue, as we do, that, "entities are outcomes rather than inputs of organizing." This means starting, not from a priori assumptions of the existence of actors or organizations, but from organizing itself, in a way that has parallels in the writings of the pragmatist theorist, George Herbert Mead. She thus writes: "Why a net rather than a network? Network assumes the existence of actors, who forge connections. Action net reverses this assumption, suggesting that connections between and among actions, when stabilized, are used to construct the identities of actors" (including, we would add, the identity of the organization itself).

This is a position that we feel comfortable with. It does not deny the idea of structure, for example, but instead places the emphasis on the structuring of the configurations of action that are most characteristic of the huge agglomerations of domains of action that are typical of modern society. It places the emphasis where, in our opinion, it should be, on the emergence of organization in communication. Where we hope this present book innovates is in making clearer than before *how* communication works to produce such organization. It is inspired by one idea, that communication is achieved through the establishment of a "thirdness," and that it is in and through the continuing reconstruction and reiteration of that thirdness in the practices of its many communities that an organization becomes present to us and is thus enabled to exist in our world, socially and materially. We thus build on our earlier work (Taylor, Cooren, Giroux, & Robichaud 1996; Taylor & Van Every 2000; Cooren, Taylor, & Van Every 2006), but in a way that is intended to take it further, to explicate the "how" of organizing as it is sited in communication. Its emphasis is on how text and conversation inform each other, and, in the process, constitute the organization itself as a communicative actor in an odd kind of dialogue with its members.

The Importance of Empirical Research

In addition to establishing a theoretical grounding, the book has a second objective, this time addressed to the practice and methodology of organizational communication research. The Alta conference in 1981 (Putnam & Pacanowsky 1983) was not limited to a rethinking of communication theory. It was also about the conduct of inquiry in a field as complex as the communicational study of organization. Its banner?: *interpretive* research, with a *critical* edge. We, in this book, interpret the Alta perspective, not so much as a reaction *against* positivism and turn *away* from functionalism, but as a return *to* an earlier celebration of pragmatism.

Until well into the twentieth century, the mainstream in sociological thought was interpretive in its orientation. It is positivism, seen in this light, that "turned" away from the established pragmatic tradition of Simmel, Weber, and others in Europe and Peirce, James, Dewey, Mead, and Goffman in North America. Positivism values method and objectivity. But method is not, and never has been, the privileged province of positivism. It was no accident, for example, that the pragmatist Charles Sanders Peirce entitled his 1903 Harvard lectures "Pragmatism as a principle and *method* of right thinking." The issue is not whether method or not, but *which* method—a debate that began before logical positivism was invented, in the polemic of nineteenth-century Europe, pitting *Verstehen* against *Erklärung*: disciplined understanding versus theory-driven explanation. Nor is objectivity seen the same way by pragmatists

(Taylor & Gurd 1996): they perceive it to be an end to work toward, part of a community of practice, not a dehumanized state of abstract cognition.

We address this issue in Chapters 1 and 2, but it is primarily in the empirical Chapters (4–8) where we illustrate what we mean by a pragmatic approach to research.

Who Was this Book Written For?

In writing this book, we had two readers in mind. In part, we were inspired by the many requests we have received from teachers of organizational communication, in the United States (Michigan, Texas, Colorado, New Jersey, New York), in Canada (Alberta, Ottawa), in Europe (France, the Netherlands, Norway, Denmark, Sweden, Finland, Italy, Portugal), and elsewhere (Latin America, notably Brazil). People were asking us for a systematic introduction to how to conduct interpretively-inspired empirical field research from the perspective of the approach that we have outlined in previous publications (Taylor & Van Every 2000; Cooren, Taylor, & Van Every 2006)—a source book, in other words, that students could use to plan and conduct such research. There exists, of course, a plethora of texts that deal with qualitative research, many of them excellent and tested in practice, but there is none that does so from the perspective we are taking: how to understand the emergence of organization in the talk and texts of its members. Similarly, there are comprehensive surveys of the literature on organizational communication (Cheney, Christensen, Zorn, & Ganesh 2004, for example), but that is not our focus.

We have not intended this book to be a review of previous research on communication, nor an introduction to the broader field of organizational communication. Our aim is instead to lay out the particular perspective that is the fruit of our own continuing investigations, as well as that of our associates and colleagues, the so-called "Montreal School," of the manifestations of organization as it enters into, and is thereby reconstituted by, the everyday life of its members. We thus focus not merely on how members of the organization realize (carry through) the latter's purposes in and through their activities, including their conversations and texts, but even more on how they simultaneously, conceptually "realize" (i.e., make *real* for themselves) the organization itself, as they go about its work (and their own). The larger portion of the book is thus given over to describing how field research based on our approach can be organized and accomplished, using the example of five recent doctoral dissertations to do so. Our goal is practical: to provide a guide to this type of research, one that will be used by teachers and students alike.

The second reader we had in mind is anyone who asks the question that is so often posed by researchers in allied disciplines who are not familiar with our field (management science, sociology, information science): "What *is* 'organizational communication,' and what do you study there?" It is a fair question, and one that the larger community of practitioners has asked itself (Corman & Poole 2000). The field, we have been periodically told, has taken a "narrative turn," or an "interpretive turn," or a "critical turn," or a "discursive turn," or a "practice turn," or a "linguistic turn." By laying out our own "turn," we hope to clarify how our approach to solving the organizational puzzle complements those other disciplines.

The Structure of Chapters

In the first three chapters, we outline our own understanding of the link from action to structure (and back). These chapters are thus theoretical. In Chapter 1, for example, we show that the making of sense, wherever people collaboratively address some task, is intrinsically *both* acting *and* structuring. The organization is already present, as what we call the "thirdness" of sensemaking, in all collective activity: understanding our singular experience as an exemplar of our common heritage of constituted meaning. At the simplest level of action, whenever "you" and "I" transform ourselves into a "we," an organization has formed. There is action but there is *also* structure and a shared meaning. The most elaborated kind of organization, with thousands of employees, operating in every continent of the globe, is merely an extension of that elementary transformation of agency into organization, the consequence of a scaling up through what we call "imbrication," which is to say domains of action that become embedded in increasingly complex webs through what Bruno Latour (1986) has termed the "powers of association."

Chapters 2 and 3 expand on this elementary insight: Chapter 2 by recognizing the fundamental role of framing a situation and the frame games it inspires; Chapter 3 by delving into how language not only supplies the modality of such construction of frames, but in how it also reflexively constitutes action and structure, as *text* and *context*.

Chapters 4 through 8 aim to illustrate and deepen our intuitive understanding of how organization gets realized in the everyday activities of people in widely differing environments, including a government-sponsored program of science awareness (Chapter 4), a large construction company, seen through the lens of its accounting system (Chapter 5), a giant hi-tech firm, caught up in the fallout of a shift in strategic planning (Chapter 6), and a successful pharmaceutical firm that managed to survive the implementation of a new centralized computer facility (Chapter 7).

Finally, we report on how competing interests of owners and developers in an oil patch were turned into more constructive cooperation, based on a shared recognition of the importance of sustained development (Chapter 8).

Chapter 9 traces retrospectively the route followed, and summarizes our conclusions.

A Word of Thanks to Our Sources

This book has one last objective, ultimately, perhaps, the most important of all. It was inspired by our ongoing conversation with a whole new generation of brilliant scholars, only now stepping up to assume leadership in the development of the field. It is their accomplishments that supplied the empirical "meat" of the book. Their geographical origin is diverse: Consuelo Vasquez, originally from Chile, who conducted her doctoral studies and is now teaching in Montreal; Bertrand Fauré and Sandrine Virgili from France, both now teaching there; Senem Güney, originally from Turkey, but trained at the University of Texas and now teaching at Albany; and Andy Blundell from Alberta, Canada, now pursuing a career in community development and teaching in that province. It is this work, and a host of others like it, that constitutes the real future of the field. We wanted to celebrate it.

To all our collaborators, we express our sincere thanks for their willingness to let us share the fruits of their labor. It has been a joy to work with them, and with many others who are currently taking up the torch, in Norway, the Netherlands, France, Brazil, Costa Rica, New Zealand, Canada, and elsewhere. The beginnings of organizational communication were in the US. This is no longer the case (Putnam & Casali 2009). The world is catching up. We will have reason to be proud if we have succeeded in bringing the accomplishments of our young colleagues, and of others with whom we maintain a continuing dialogue, to the attention of a wider audience.

Suggested Supplementary Readings

For a perceptive analysis of trends in current organizational communication research see Fairhurst and Putnam (2004). Jian, Schmisseur, & Fairhurst (2008) explore in even greater depth the parallels and differences between the active field of discourse analysis and research in organizational communication. Both articles are accessible and highly recommended. Read also the responses to the latter article in the same issue of *Discourse and Communication*. Also useful as background: Corman & Poole (2000) and Taylor, Flanagin, Cheney, & Seibold (2001).

For background on the approach developed in this book, see Brummans' chapter on the Montreal School, in Cooren, Taylor, & Van Every (2006). Taylor & Gurd (1996) explore both the parallels and differences in the genesis of the school compared with the mainstream interpretive approach initiated in the Alta conferences in the early 1980s, as described in Putnam & Pacanowsky (1983).

Part One

Theory

Chapter 1

The Premise of Organization as Thirdness

Our answer to the puzzle of organization, the theme of our prologue: how can it be at one and the same time *both* structure *and* action? Organization, we will propose, in response, is what we call the thirdness that must be present in every relationship making up the fabric of an organization.

The agenda of this chapter is thus devoted to a single objective: to set out in its essence our hypothesis of organization-as-thirdness. Future chapters will elaborate the implications of adopting such a hypothesis, emphasizing the role of language in communication and exemplified in empirical research taking the form of several case studies. In this chapter, however, we limit ourselves to the essentials: what thirdness is, how it might explain organization, and how it works, in practice. We begin, not by a consideration of organization but instead by focusing on the elementary act of communication that supports cooperative work. Only when we have begun to see how it is that organization is not something outside of communication, but an intrinsic property of it, can we then take the next step: to scale up to more complex processes of organizing, and see how they in turn constitute the more elaborate constructions that we think of as "organizations."

Preliminary Remarks: Connecting to Weick's View of Enactment

In 1979, Karl Weick published a book entitled *The Social Psychology of Organizing*. In it, he laid out a thesis, namely that organization exists in and through its enactment. Organization, he argued, emerges circumstantially in its practices in two ways, conceptually and proactively. Conceptually, there is emergence in the categories that allow people to see meaning in their experience and constitute their way of making sense of what they encounter in their daily activities: a mapping of impressions to established ideas, and vice versa. Proactively, there is emergence in how they react to their environment in the way they do. The resulting interaction is thus simultaneously material (they deal with a real world occupied by real objects), social (sensemaking is a collective achievement), and ideational (the complexity of experience is dealt with cognitively: people retrospectively fit their experience to pre-established categories that language furnishes—"cognitive maps"—thereby giving it a "sense").

Weick, in this work, was perpetuating and refining a tradition that had its source in a philosophical stream of thought called *pragmatism*. The original pragmatist was a brilliant but eccentric American intellectual, Charles Sanders Peirce, whose writing dates from the end of the nineteenth century and the beginning of the twentieth. His work can be understood, in one sense, as a reaction against the overly rationalist stream of European thought of the time, which drew its inspiration most notably from Kant and Hegel (although Peirce saw himself as extending rather than refuting their insights). The rationale for pragmatism, well illustrated by Weick's work, is that knowledge does not exist in some abstract space of pure logic, or eternal categories, but is better seen as the instrumentality that allows us to get on with our life: make sense of our experience.

Any time there is a mismatch between knowledge and experience, Peirce argued, doubt will be generated, and it is doubt that impels us to question our ideas and seek new ways of accounting for what we are experiencing. If we do not doubt our ideas, they will remain invisible to us, what a later tradition would call "black-boxed" (Latour 1987)— out of our immediate consciousness and yet still operative in determining how we see things. Doubt, on the other hand, leads us to open ourselves up to a dialogue with others, in the quest for a resolution of our uncertainty.

For Peirce, science itself conforms to the same logic: it too is driven by the impulse to question explanations that, on close examination, have proven, as a result of empirical investigation, to be of dubious validity. The scientific quest is thus neither quite deductive (a purely logical inferential procedure, inspired by an undisputed set of premises) nor inductive (simply a classification of our impressions). It is abductive: a reconciliation of ideas and experience in the endless quest to resolve our doubts by finding a convincing explanation, a plausible generalization of what our experience means (Taylor & Gurd 1996). Abductive logic is thus not "transcendental," a search for an unchanging or universal truth, but "constitutive" (Maturana 1997). It is objective only in the sense that it resolves doubt within the bounds of a discipline whose procedures serve to legitimate the validity of the conclusion. Knowledge, conceived in this way, is the product of a practice, a "making sense" of experience within the domain of a community of practice such as is found in the construction industry (Chapter 5) or technology development (Chapter 6): simultaneously acting and understanding.

Abduction

Since the principle of abduction goes to the heart of the approach to research that motivated the writing of this book, we make a short detour here to explain what is special about it. Deduction presumes you are starting from a theory you and others have already worked out, from which you derive hypotheses that can be tested against people's experienced reality by accumulating data that either confirm or disconfirm those hypotheses. Induction implies the inverse: collecting a quantity of data and then patiently sifting through them, using an established methodology, until regularity is detected. Abduction, however, reduces neither to deduction nor to induction. Both methodologies privilege the categories and explanations of the *researchers* and relegate "informants" to the status of objects to be studied, like the cells of the brain, or the marine life of an ocean, or the components of urban pollution. Abduction presumes that the "subjects" of the research are themselves making sense. Research then comes to mean entering intuitively, but in a disciplined way, into the reality that is the consequence of its purposive construction by those who live in the world being studied. Abduction is also about confronting doubt and establishing belief, but its object is a world that is already informed by sense prior to being observed by the researcher.

Peirce's idea of abduction has been compared with the intuitive leaps that identified the method of that singular nineteenth-century fictional detective, Sherlock Holmes (Eco & Sebeok 1983). Peirce's method, like that of Holmes, rejects neither induction nor deduction in that it privileges both (1) an accumulation of the particulars of a situation, through careful observation, and (2) a willingness to probe beneath its surface to discover, either through intuition or understanding, the hidden order those particulars no more than hint at. As the examples of empirical research described in Chapters 4–8 illustrate, that means for us embedding oneself in a situation and in the community that lives it, first to meticulously accumulate (and if possible record) observations, and, second, to reach beyond the experience of the moment to comprehend intuitively and theoretically the patterned network of interdependent relationships that give events their meaning for those who are involved. It is how Peirce imagined the way to the resolution of doubt.

Practically speaking, pragmatism positions the analyst, as Chapters 4–8 illustrate, in the role of a detective: confronted with a host of facts that call for an explanation, and facing the challenge of finding their hidden pattern. That "pattern" is what we understand by organization. Rather than start from an a priori conventional image of organization, the researcher must strive to discover, empirically, the principles of its construction. The challenge for the investigator, as it was for Sherlock Holmes, is to discover the hidden order obscured by sequences of events whose significance may have escaped others who may be imprisoned in conventional ways of thinking—a clichéd idea of organization that treats it as a black box.

Weick's concept of enactment is abductive in spirit. So do we intend the approach to be that we develop in this book. We mean it to serve as a guide to the people who undertake research in this manner: confronting—even welcoming—the "doubt" that surfaces in their investigations.

With this in mind, let us now turn to elucidate the idea of thirdness.

What is "Thirdness"?

The concept of thirdness, we should make clear, is not new. Indeed, far from it. It too was innovated by Peirce. Peirce, the pragmatist, is also remembered as the person who developed a discipline that he called "semiotics." (Semiotics is the theory of signs, where he defined "sign" as "something which stands to somebody for something in some respect or capacity" (Peirce 1940/1955: 99), a definition that includes but is not limited to spoken language.) For this second Peirce, the semiotician, there are three "modes of being" (Peirce 1940/1955: 75). The first he termed "the actuality of an event" (p. 75). It occurs, to use his own words, in a *here* and *now* (he used italics for "here" and "now" in the original text). Firstness emerges, he wrote, "in its relations to the universe of existents" (p. 75). It is "something *brute*. There is no reason for it" (p. 76, again emphasis in the original). Whatever it is, it is just *here*. In and of itself it has no meaning.

Think about the garden behind your house. The "garden" in its firstness is not a garden at all (it doesn't become a garden until you begin to think of it as such and treat it accordingly). It is merely soil, lying there, inert (or teeming with hidden life, if you prefer). It only starts to take on a meaning for you when you focus your attention on it and act on it in some way. To cite Peirce,

> For as long as things do not act upon one another there is no sense or meaning in saying that they have any being, unless it be that they are such in themselves that they may perhaps come into relation with others.

Taking on a kind of significance will begin when you set about digging and hoeing the soil (one condition for enactment, to put the idea in Weick's terms, is to act). Now a relationship exists: your activity links your body to the soil. Again, however, the relationship merely consists of two connected instances of materiality. The second, *you*, is acting on the first, *the soil*, brought into what Peirce called a "relationship" by the action that connects one to the other.

That, however, is not yet gardening. It is merely one body, yours, connecting, materially, with another, that of the garden. *Gardening* implies something more: a sustained practice that you have had to learn how to do. It is in that "knowing how to do" of gardening that thirdness resides. Thirdness, for Peirce, is "the mode of being which *consists* in the fact that future facts of secondness will take on a determinate general character" (p. 77, emphasis in the original). When you take tools outside and dig up the soil, or perhaps when discussing with a friend where you should put the plants, you are now understanding what is occurring within the wider terms or rules of a general project known in our society as "gardening." You are drawing on your own and other people's past experience of how a gardening project unfolds (or should unfold). You understand what you are doing in the light of a generalization about gardening (Peirce called it a "law"): what it is, and how to do it. (You could even buy a manual that explains all the finer points: "Gardening for dummies!")

You are thus able to make sense of it in a way that mindlessly going out and randomly digging some holes in a site does not afford. That is still only secondness in relation to firstness. As Peirce observes, "every genuine triadic relation involves meaning, as meaning is obviously a triadic relation . . . a triadic relation is inexpressible by means of dyadic relations alone" (p. 91).

Complications that Ensue when We Try to Apply Peirce's Idea to Communication

Everything that follows in this book is an elaboration on this elementary idea of thirdness. There is, however, a caution that we should introduce before we go any further. This is not a book about semiotics, even though one of our preoccupations throughout will be to take account of the role of language in organization. Peirce, as we said, invented the science he called semiotics. His Swiss contemporary, Ferdinand de Saussure, writing at roughly the same time, also proposed a new science of signs (including language) that he called "semiology" (which he defined as the "science that studies the life of signs in social life"). Semiology, Saussure-style, was absorbed into the rapidly developing science of formal linguistics. It was seen as an exemplar of structuralism, or the logical foundation of languages exemplified in a formal grammar. Peirce's views had much less resonance, especially in the early twentieth century, when an intellectual infatuation with logical positivism, the most rationalist and least pragmatic of all approaches to communication, predominated in European philosophy. For decades, when the ideas of Peirce the *semiotician* received any attention at all, they tended to be classified as a mere variant of semiology. The philosophical roots of his semiotics in pragmatics were obscured. (Thibault (1997) has argued that Saussure's own pragmatic side, his emphasis on *parole* as opposed to *langue*, also got discarded along the way by the logic-driven structuralists.)

We are certainly not concerned to build a syntactic/semantic or a cognitively grounded "system." Our focus on thirdness aims to restore its pragmatic, not its cognitive or structuralist, connotations: to explain findings that recent investigations into organization have brought to our attention.

Adding in Communication

Now for the issue we are exploring. Since the topic of this book is organization, and since organization implies a network of relationships involving many human actors, as well as their tools, tasks, and objects of attention, the Peircian presentation of thirdness offered above has a missing dimension: it involves only *one* actor (a "second") relating to *one* object (a "first"). In this respect, Peirce's analysis was still set within the prevailing Western tradition of seeing meaning as an extension of individual consciousness and practice, rather than as a by-product of communication between people. For organization to even exist in the way we will be using that word, however, as a composition of human and non-human relationships, i.e., an *organization* (in the full sense of that word), there must be more than one human actor relating to a shared object. An organization implies an association of human actors, all of whom nevertheless are focusing their attention on the same objects: that is the *sine qua non* of all organized collaboration.

The reader will immediately see the problem. An actor–object relationship involving only *one* person constitutes a firstness–secondness couplet: individual work, for example. Each such relationship implies a thirdness (otherwise the activity has no meaning: it is merely activity, or what Kenneth Burke (1966) called "motion"—behavior, in other words, as opposed to action). The question that is now posed to us is this: if there are instead *two* people (or more than two)—two gardeners working on the same garden, and they relate to (the same) *one* object— are we to attribute to both (or all) of them the *same* thirdness? Why should we? They are all sensemakers, are they not? Why would we imagine that any such two or more people would spontaneously make the same sense of what they are doing together? And if they do not, aren't the people working the garden likely to be doing so at cross-purposes: because they make sense of what they are doing differently, will they not cancel out each other's efforts? ("That plant should go here." "No, not here, over there.") Conversely, as they go about their work in a smoothly coordinated way, surely, we say to ourselves, they must be organized! They must be making the *same* sense.

Even to exist, it would seem, pursuing Peirce's logic to its conclusion in a context that he did not himself much explore, organization implies a unique thirdness, a unifying fabric of generalizations and explanations. But, if the two or more individuals *are* organized, and if they *do* share a single thirdness, or interpretation of what they are doing, how did they accomplish that agreement? Especially, as we know is often the case, if they have different identities, reflecting different interests and skills: the *sine qua non* of any very complex organization.

Here is the problem, this time formulated slightly differently. We know that distinguishing between a first and a second is Peirce's initial move in explaining meaning: one actor, one object. Let us now suppose (as an exercise in organizational reasoning) that we take one of the two gardeners as the object, or firstness (i.e., that person, otherwise merely an "existent," that is to say the one who is to be acted on, in the absence of which he or she is no more than a potentiality, communicatively speaking), and the other as a secondness (he or she who is doing the acting and the sensemaking). Doesn't their joint second-to-first relationship then *itself* imply a new thirdness, namely how to read the meaning of their second-to-first association, now seen as a collaborative interpersonal event—a thirdness that may be thought of as a "law" of human relationship (a general theory of employer–employee relations, for example)?

Surely there is a different dimension of thirdness here that Peirce did not address, namely how to interpret those "laws" of human relationship. Otherwise, once again cooperative efforts would have no meaning to the people involved, or indeed to us. (All we are doing here is pursuing Peirce's reasoning about the origin of meaning by applying it to a communicative context, as he did not.)

The Explanatory Challenge We Now Address

Collaboration that Is Grounded in a Practice

It doesn't matter, it seems, how we interpret first and second, human versus non-human, or human versus human: if the first–second relationship is to have any meaning, it must be because of a thirdness. So, this implies that for two people to constitute an organization, abstracting from their respective orientations to an objective world they both relate to, one person is a first (that one who is *acted on*), and the other is a second (the one who is *doing the acting on*). Since each is also an actor in a physical world, the relationship to each other and to the world beyond must have two dimensions: subject-to-object (both potentially relating to the same object), and also subject-to-subject (also obliged to relate to each other, but now as second to first). Thirdness no longer has the same connotation it did initially, as merely acting in a material universe of gardens (or whatever other domain we choose, as long as it is a real physical environment made of non-human objects). Now there is a second facet of organizing, in that thirdness also gives meaning to interpersonal relations: inter-human as well as to subject–object association. We could further assume, if we wished, that each of those facets, in turn, is dependent on the other: good gardening means more than getting the operations right; it also means a cooperative effort on the part of the gardeners. Vice versa, success at doing the gardening skillfully presumably indexes and promotes cordial relationships between those involved. There is feedback. The relationship is reflexive (a topic we address in Chapter 3).

Inter-Group Collaboration

A second dimension of organizational collaboration is still being glossed over, however. Today's large organizations are not merely collections of individuals sorting out their interpersonal relations in the search for tolerable modes of collaboration that resolve the firstness–secondness puzzle, in a context of activity directed to dealing with an object. They are also compositions of *groupings* of such actors, forming networks whose nodes are local organizations that collectively address specialized tasks requiring technical skills of a high order (and therefore whose "thirdnesses" do not match up because their objects of attention, and how the latter are interpreted, differ).

An extension of Peirce's notion of thirdness thus raises two questions for organizational analysis. The first is this: if collaborative action involving more than one person implies a secondness-to-firstness precedence (one person acting, the other being acted on), why on earth would one of the two human actors take on the passive role of firstness, to be no more than he or she who is being acted on? Nobody should object to being the secondness, we are tempted to speculate: the one who *acts on* something or someone. That is surely how we all spontaneously would like to think of ourselves, as people who are proactive, constructive, creative. But to be merely the one who is acted on? That is definitely a less flattering prospect. So, empirically speaking, how *do* people work out their firstness/secondness? Said otherwise, how do they establish precedence?

That is one complication. But there is a second, as well. Just as, earlier, making a shift from one person concentrating on one object to two people focused on the same object necessitated a re-thinking of the role of thirdness in human affairs (and, even more important, our conception of thirdness as such), so now we are obliged to take into account the fact that any organization of some size must link up multiple communities of such relationships, each of them, if it has found its own *modus vivendi*, already internally structured, with its *own* established thirdness, or way of understanding its context. The same line of reasoning as before should thus apply. For the organization to exist, assuming that organization is by definition a network of such distinct, locally grounded relational groupings, then we should have to postulate a kind of super-thirdness, namely an over-arching thirdness that constitutes the meaning, not only of all the individual intra-group activities, but also of all the groupings of groups, and groupings of groupings, that arise as the "organization" pursues its goals.

Collaboration as Downlinking (Practice) and Uplinking (Coordination)

We could interpret these two as yet unexplained dimensions of organizational collaboration as the *downlink* question (how having to deal with a material world affects interpersonal accommodations, and, vice versa, how collaboration impacts on workplace modes of practice) and the *uplink* question (how the respective local organizations are reconciled to each other and to their work as part of an encompassing larger network of communities of work). We use the term "downlink" to indicate where activities manifest themselves, concretely, in dealing with a certain situation—planting shrubs, for example—as opposed to "uplink," which implies a preoccupation with clarifying and stating the global intentions of the organization as a whole—running a landscape operation with multiple teams, for instance. It is coordinating many activities, and the thirdness that is thereby implied, that establishes the organization as *itself* an actor. Thirdness is *not* to be confused, we emphasize, with context; thirdness is what gives meaning to activities, *and to the context they occur in*. It constitutes them as a practice, if we were to think of such a sharing of understanding about what one is doing, and with whom, in institutional terms.

Toward an Explanation

Our answer to the organizational puzzle we posed at the outset can now be summed up in a nutshell: organization is a collectively recognized thirdness, namely that which integrates all the activities making up a complex organization by giving them a sense. Seen this way, organization-as-thirdness refers to those sets of understandings, worked out in communication, that account for the meaningfulness of people's collaborative efforts: both how to interpret their relationship to the object that occupies their attention, and how to relate to each other as collaborators, in the small and in the large. As pragmatists, we assume no transcendental, eternally-true-for-all-times-and-places authenticity in this or that particular thirdness. That would be deductive, not abductive, thinking. Any given organization is a contingent, "for-now" accommodation to a set of circumstances, both external and internal, for which its immanent thirdness constitutes, for the moment, a stable basis of meaning for people's collaborative efforts. It provides both the semantic and pragmatic underpinning of the activity of a certain community of people, in a certain time and place, and engaged in a common enterprise. The system of meaning thus achieved will no longer be stable, we further hypothesize, when it becomes incompatible with those people's experience. When that happens, doubt will arise, and the authority of the organization will be undermined to a greater or lesser degree. Once doubt enters the picture, the search for a new stasis—a new foundation of thirdness—is on.

There is, however, doubt and DOUBT! In a very large organization, with many communities, linked more or less tightly with each other, it would be astonishing if (lower-case) doubt did not arise pretty much on a daily basis, somewhere in the network of relationships. The empirical sections of the book, beginning in Chapter 4, will explore, in a variety of organizational settings and situations, the dynamics of doubt and the search for the re-stabilization to be found in a new shared basis of thirdness. None of the research reported in this book documents the total failure of organization due to DOUBT (upper case), although we all know it too sometimes happens. Projects fail. Organizations do collapse and disappear. That is itself a topic worth addressing (Kirsch & Neff 2008), but we do not take it up for study in this book.

Our own immediate attention is directed to the development of a hypothesis that, where organization is concerned, the second-to-first relationship that Peirce perceived to be the crucial ground of meaning can be construed in another way, as the establishment of agency, or in other words one actor acting *for* another. It is in the construction of agency that organization discovers its *raison d'être* or thirdness, as both the ultimate source of agency, and that which informs the agency relationship with meaning—and authority. In the sections that follow, we first discuss the dynamics of agency and the mobilization of agents. Since an organization is not a human agent, we also explore the communicative processes of the establishment of authority and what we call the authoring of the organization.

Organization as a Thirdness: Establishing its Agency and its Authority

In 1994, Bruno Latour, writing in the tradition of the sociological study of science and technology, proposed that we conceptualize agency as the enrolment or mobilization of agents. Imagine, he suggested, an actor who has an objective, let us say a medical researcher seeking a treatment for bone deterioration. By him or herself alone, unaided by technology, the way to a solution is blocked. To achieve his or her objective, a treatment for bone disease (suppose we call the latter X), the scientist (B) is obliged to enlist another actor, for example stem cells (the "real" or effective actor in this mini-drama is thus A, the cells). To B's delight, and that of the research center where the scientist is employed (not to mention the medical community at large), the stem cells demonstrate a remarkable capacity to regenerate the injured or diseased bones. B's objective X has been attained, through the mobilization of A's agency.

The reasoning turns on the concept of *agent*. As even a cursory consultation of any dictionary will confirm, an agent is not merely that which acts, an actor; it is also that which acts *for*. A is the indispensable intermediary that enables B to act *on*, and *in*, a world: it is B's agent acting for him or her. Otherwise, B, the scientist, is frustrated in his or her quest.

The A–X relationship is the *sine qua non*, as Peirce explained, for any attribution of thirdness: an object, X (a firstness), and an entity, A, that acts on the object (a secondness), thus constituting a second-to-first couplet. What we have added in the stem cell example is a third person, an initiator, and a beneficiary, B (the scientist), whose objective can only be attained by the intervention of A acting on X. There is therefore one second–first relationship, A–X (stem cells, bones), now embedded within—a sub-set of—another second–first relationship, B–A (experimenter, stem cells). We term such embedding *imbrication*.

Imbrication Explained

Now, the crucial step to explaining organization. Note that, if we concentrate our immediate attention strictly on the interaction of stem cells and bones, A–X, *then the materiality of the scientist, B, is for the moment made irrelevant*. His or her "presence" in the actual events of the experiment (stem cell acting on bones) is merely that which furnishes its *purpose*, an immaterial thirdness or *meaning* that explains for us (and for the experimenter) what is going on. This is how we understand experimentation (the parallel with our earlier gardening example should be self-evident): the stem cell–bone interaction is given meaning for us by its *being* an "experiment." B, the experimenter, as the material agent who caused the experiment to occur in the first place, becomes, *in this embedded context*, only a conceptual thirdness: the reason *behind*, or the explanation *for*, the stem cell-and-bone drama now unfolding before us in the laboratory. The purposeful experimenter, in all his or her materiality, is for the moment backgrounded: reduced to a presumed scientific objective, along with those of the community of scientists he or she belongs to (not to mention the patients who hopefully await the outcome of the research).

We perceive the setting; *we* take the perspective. The stem cells (presumably!) are quite unconscious of all this. *They* merely act in the way they have been programmed to do, genetically, by nature. They do not need to understand anything about medical research to act. The scientist must (otherwise it would not be medical research).

Re-Framing Activity Changes Our Perception of the Materiality of Thirdness

If we shift our attention elsewhere than what is happening, materially, in the laboratory, to now concentrate instead on the perspective of the scientist who is accordingly perceived to be the actor, the thirdness that made it an "experiment" has been materialized: located in his or her person—that of an experimenter. What had seemed immaterial before, as long as our attention was limited to what the stem cell was doing— thirdness as merely a reason or explanation for what was happening in the lab—is made concrete by its embodiment in the person of the scientist, who is also, like the cells, an actor. All that has occurred is a shift in register, from attention to the actions of agent A (the stem cells) to those of the principal who mobilized the agent: B, the experimenter.

It is this shift of register, and thus our perception of where thirdness resides, that explains how *organization* emerges in communication. To see why, let us focus this time on the scientist and his or her relationship, no longer to the stem cells, but instead as himself or herself being a secondness who indeed manipulates the stem cells, but now in the context of an encompassing practice embodied in a scientific community—a new thirdness that now gives meaning to *his* or *her* actions. What we had before identified as the beneficiary B of the activity of the stem cells (the scientist) is now seen differently, as an agent acting for someone else, an A: initially, for example, the research center where he or she works (of course, the center could itself be seen as acting for a university, were we to extend the horizon even further). The secondness-to-firstness relationship that now becomes salient to us has changed level again, what we will describe below as a shift of frame: no longer a non-human actor acting on a non-human object (stem cell, bone); nor a human actor on a non-human actor (scientist, stem cell); but an organization acting on a human actor (research center, scientist). In this new imbrication, the research center can be interpreted as the beneficiary B (it will attract more research funds, for example, if the research the scientist is doing is successful). The center also becomes, in the context of the experiment, a thirdness, because it supplies the reason motivating, and thereby making sense of, the scientist's activities in the lab (he or she is carrying out its mandate, as an institution that furnishes credentials and access to resources).

Formalizing Imbrication

If we again extended the imbrication frame even further, we could then postulate one organization acting for another organization as also an A to a B (research center as an agent of the university, for example). If we were to formalize this successive embedding, we have a pattern of imbrication something like this:

- A–X (stem cell–bone);
- B [A–X] (stem cell–bone, in the context of an experiment);
- B [A/B [A–X]] (experimenter–experiment, in the context of a research center);
- B [A/B [A/B [A–X]]] (research center in the context of a university);
- B [A/B [A/B [A/B [A–X]]]] (university in the context of society);
- etc.

Framing

How we "read" what happens in the laboratory thus depends on how the reporter or observer chooses (with apologies to Erving Goffman, who invented the term) to *frame* the activity (more on his idea of frame in Chapter 2). Each pair of brackets defines a frame. Uplinking and downlinking from one frame to another implies pragmatically, however, more than an abstract exercise in logic. This is because each frame engenders, in the context of a practice, its own appropriate mode of discourse. The scientist uses a different kind of language in the laboratory, speaking to colleagues or an assistant there, than he or she does when he or she is interacting with colleagues doing other kinds of research in the center, or dealing with the administration, or talking to a reporter. These are not merely transpositions from one level to another. The shifts imply different modes of being—different domains of enactment. They imply, according to Goffman, *rekeying* to adapt to a new frame as the context is altered (some surprising organizational implications of these shifts of frame are explored in Chapter 5).

One of these manipulations, however, namely that which involves the establishment of a second-to-first delegation of agency linking an organization and an individual, differs from the others in a crucial respect. To conduct the experiment in the laboratory, the scientist had to intervene *physically*: collect the stem cells and grow a culture. The stem cells did not need to be moved by an intention to act; they do what they do. Intentionality is irrelevant, as long as we consider them.

The organization, however, cannot enlist the scientist in this same way, because it *cannot* act physically on him or her. The scientist, unlike the stem cell, must be motivated if he or she is to be mobilized. The organization can therefore only recruit *human beings*, because it is only they who can be motivated to act, with an intention, even a passion (for research, for example), arrived at through their self-conscious awareness that they are agents. Unless it can recruit *human* agents, the organization cannot emerge as a thirdness. It will be, as Latour put it, blocked. Its way will be barred. The only way for the center to enlist the scientist is to *communicate* with him or her, and to do so by using language. (How *language* works to enlist agents is the topic of Chapter 3.)

The Organization as Actor (and Ultimate Thirdness)

We have arrived at the essence of why there is an organizational puzzle.

On the one hand, if humans are the agents (those who act, the As) and the organization is the beneficiary B, then, following the same logic as before, we must attribute to the organization the property of having an intention (otherwise there would be no thirdness). It is the reason for, and conceptual presence behind, the scientist's experiments. The organization, however, because it is not an innately material agent— unlike the individual, located in a *here* and *now*, manifesting itself in flesh and blood—has *in and of itself* no alternative other than to mobilize human agents to realize its purposes. *It* cannot physically go out and collect the stem cells, much less grow them in the laboratory. If it cannot mobilize agents, human and non-human, to do so, *it* cannot be active in the world. Its purposes will never rise to the surface. It will then not even exist (a research center with no researchers? Nonsense). Since the human beings it mobilizes *are* grounded in materiality (they *do* have bodies, they *do* have intentions), they in turn are able to mobilize a variety of other agents that consist of tools, technologies, buildings, reports, and so on, which then magnify the power of the source, the organization, to act through its emissaries. By recruiting a great number of As, what Cooren (2006) calls a "plenum" of agents, the organization B will have constructed a network of actors, both human and non-human, involving many imbricated layers of delegation. The organization will have thereby established itself as an authentic actor, now materially and visibly extended in the real world, in the same way as scientists must also be if they are to be recognized as "scientists" (we know, after all, that people *are* scientists only because it is they who mobilize certain kinds of agents, or "actants," such as stem cells).[1]

---

1   We use the term *actants* in place of *actors* in order to emphasize that the "actors" in question are not necessarily human. Stem cells, for example, act, but they are not "actors" in the usual sense of that term.

The Authoring of Organization

Another puzzle now confronts us, however. Since the organization, B, is *not* a human agent, nor does it *really* have intentions, how does it formulate its objectives so that A will be able to recognize them as such? How, since it cannot ever use language to speak for itself, nor write a single sentence, does it manage to mobilize a network of actors that, in and through *their* actions, constitute *it* as an agent in its own right?

Two steps are involved. First, the organizational B must be recreated as the equivalent of a person so that it can enter human communication as an actor on the same terms as others. This is the sense of the court decision in 1886 that we referred to in the prologue. The organization is constituted as a "legal" person. We treat it *as if* it genuinely incorporated human motive and intentionality, like everyone else. We attribute to it human-like motivations of purpose, attitude, or emotion: "U.S. lumber group says . . . ," "The Coalition for Fair Lumber announced . . . ," "Penn West Energy Trust hopes . . . ," "Magna International Inc warned . . . ," "Stelco yesterday turned up the rhetoric sharply . . . ," "Sleeman Breweries Ltd said . . . ," "Washington says . . . ," "Ottawa said it believes . . . ," "3ComCorp announced . . . ," "The European Union aims to present its strategy . . ." (all examples taken from a single issue of one daily newspaper).

Second, to communicate its intentions and attitudes to its agents, the organization will have to count on someone (an A, or human actor) who is delegated, or who undertakes, to write and/or speak *for* it. But, on the same logic as before, that person is no more than its agent: a fallible human being. Yet, it is by the authoring of the perceptions and intentions of the organization (B) by someone (A), its agent, that organizational authority is established: a second-to-first relationship of the organization with all its agents, justified by a recognition of the legitimacy and authenticity of its mission and accomplished by its communicating with them.

The translation of the virtual intentions of the organization into the real words of its spokesperson(s) is, to reiterate the point, what establishes the organization as the source of an entire chain of agency. It further constitutes those to whom its purposes are addressed as being its agents. It thus renders their actions meaningful by supplying a thirdness that justifies their activities. Individual members and their groups as firstness; organizations (materialized by agents who author their intentions) as secondness; the purpose of the organization as the immaterial meaning *behind* those intentions, as thirdness—Peirce's "law." The organization is thus, at one and the same time, like the scientist, immaterial (a reason) and materialized (a tangible presence in the world of human actors, rendered visible there by its artifactual extensions, starting with the people who voice its intentions). This is what authoring accomplishes, because

it is in this way that the organization recruits its agents, and thus trans-
mutes itself into a powerful social actor and material presence in the
arena of public activities.

Motivating the Organization's Agents

This authored chain of agency then poses the question of volition: why
would the recipients of organizational agency buy into such an assertion
of authority. Why do they see it as being legitimate, since it constitutes
them as a first (*acted*-on) to the organizational second (*acting*-on-them)?
Why do all those As do what B is asking them to do: willingly take on
the role of firstness that we earlier described as so unappealing?

The answer given by Latour is that the action of A on X will not only
achieve B's objective; there are other objectives that may also be realized—
other Xs that may benefit the actor A as well as the beneficiary B. The
scientist in our example has his or her own objectives in conducting the
experiment. Up to this point, we have been emphasizing only one
dimension of agency: the indispensability of agent A to the furthering of
B's objectives. We can now state the corollary: *B is as indispensable to A
as A was to B*. It is by giving allegiance to B that A accomplishes a whole
spectrum of other objectives: a salary to support a standard of living;
status and prestige that define a social position; an authority to direct
activities of other human agents; a personal satisfaction in accomplishing
remarkable things that would have been impossible otherwise. And above
all, the delegation supplies a meaning to his or her actions.

This is also the answer to the question we posed earlier. Why do
people accept to be the firstness to the secondness of someone else (now
assuming this "someone else" to be the organization)? It is because, in
so doing, it simultaneously constitutes *them* as a secondness and thirdness
in their downlinked world. A syncretism is involved: each party to the
arrangement, the organization and its members, is constituted as an actor
in and by this mutuality. It is a quasi-Faustian deal: a tit-for-tat
arrangement, where each party achieves its ends through a mutual
accommodation. The organization has now been constituted as an actant.
But so have its members.

Authority

The keystone on which this entire analysis rests is authority: constituting
the organization as author of a text that, in turn, in acting for the organization, disseminates an understanding of its purposes and intentions. In
the absence of an authoring of the organization's intentions—transcribing
them into text, as we argue in Chapter 3—the entire chain of imbrication
is left without a common point of reference: its rationale dissolved,

fragmented into a kaleidoscope of diverse and incompatible thirdnesses. Chapter 2 therefore addresses the issue of authority and begins to explore how it is constructed in and through people's ongoing conversations and textual inscriptions. Those communicative activities, we will argue, are best seen as a "frame game," as people do their best to have their perspective accepted, not merely as *a* perspective, but as *the* perspective: a constitution of authority.

A Caution and a Clarification

We began our explanation for the emergence of organization by citing the concept of thirdness, as that which gives human activity meaning by seeing any *particular* event or object as an instance of a *general* concept or common understanding. Mindlessly working the soil is one thing. Gardening is another, because gardening is a practice that we have to learn if we are to do it skillfully. Conducting scientific experiments is another: to the mere observer watching the scientist at work, what he or she does has no real meaning until it is explained. Complex organization is a patchwork of practices, and therefore of modes of understanding.

That is one way we used the term "thirdness," reflecting only our understanding of what Peirce was telling us. Peirce, however, was not a student of communication. Nor was he preoccupied with understanding organization. We have had to innovate by giving thirdness a second meaning that is distinct from that of Peirce. The second connotation of thirdness we have introduced *embodies* it by re-locating it in the person of an actor. Whether one thinks of thirdness as explanation or reason, a kind of cognitive map that people use to guide their actions, or as the third person in a triad of actors, as we have just been arguing, depends on how you have framed any given event. To this explanation we have now added one additional clarification, that, in the physical absence of the person who incorporates organizational authority, a text can act as emissary.

Reading this, the reader might be tempted to think we have been deliberately magnifying complications. It is exactly the opposite. What we are seeking is not the most complex, but the simplest possible, explanation of organization. Unless we are ready to believe that it is some clever strategist, sitting in his or her comfortable quarters at Head Office, who designed the organizational structure, we are obliged to abandon our old prejudice of seeing organization as a kind of machine. We have to be bolder. The fact is that *everyone* who belongs to an organization is a strategist, and they are often as clever and sometimes even better educated than their hierarchical peers, especially in an economy where so many of the personnel are trained professionals and technicians. So, explaining the organization means comprehending how these people, as a complex action net (Czarniawska forthcoming), have *collectively* created it.

We understand that, in the transposition from thirdness-as-script, or why *individual* agents do what they do the way they do, to thirdness-as-actor, how purpose emerges in collective enterprise, we run the risk of creating a confusion. Is thirdness the conceptual basis that gives an activity a meaning, or is it literally the third person in an interpersonal conversation directed to some activity? Both, we answer. Why?

The reason is this. As Peirce understood thirdness, it was a framework of understanding, a "law" or "generality," that is the *conceptual* grounding for some individual's enactment of the environment he or she confronts. But then there is no organization at all. People converse with each other, perhaps, and they may influence each other's way of thinking, but everyone remains an independent actor, not a constituent of organization. For there to be organization, there must be coordination of action. But, for the action still to be meaningful, there must be a *single* thirdness, or at least an approximation: an agreed-upon program, project, mission, or script. The simplest explanation we could think of that would explain how this shift from individual to organizational is accomplished is to see it as one actor acting *for* another as his or her agent. Then, the plan or script is located in one person, while the other becomes responsible for its execution. All that the notion of imbrication does is to see the delegation of responsibility as the key mechanism explaining the emergence of more complex forms of organizing.

We do not assume that, because one actor accepts to be the agent for another, at the point of execution of a task, he or she has thus abandoned the right to make his or her own assessment of the arrangement. On the contrary. It is precisely this tension between an acceptance, for the moment, of authority as lodged in another, and a continuing sense of judgmental autonomy, that explains the principle of why each organization unfolds the way it does (the topic of our empirical Chapters 4–8).

Imbrication, we will discover in later chapters, generates its own internal dynamic. If it is one person acting for another, then it is *I* who cede to *you* the responsibility for defining the situation and taking decisions. The relationship is interpersonal. If there are three agencies involved, however, then both *you* and *I* are ceding to *him, her,* or *them* the authority for taking responsibility for our collective actions. When this extension occurs, we have transitioned from a local conversation and dialogue, where the assignment of authority is worked out interactively, to an extended arena of action, where the delegation of authority from one agency to another must be mediated by some kind of text, image, or whatever. Only in this extension via mediation can the larger units of organization we are familiar with emerge. But mediation brings with it complications, as the field studies in later chapters illustrate.

A Concluding Note

In this chapter, we have deliberately over-simplified the emergence of organizational authority, conceived as the thirdness that gives ultimate meaning to a diversified set of activities, typical of our world. We are aware, for example, that, if it was a huge corporation preoccupied with gardening, there would almost certainly be a landscape architect, a fertilization coordinator, a pruning engineer, a bush manager, and a pollination habitat maintenance specialist (more commonly referred to as a beekeeper!) (Andy Blundell, personal communication). But the same issue would arise: how to reconcile all these perspectives to produce a coherent result, one that conformed to the principles of good gardening. The usual way of thinking would postulate an overall project supervisor who organized the human and the non-human actors, to produce a harmonious outcome. The empirical research that makes up the bulk of this book does not confirm this simplifying assumption. What emerges from the field research we report on is something that has more the appearance of a complex game, where competing ways of framing the project collide with each other, generating a significant amount of friction. It is through this trial by fire that the organizational intention is forged, not uniquely through a unilateral assumption of unchecked authority. Chapter 2 establishes the theoretical grounds for this by examining the idea of a frame game: namely, how each actor in the arena of action constructs his or her thirdness, and manages or fails to have it prevail as *the* right way to think.

Suggested Supplementary Readings

Strongly recommended: Chapters 1 and 2 of Weick's *Sensemaking in Organizations* (1995).

The concept of imbrication was originally developed in Taylor's paper published in *The American Journal of Semiotics* (2001). For a brief background analysis of its relationship to organizational coorientation theory, see his analysis in the *Encyclopedia of Communication* (2009). Also relevant is Chapter 9 of May and Mumby's *Engaging Organizational Communication: Theory and Research* (Taylor 2005).

John Dewey's introductory chapter in the classic *Logic: The Theory of Inquiry* (1938) is readable and still relevant.

Bertilsson's 2004 article on Peirce offers a quite accessible guide to some of Peirce's principles of understanding. Robichaud's 2006 chapter in Cooren, Taylor, & Van Every provides a lucid explanation of thirdness.

Chapter 2

The Frame Game

How Playing *on* the Game While Playing *in* It Establishes and Distributes Organizational Authority

In Chapter 1, we sketched an image of an organization as a configuration of domains of action, linked to each other through the interlocking of delegations of agency that we called *imbrication*. In this chapter, we examine imbrication from the perspective of the communication processes that are constituted by, and in turn constitute, the linking. In doing so, we aim to illustrate the dynamic of organizing—imbrication as it is "enacted" in the hurly-burly of organizational life. Inevitably, we argue, because organizing involves establishing a delegation and distribution of agency—the goal being to have acceptance of a kind of organizational "map" that claims the authority to designate who is responsible for what—imbrication invites game-playing. Organizational games, what they are, and how they are played thus form the topic of the chapter. Our second purpose, from this analysis, is to establish a reasoned basis for the conduct of field research, as exemplified in later chapters: how to understand the imbrication that leads to a chaining of agency empirically, now from the point of view of an observing researcher.

The chapter is divided into four parts. In the first, we present three different conceptions of what a game is. As we do so, we will be exploring a view of organization as a domain of organizing, which we identify as "playing a frame game." In the second section of the chapter, we consider an implication of imbrication: the role of organization as what we term the absent (but present in the conversation) third party: the organization itself. In the third part of the chapter, we identify a variety of frame games. Finally, in part four, we consider the topic of how to conduct research in the situated organization.

Games as Situated Organizing

Von Neumann's Theory of Games[2]

Game theory was the brainchild of one of the most brilliant mathematicians of the twentieth century (some said of all time), John von Neumann (he was the same man who, among other notable achievements, seems to have written the first software for a fully functional digital computer). Von Neumann conceived of the communication situation as people engaged in a game, with potential winners and losers. Each player chooses a move in turn, and eventually there is an outcome. There is a reward, and it may be positive or negative, depending on the result: one can win and the other lose; both may win (in the sense of improving their situation); or both may lose (both end up worse off than when they began). By tracking people's choices as they play the game, you, the observer, can analyze their strategies as optimal or sub-optimal. You can also, and here was the appeal for a mathematician, "solve" the game.[3] The analyst can identify a best strategy for each player: the one that maximizes their gains and/or minimizes their losses.

Von Neumann's austere, formalized image of a game is, however, insensitive to realistic context and situational detail. The people are mere abstractions—the "players." The social or material context is irrelevant to the unfolding of the action. There is no object beyond the game, other than to succeed at it. The game is hermetic: self-contained, incapable of evolving from within. If we assumed the organization to be a pre-determined structure of roles and positions, without adaptability, then it could indeed be translated into a von Neumann game. If, however, as we do, we view organization as dynamic, emergent in and through communication, we need to take account of situation. For that we must turn to a different literature, that of pragmatism.

Situation and Why it Is Important: The Pragmatist View

The original proponents of a pragmatist way of thinking, as we have seen in Chapter 1, were C. S. Peirce and his contemporaries, William James, John Dewey, Charles Horton Cooley, and George Herbert Mead (although their respective interpretations of what pragmatism *is*, exactly, were far from identical). Peirce and Dewey were logicians and both published extensive treatments of their theories of logic. Their versions were, however, very much at odds with a concurrent tradition associated with such names as Frege, Russell and Whitehead, Brouwer, Tarski, and others. Lord Russell and Dewey, in fact, engaged in a heated polemic, with Russell pouring scorn on what he considered to be the fuzziness

---

2   The essential text is that of von Neumann and Morgenstern (1947 [1944]) but von Neumann's first treatment of games actually dates back to 1928. Von Neumann and Morgenstern's book is, however, the definitive version.

3   In principle, that is. The classic "solution" to a many-player (or "N-person") game is called a "Nash equilibrium," after its discoverer, John Nash. Recent work suggests, however, that the solution "is considered too difficult for practical computations" (Kalai 2009, based on work by Daskalakis, Goldberg, & Papadimitriou 2009).

of "Doctor" Dewey's ideas, and the latter responding in kind, giving as good as he got: pointing out all that Russell was glossing over.

Von Neumann was an inheritor of that tradition of formal logic originating in Frege and Russell. Pragmatism, however, sees logic differently, in a way that takes account of the role of situation in its constitution.

The difference between the two traditions, to oversimplify, is this. Classical logic, as interpreted by Frege, Russell and Whitehead, and others, has roots that can be traced back to Aristotle and the Greeks. If x implies y and a is an x, then, by extension, a must also be a y. It is a logic that is built up out of propositions that are either "true" or "false" and are linked to each other by a chain of implications. The root is mathematical, but there are also parallels with formal linguistic sentence analysis.

The movement known as "logical positivism" that developed in Vienna in the early twentieth century argued that some such system of logic is also the proper basis of scientific research (it is one reason why, for example, statistics has become the standard tool of the social sciences in contemporary research). Positivist research is based on the premise that, since a certain theory says that proposition A implies proposition B (the hypothesis), then, if you can find instances of a and b that either confirm, fail to confirm, or reject the hypothesis, statistically, then you are being "scientific" (Taylor & Gurd 1996).

Pragmatism in Dewey's Interpretation

Dewey proposed an alternative premise. His point of departure is the situation as *experienced* by someone who is resolving a doubt as to the validity of something that had previously been taken for granted. The horizon widens from no more than that which is being "objectively" observed (the "by whom" left *under*-stated) to now focus on the person who is doing the observing—a von Neumann, for example. Knowledge ceases to be a depersonalized, abstract entity grounded in formal logic and becomes instead the knowledge *of* someone, *with* a history, located *in* a society, and *about* something. As T. Burke (1994: 22) has observed, "Dewey followed Peirce in focusing his logical theory around the epistemological notion of inquiry, rather than on a study of syntax and formal proof procedures." In doing so, Dewey aimed to highlight situation, not to reduce it simply to references to the elements in a context, or the seeming "facts."

Situations, however, are, by definition even, emotionally loaded. According to T. Burke (1990: 22), writing about Dewey's ideas:

> Situations, occurring in the ongoing activities of some given organism/environment system, are instances or episodes (or "fields")

of disequilibrium, instability, imbalance, disintegration, disturbance, dysfunction, breakdown, etc.

Standard game theory assumes (to the extent that it makes any assumption at all on this score) a "neutral" point of view: that of an "objective" analyst. Pragmatism is different. As T. Burke (1990: 236) remarks,

> Inquiry, in general terms, is the resolution of uncertainty on the part of some inquiring agent. A situation in Dewey's view is problematic insofar as it is a locus of uncertainty within the overall conduct of normal affairs. Inquiry consists in transforming a situation into one that is not problematic ... This conception of inquiry has to be understood not so much as cognitive problem-solving but more generally in terms of an adaptive stabilization propensity of organism/environment systems.

Weick's concept of *enactment* (Weick 1979, 1995) furnishes an illustration of how pragmatism interprets situation. For Weick, as for Dewey, the environment is always under construction: a product, but also a determinant, of the sensemaking processes of organizational members. It is not an exercise in abstract logic but a result of what Pickering (1995) calls "a dance of agency": grounded in practice and not merely in cognition.

Focus and Frames

It is Barwise (1989: 224–225), writing in the same tradition as Burke, who provides the link to our earlier discussion of imbrication (Chapter 1). He emphasizes the role of *focus* in defining a situation, and furthermore focus and situation as constituting the perspective of an agent, or what we have called a "frame." The consequence of this is so important to our discussion that it is worth citing him at some length:

> It is virtually a tautology to observe that inquiry, which is what I take fact finding to be, always takes place by a cognitive agent embedded in an environment. The facts discovered, by whatever means, serve to classify the current focus situation as being one way or another. The point here is that facts are always facts concerning a portion of an agent's embedding environment, namely, the current focus situation. But the facts are not themselves situations, that is, portions of the world. Rather, they arise out of the interaction of an inquiring agent and his embedding environment. (p. 225)

This is a radical move away from a view of truth as merely interconnected objective facts, linked by rules of implication: the cornerstone of positivist research. For a communication-oriented investigator, it opens up a very different view on organization, and on inquiry into organizational process. That "view" comes, in other words, with an implication that we take to be fundamental to the conduct of inquiry: there *is* no "objective" perspective on organization—it all depends on how the situation is read, by whom, and what they focus on. The "situation" of the stem cell (Chapter 1) was one thing, when we focused on it as it affected bone structure. Turning our attention to the experimenter highlighted another situation, because our focus had shifted. A re-framing was implied: seeing the situation through a different lens. Furthermore, it is a "situation" for the stem cell experimenter, presumably, because something is not quite going right and needs to be dealt with: a mistake had been made, perhaps, endangering the validity of the experiment, or the equipment has broken down. The research center administrator, we could speculate, confronts a different situation from that of the scientist, perhaps a budget crunch. The research that the experimenter is engaged in, seen from the perspective of the center's funding, now takes on a different connotation for the manager from that of the scientist in the laboratory: it could even, perhaps, open the door to new funding.

To reiterate, there is no magical vantage point from which to investigate the organization, one where we, as observers or "inquirers," can position ourselves as being in the "right" place, with the "right" focus. But the same principle applies equally to the members themselves: they too experience their organization as situations, and the "facts" they each separately bring into focus are never going to be colored the same way. The person who declares that such-and-such is what the organization is doing, or wants to do, manages to arrive at this perception by highlighting certain traits of the context that appear to him or her to be salient, while ignoring others. The "facts" they thus present as gospel truth are what constitute it as a "situation" (for them). There is no reason to suppose, however, that the sensemaker's neighbor, although ostensibly located in the "same" situation, is necessarily focusing on the same "facts," or even shares the same perception of what the situation is. In fact, the contrary is often the more plausible case, where management is concerned. Even managers who work together every day may see the situation differently, if only because they have contrasting responsibilities. Nor is it always easy to envisage how their respective visions might be reconciled, other than practically, through negotiation, as they play the management game (Cooren & Taylor 2000; Katambwe & Taylor 2006; Taylor & Robichaud 2007; Taylor & Virgili 2008).

Erving Goffman's conceptualization of games, coming as it was out of the pragmatist tradition at the University of Chicago, was thus quite different from von Neumann's, even though it was ostensibly inspired by his reading of the latter's theory.

Goffman's Interpretation of Game Theory

Von Neumann's interest in game theory was that of a mathematician and logician. Games, however, are also typically social encounters (bridge players will understand). The sociologist, Erving Goffman, made a connection between the abstract theory of games and its application to actual social practice in a book published in 1959 and entitled *The Presentation of Self in Everyday Life* (he later expanded his ideas in other books, *Strategic Interaction*, 1969; *Frame Analysis*, 1974; and *Forms of Talk*, 1981).

Imagine, Goffman (1959) began in his first chapter, a situation where "an individual enters the presence of others." The people there are going to seek information about him or her: "socio-economic status, conception of self, attitude toward them, competence, trustworthiness." The gleaning of information that people now make, face to face with the other person, has one purpose: to predict "what he will expect of them and what they may expect of him." Only when armed with this information will they "know how best to act in order to call forth a desired response" (p. 1).

That is just the beginning. The interaction continues. It is, as Goffman put it, "a kind of information game—a potentially infinite cycle of concealment, discovery, false revelation, and rediscovery" (p. 8).

An information game is thus defined as an interplay of *expression* (speaking and acting) and *impression* (trying to read the game plan of the other based on his or her words and actions): an open-ended process composed of moves and counter-moves. As in any game, you assume that the other person has his or her own objectives and agenda. Your task is to "read" what he or she is up to, based on your interpretation of the explicit moves your opposite number makes.

Precedence, or what we called in the previous chapter the social dimension of the second-to-first relationship, is up for grabs. The game is about whose interpretation will dominate. Each person tries to create "a definition of the situation" (Goffman 1959: 4) that will best serve his or her own interests. Whenever you commit yourself to communication you are thus defining, implicitly, the situation as you experience it. But when the next person speaks, their definition of the situation builds on, and, if it becomes accepted, incorporates yours as a component. One person's *expressions* are now read, and translated into someone else's *impressions*: something to be reconstructed in the meaning system of the hearer, who in turn must project his or her own vision.

A kind of metacommunicational dynamic (we will explain the concept of metacommunication later) is therefore intrinsic to the expression–

impression interplay: a dynamic involving whose interpretation of the situation will become the accepted one as the conversation unfolds. As Goffman put it, "We live by inference" (1959: 3). "Of course," he wrote, we also "live by inference in [our] dealings with the physical world, but it is only in the world of social interaction that the objects about which [we] make inferences will purposely facilitate and hinder this inferential process" (1959: 3).

The Information Game and Thirdness

There is a consequence in the wider arena of organizational sensemaking that Goffman did not delve into, but that his analysis suggests. If, as we have observed, the "definition of the situation" is how one manager, let us say a CEO, is constructing in his or her talk the intention of the organization he or she has been authorized to embody, then we can interpret Goffman as saying that such a definition is susceptible to an unlimited sequence of subsequent reinterpretations. Goffman's "definition of the situation" can therefore be construed as an evocation of thirdness, as Peirce understood that term, because it aims to establish what the context is, and people's implied identity within it: make sense *of* the interaction from *within* the interaction.

For Goffman, that reinterpretation process is exactly what is at stake. As a result, the managerial meta-conversation, as he perceived it, lacks the kind of closure that work in a real material environment imposes. The gardener's garden flourishes, or withers. The scientist's experiment succeeds, or fails. The executive's interventions are not quite so easy to evaluate, however, because his or her words are themselves one further move in a game of expressions and impressions. They may, for example, claim to be *ex*pressed in a document (a plan, a strategy, a budget, a contract). The document means nothing, however, until it is read and interpreted—*im*pressed—by those to whom it is addressed.

When the competition to establish the situation so that it conforms to one's own agenda is thought of as playing a game, it sounds like a formula for permanent managerial conflict. It might be, except that we are forgetting a precondition of all games: the role of the game itself. If the game stopped, all pretension to sociality would collapse, and interaction would deteriorate into chaos. Everybody, therefore, has a stake in keeping the game going, because otherwise winning it has no meaning. So the "players" in the organization's conversational exchanges live with a constraint: play the game, do so in a way that is advantageous in asserting your own identity, but don't push the limits so far that the game ends. Live with some residual ambiguity (Eisenberg 2007).

Anyway, as Goffman observed, things settle down: "Ordinarily the definitions of the situation projected by the several different participants are sufficiently attuned to one another so that open contradiction will not occur" (1959: 9). This is especially true where people meet and interact every day, because, after a while, they more or less understand each other's game. They can relax. They may not always agree, but there are many areas where they do (and they may later need the others as allies). Except, of course, they can never be totally sure they really *do* know everything that is behind other people's behavior. If they did, there would be no stories of misunderstanding, deception, and betrayal: no novels, films, or TV dramas that delve into the intricacies of human motive and behavior.

From this analysis, Goffman constructed his own interpretation of human interaction. Face-to-face interaction, he wrote, "may be roughly defined as the reciprocal influence of individuals upon one another's actions when in one another's immediate physical presence" (1959: 15). There is ambiguity, but it can be tolerated. Indeed, a measure of ambiguity seems, on Goffman's analysis, to be indispensable to continued harmonious interaction.

Organizational discourse is thus always potentially game-oriented: how one *expresses* oneself is the source of the *impressions* others are forming, and vice versa. Communication is not merely an "exchange or flow of information," as it has often been construed in the literature. It involves as well the construction of a relationship in which the partners are both united by their collaboration in maintaining the game, and yet divided by their separate agendas and identities. Each acts, but always, even in the absence of an explicit strategy, within a structured arena that they are themselves reconstructing by their continued playing.

Goffman recognized that such interdependence has its own logic, in that, as the relationships which working together in some environment continue to develop, the continuity that this implies becomes itself a kind of thirdness. Once everyone shares roughly the same interpretation of the context within which they are interacting, a collective thirdness is on its way to being established. Not all the rules of a game need to be written down. The customary practices that grow up over time themselves *become* the rules—a self-generating law of meaning. To use a different terminology, the practices take on an institutional coloring, with all the elasticity, resistance to change, which that implies.

Goffman's analysis, even though it limits itself to interpersonal interaction and ignores any larger organizational context, can also be seen as one way to understand the link between organizational context and communication. What people are doing when they interact with each other, whether in face-to-face interaction or in the extended text-mediated networks of an organization, is trying to have *their* framing of the situation accepted. This is because, by doing so, they establish reciprocal identities and purposes—impose *their* interpretation of thirdness, in a word. If their frame becomes the norm, then they will also have established their authority. That is why we use the expression "frame game."

What Goffman introduced that had been missing in the von Neumann version of a game was the salience of situation. But Goffman also signaled the central role of metacommunication (although that was not a term he used)—communication that takes itself as its topic—in interactive sequences where identity and interest are being affirmed and/or asserted. Before we address that implication of his thought, however, we need to present a third conception of game: a "language game."

Wittgenstein's Concept of a Game—a "Language Game"

There is, historically, a third way of thinking about a game, now from a different communicational point of view than either von Neumann's or Goffman's. It was that of a brilliant and tragic European philosopher whose most influential work appeared only after his death—1958 in its English translation—Ludwig Wittgenstein. He introduced the concept of a "language game" (Wittgenstein 1958: 11).

His innovation was radical because it contradicts, and is subtler than, our usual notion of what language is and how it works. Traditional views of language, in linguistics but also in the social sciences, pictured it as a set of symbolic constructions that refer to things. Philosophers were accordingly prone to long disquisitions on whether the expression "the present king of France" referred to something or not, and therefore whether the phrase could be said to have any meaning, since France has not had a king since the eighteenth century and does not have one now. The phrase thus refers to nothing real. Or, another example, what does the word "unicorn" refer to? Since there *are* no unicorns, they are a mythical construction, and the word therefore does not have an actual reference. Or does it?

It was the kind of arcane issue traditional philosophers of language could get their teeth into!

Wittgenstein brushed this debate aside. Instead, in his interpretation, "the speaking of language is part of an activity" (1958: 11). "To imagine a language," he wrote, "means to imagine a form of life" (1958: 8). Words are "tools" (1958: 6). If you want to know what a word or an expression *means*, therefore, don't turn to the dictionary: go *look* and *listen* to find out how people use it in *some context*, in the act of accomplishing *something*. Or perhaps we should have phrased that the other way around: it is the compilers of dictionaries who are continually confronted with the challenge of keeping up with how people are now using (or no longer using) such-and-such an expression. The games of language are thus practices, ways of doing an activity: things like "giving orders, and obeying them, describing the appearance of an object, or giving its measurements ... reporting an event, speculating about an event ... making a joke; telling it ..." (1958: 11).

The importance of grasping Wittgenstein's reasoning, for an organizational communication theorist and researcher, is this. We share a language when (and because) we share a domain of practice, a "form of life." If we don't participate in the same practice, then it is not the same form of life, and, even when we use the "same" words, they do not mean the same! As Wittgenstein put it, "Language is a labyrinth of paths. You approach from one side and know your way about; you approach the same place from another side and no longer know your way about" (p. 82).

"Labyrinth of paths"? It sounds suspiciously like a map—the kind of "map" that people are implicitly using as they react to a situation, to guide their navigation of it, as they thread their way through its pathways: home, work, leisure, family, all those patterned occasions that make their experience meaningful.

We will come back shortly to the importance of language as furnishing a map where people are enabled to make sense of their experience, and why it has organizational significance. First, however, we need to conclude our discussion of the dynamic of games, now from the perspective of a different observer, Gregory Bateson.

Bateson and Metacommunication

What Wittgenstein adds to our understanding of human interaction, which is at best merely implicit in Goffman, is this. Goffman saw the game of organizing as an ongoing interplay of expression–impression. Wittgenstein understood this differently, as a dynamic that is constituted in language. Language accomplishes a fundamental shift. On the one hand, as Wittgenstein insisted from the outset, it is an instrumentality for people who do things, a builder and his assistant, for example, as they coordinate their actions to get their work done (this is his point of departure in his book). On the other hand, both builder and assistant are themselves constructions of language, fully as much as is what they are doing. People, in other words, both are components *in* a situation, and yet simultaneously constitute the parameters *of* that same situation.

It was Bateson (1935, 1972) who saw the organizational implications of this enablement of language, and its strategic consequences, as an effect of what he called "metacommunication." He first introduced the concept of metacommunication to explain his findings as an anthropologist, studying inter-tribal relationships, in the South Pacific. It was later adopted by a branch of family analysis, known as the Palo Alto school (Watzlawick, Beavin, & Jackson 1967), where it became a key unit of analysis of family dynamics. Metacommunication, as Bateson had conceived the idea, is the folding back of a conversation on itself: taking itself as its topic. People, as he saw it, are always *both* communicating *and* metacommunicating.

Bateson's inspiration for the idea of metacommunication originated in his reading of explorations in formal logic, exemplified by one of the oldest of all logical puzzles, the so-called "Cretan paradox." Put simply, the paradox is illustrated by the assertion: "I am lying." If you are *really* lying, it follows logically, then actually you are telling the truth, since, if what you said ("I am lying") is *true*, then you cannot be actually lying, since what you said *is* true. You are telling the truth: you *are* lying. Since, on the other hand, you *are* telling the truth, then you must be lying, because you said you were, and, since you were telling the *truth,* what you said ("I am lying") must be true!

One's head buzzes!

The paradox arises because you are *saying something* about yourself *saying something*. It is the self-reference that is the problem. Bateson's innovation was to realize that paradox is a parasite that potentially infects all acts of communication, simply because communication is enabled by language, and language is always inherently capable of doubling back on itself to say things about itself, true *and* false.

One way to conceptualize metacommunication, to again draw on Goffman's work, is to think of it as framing. As long as the conversation is in an already established and shared (and thus out-of-consciousness) frame, there is nothing "meta" about it. It is just people talking in a jointly maintained and well-understood situation where they confront some problem or challenge (or maybe, alternatively, they are just chatting idly; the difference is not crucial). When one of them takes their own *in*-frame communication as their topic, however, they thereby step *out*-of-frame, since in commenting on their own conversation they have introduced a new frame, that of an external observer, someone commenting *on* their interaction as if they stood outside it. It is as though now they are simultaneously *in* and *out*. Our imaginary stem cell looks the scientist in the eye and says, "You are not doing the experiment right, boss; you need to start over. Here is how you *should* be dealing with me and the bones . . ." The cell, which we have previously thought of as merely an agent mobilized by the researcher in seeking a treatment for bone disease, has stepped out of that frame and, metacommunicatively, introduced a different one where now it is the *cell* who is the expert, and the experimenter is merely an agent. Since the two are doing this shifting of perspective from *within* a single shared frame, they now become simultaneously *in*-frame and *out*-of-frame: *in* it, but now reflexively taking *it* as topic. The cell is playing a "frame game": playing *on* the game while still playing *in* it.

People do this all the time: they say, "What I meant was x, y (or whatever)," or "I hope you didn't mean to imply z!" It is all about establishing an understanding, not merely conceptual, but practical: configuring not only the objects of attention people address, but themselves as well, as agents who relate to each other, forming as they do a situated mini-organization.

Sometimes, however, metacommunication is more complicated—contestatory.

Schismogenesis

Bateson (1935, 1972) called any breakdown of understanding leading to more or less overt, more or less veiled, conflict, *schismogenesis*, or a collapse of sociality and the opening up of a gulf of misunderstanding.

Symmetrical schismogenesis, as Bateson observed it in his research on tribal territorial conflict, occurs when one party makes an aggressive interactive move that is countered by an even more aggressive response, which in turn motivates an even stronger response, and so on. Neither party backs down, and the contest escalates.

Complementary schismogenesis occurs when one party assumes a primary or "one-up" position and the other abjectly accepts the corresponding inferior, "one-down" position (Watzlawick, Beavin, & Jackson 1967), thus inviting abuse of authority on the part of the other.

Both kinds of schismogenesis, although mutually constructed in and by people's interactions, have dysfunctional consequences, either because the organization's discourse becomes riven by destructive controversy, or when those who are "down" are no longer capable of influencing those who are "up." Either way, it is the organization itself that is at risk, since the accommodation that is indispensable to productive collaboration is lost. The reason for this inherent fragility of all human organization is that organizing, using language or not, always implies precedence, as one of Bateson's disciples, Haley (1976), observed:

> When one is observing people who have a history and a future together, one sees that they follow organized ways of behaving with one another. If there is any generalization that applies to men and other animals, it is that all creatures capable of learning are compelled to organize. To be organized means to follow patterned, redundant ways of behaving and to exist in a hierarchy. Creatures that organize together form a status, or power, hierarchy with someone above him and someone below him. Although groups will have more than one hierarchy because of different functions, the existence of hierarchy is inevitable because it is in the nature of organization that it be hierarchical. We may dream of a society in which all creatures are

equal, but on this earth there is status and precedence and inequality among all creatures. (pp. 100–101)

Schismogenesis is not inevitable, of course. There is another possibility, which Bateson calls *reciprocity*. Here is how he explains it: "In every single instance the behavior is asymmetrical, but symmetry is regained over a large number of instances" (1972: 69). People find a compromise, in other words, and the organization goes on. How this give-and-take is accomplished, in practice, is a topic that is addressed in every one of the later chapters where field research is described.

To Summarize

We have presented three conceptions of game, from three quite distinct perspectives. Rather than treat them as different theories, however, we view them instead as complementary dimensions of a more comprehensive view of games. Von Neumann concentrated on the patterning of successive "moves." Goffman was fascinated by the up-close move-making that is illustrated best in interpersonal communication. Wittgenstein reminded us that moves involve the expert use of language and are only made comprehensible when we take account of the grounding of all language use in a practice (and vice versa). Von Neumann told us that organizational process—the game—has a structure. Goffman modified this view by showing us that the structure emerges in process and, since the process is continually generating its own restructuring from within the game framework (and that of the organization), it is malleable. Bateson added the insight that people, using language, are actually capable of consciously re-writing the game they are playing in, by "meta-ing" it.

All three perspectives are essential to organizational communication analysis. Each furnishes clues to the process view of organization, as "organizing." As Chapters 4–8 will illustrate, games get played out over time (von Neumann) and they are intensely involving at the level of interpersonal interaction (Goffman). Because language games are grounded in a practice that they both index and constitute, the language use that different communities develop also implies that the meaning of words is not directly transferable from one situation to another (Wittgenstein, Bateson).

What we have been addressing to this point, however, is merely the dynamic of *organizing*. We have described it as game-playing, since there is a stake. Each of those involved is establishing, as Goffman described, their position with respect to the others: all of them presenting and defending a "face" (in the sense of status). They communicate, and as they do, Wittgenstein argued, they are constituting reality for themselves, both with respect to an external world, and to themselves as an essential component of that world. It is a vulnerable constitution of society, however, since, as Bateson argued, it incorporates, intrinsically, the potential for breakdown—a tendency to schismogenesis.

Von Neumann, Goffman, Wittgenstein, and Bateson demonstrated the contingency of organizing: its inherently *situated* character. The image of organization that emerges is that of a configuration of agencies and objects that is continually under construction. What none of their analysis addresses, however, is the issue of how the organization as an *entity* emerges in this inter-weaving of conversation: how it becomes an actor in its own right, with its own identity and "personality," with attitudes and purposes that it too asserts in the ongoing talk of people—not merely constituting the "game," but the players in it as well (illustrating reflexivity, a topic addressed in Chapter 3). We have, in other words, established organization as situated, but we have not yet explained it as source of, and justification for, the chain of imbrications.

The Organization as the Absent (but Present) Third Party

Let us return for a moment to a context that we alluded to in Chapter 1: gardening. Suppose two people are involved (if there were fewer than two, there would be no need for communication). The first is the owner of a large property. She has realized that the land at the rear of her house would make a beautiful garden. Having herself no taste for, nor experience in, gardening on this scale, she decides to employ a specialist (let us make it a *he* for convenience of reference—the gender of the two is irrelevant). They are now partners in a transaction where he is her agent, but she depends on his experience and skill. She has a subjective investment in the future garden because it is an extension of her personality. It *belongs* to her. His actions will therefore have consequences for her, positive and/or negative.

The gardener, on the other hand, will be treating the garden as *his* object. However, since it was *she* who hired *him*, she was thus acting *on* him, making him *her* object—an agent. Their relationship is what we meant by imbricated: one relationship, gardener acting on garden, embedding within another, owner of garden acting on gardener.

Because the gardener acts on the garden, alternatively, *she*, by a slight extension of the logic of the situation, as its owner, becomes *his* object. And since *he* is *her* object (*she* employed him and thus acted on *him*: he is here at her bidding), the snake seems to be swallowing itself!

They each, owner and gardener, see the project through a different lens, with a different focus. Neither view is logically reducible to the other, even though each is the indispensable complement to the other. It is the same garden but yet, since it is not framed in the same way, it is not exactly the "same." There are two independently constituted situations: the owner's and the gardener's. Since each is contingent on the other, the mutuality becomes itself, metacommunicatively, also a situation: what we have earlier described as an effect of "worldview" (Taylor 1993; Taylor, Gurd, & Bardini 1997). The two interlocked agencies, owner and gardener, thus constitute a mini-organization of their own.

Now, however, let us introduce a complication.

While the work is going on, the owner will be absent from her home on an extended trip, and so she hires someone, an agent, to represent her in all further dealings with the gardening specialist. There is a written contract that specifies the work to be done, when and for how much, duly negotiated and signed in the presence of a notary. Just before she leaves, she hands the contract over to her delegated agent, with instructions to make sure the gardener's work is in conformity with the agreed-upon terms. For convenience sake, let us illustrate this relationship graphically: X is the garden; A[X is the gardener; A*/B is the interaction between delegated agent and specialist gardener; and B*[A* is the owner's relationship with her agent. The composite relationship reads as follows:

B*[A*/B[A–X]]

Note that, in the actual conversation involving gardener and owner representative, neither the garden itself (being inert) nor the owner (being absent) participate overtly: the garden because it cannot (it is merely the object to be addressed), and the owner because she is not physically present and so cannot join the conversation. Because of her interest in the garden, she has become an "absent (but present) third party" in the ensuing arena of interaction between her agent and the gardener.

Why Imbrication Typically Produces Frame Games

Suppose now that the owner's agent complains to the gardener that, according to the agreement, the latter specifies Himalayan violets in such-and-such a location, and he has failed to live up to his commitment. The gardener expostulates that his opposite number obviously knows nothing about gardening: violets can only be planted in the spring, and it is, through no fault of his, totally the wrong time of the year now, so instead the gardener has filled in temporarily with a substitute and he has had to absorb the additional cost himself. "I'm sorry," retorts the owner rep, "I have my marching orders, and you are going to have to respect the terms of the agreement."

They are playing a frame game. Each has evoked a frame that justifies an interpretation: B[A–X] in the gardener's case; B*[A* where the delegated spokesperson is concerned. In the resulting impasse, the owner has become an absent third party, made present, however, in the signed agreement, which is, as Goffman showed, open to interpretation, like any other token of communication. Since *no* written agreement, however elaborated, can ever capture every contingency, there is ample room left for ambiguity and disagreement—and an ensuing game.

Now suppose that, instead of the owner being an individual, the property belongs to a limited company, a firm. The company, unlike the woman who owned the property, is *never* going to "return home." It can only *ever* be present in the agent–gardener frame game as an absent third party: rendered present in their talk because they evoke it continually as furnishing the justification for their own position. Each claims the organization as the basis for its rationale and the justification for its interpretation: the gardener because he is thinking first and foremost, he protests, of the welfare of the garden and therefore of the owner; the delegated agent because she is assuming, as its representative, the owner's perspective.

The third party, the organization, is present only in the sense that it furnishes the rationale for each of their interpretations. And yet the organization *itself*—that enigmatic sphinx!—is forever silent; it invariably leaves the enunciation of *its* thirdness to its spokespersons. The result is a situation pregnant with the potential for conflict (a dispute that could even end up in small claims court) or abuse (the gardener, for example, cheats, and the owner's agent lets him get away with it). Bateson, as we have seen, had a name for this kind of breakdown of relationship: schismogenesis.

How the Organization Becomes Present in the Conversation Even in its Absence

Let us now pick up the thread we left undeveloped at the end of our discussion of Wittgenstein's work: language as a "labyrinth of paths," or how to "know your way about." Think of the gardener's image of his project: he knows, from experience, "his way about gardening." The owner's agent, to use Wittgenstein's phrase again, is "approaching the same place from another side" and so she "no longer knows the same way about" that the gardener had in mind. Their dispute over whose interpretation of "the way about" can only be resolved by an adjudication involving the absent third party. That "party," however, only becomes present vicariously in the written agreement that specified, in whatever detail, the pathways the project should follow.

Such a "labyrinth of paths," enabling people to "know their way about," is what we term a *map*. The stake of every organizational frame game thus becomes, as our example illustrates, interpreting and authenticating the organizational "map." It becomes a frame game because maps only work through being read and interpreted.

An organizational map can claim to govern the actions of every member and every community, however, only when it has been *legitimated* as the authentic statement of the organization's intention and understanding (like the contract the owner wrote with the gardener). And since the map defines, not only pathways, but also identities, domains of authority, and statuses, it follows that everyone involved has a stake in its authoring.

As long as interaction is strictly local, mediated by the usual modes of conversation, the "map" need not be written down, any more than it was for the gardener, who knows his trade so well that the "map" has been internalized. It is when he enters into conversation with others who do not share his experience that an issue is raised. Now there must be an explicit documentary inscription of some kind that people in different circumstances can all consult. The map constitutes their common frame of reference: how they will resolve their differences. What our gardening example was also meant to show, however, is that, no matter how meticulously constructed, the "map" never quite corresponds to the territory (Weick 1979). The disparity between map and reality is what triggers a frame game. Interpreting the map in your favor is how you establish your area of discretion, and your authority.

So let's see what we know generally about maps (for a more extended discussion, see our 2000 book, *The Emergent Organization*, Chapter 9, based on Wood 1992).

Maps

First, what distinguishes a "real" map, as opposed to its virtual equivalent (merely "what people know"), is that it must be inscribed on some permanent, or at least semi-permanent, medium: paper, typically, although there are other kinds of materialization that work just as well, such as Websites, GPS, and signage. To write the representation down, however, constitutes a very considerable reduction in complexity from the infinitely greater capacity of the human experience, as people have internalized it. Some things must be highlighted, others ignored. Its advantage is that the representation, having been written down, can now become a reference for many, many people. It is no longer one person's idiosyncratic experience of a place. It claims objectivity: what *everybody* knows. It claims *authority*.

Second, however, since maps are artifacts (somebody had to have drawn them), there had to have been a map-maker—an *author*. That which is to be mapped had to have been seen from a perspective, that of its author.

Third (and this is the crucial point for our understanding of organizational games), once the map exists—has been authored—the author, the map-maker, must disappear from view: literally vanish from sight. Only in this way can the map be "naturalized": becoming "what everybody knows," and not merely how one person sees the situation. (Note the advantage of anonymity: you can argue with a map-maker. It is not so easy to argue with a map. It doesn't answer back. It just sits there: immobile, impervious to influence—and imperious in its seeming omniscience, like the notarized agreement the owner and the gardener signed.)

To understand the implications of naturalization, think back again to our characterization of the experiment in stem cell research. As long as we excluded the person of the experimenter from view, then what made it an "experiment" was that it conformed to certain general properties of scientific research that we know about. Thirdness was no more than what we understand to be the "law" of such research, and how it unfolds. The minute, however, we enlarged the frame to include the experimenter, the thirdness now appeared to be embodied in his or her person, and his or her interpretation is open to questioning because it *is* a perspective, not an objective reality.

It works the same with maps. They claim to embody the general knowledge belonging to everybody. Until, of course, we peek behind the screen of the map to ask about the motives and competence of the hidden map-maker. The map claims the authority of thirdness, as we have been thinking of it in Chapter 1: that which gives meaning to the situation. If, instead, we pull back the curtain to highlight the maker of the map, he or she becomes a fallible human being: not the wonderful Wizard of Oz, but merely a "little old man from Omaha."

So making the map is a source of real power—of covert *authority*. Because it is infallible, it is a way to avoid debate, or to have one's motives or knowledge interrogated.

Fourth, organizational maps identify ownership, at a location. "This is where Research and Development takes place; here Sales is located; this is where Policy is developed." Ownership, in turn, establishes the ground for claims of authority, as again any bureaucrat knows: "I'm in charge of this file." Authoring a map, and having it naturalized, is one way that authority can be selectively distributed among members, and thus constitute them as a hierarchy (with, to be sure, the author–map-maker at the summit).

Fifth, and finally, if maps are to claim authority (and in this way consolidate the authority of the author), they must nevertheless be socially validated. They have to be *recognized* as legitimate, taken-for-granted repesentations if they are to work. They may start as artifacts but, until they are accorded the status of facts, they are no more than opinion.

What we will discover, in later chapters, is that validation is a process, and that, as a result, maps are continually in the process of reconstruction, if only because the lived variety of any very large organization is so extensive that it resists being easily reduced to standardization.

We will encounter a variety of maps in Part Two, as we describe field research: a campaign plan; a poster; a formal budget and the accounts that it subsequently exacts; a corporate plan for product development (actually referred to in that organization as a "roadmap"); a software system designed to integrate all the operations of a manufacturing company; and a regional land-use map (again specified as a map), meant to ease relations between landowners and drill operations by petroleum companies.

Summary

Our initial version of the organizational "game" portrayed it as process, but, as we saw, process, because it involves precedence, is susceptible to schismogenesis. What we have now added to this initial formulation is that organization is not merely the context of a game, but simultaneously a player in it. It enters its own game, however, only as an absent third person, made present in its evocation by those who do play in it. It is the indispensable third person, the arbiter—referee, judge, umpire—to whom disputes may be referred for adjudication. It is in this way that order and continuity are sustained. Since, however, the organization can only be present in its conversations through a textual evocation of its judgments, the frame game consists in authoring and naturalizing its text (what we have called the "organizational map"): a reflexive loop, described in Chapter 3.

Initially, it may seem a stretch to think of the organization as the third person in its own conversations, even though that is what we do spontaneously whenever we assert, for example, that Company A's position in such-and-such a marketplace is being threatened by Company B, as if it were like "Margaret's" role in the company being undermined by "Vincent." But, as we will argue in Chapter 3, citing the pragmatist George Herbert Mead, that is the point: our identities are all contingent on the organizing process. As Goffman understood, in the absence of the game there *is* no sociality—nor personality.

Varieties of Organizational Frame Games

In large organizations, the frame game is played out interactively in conversational exchanges, both mediated and face-to-face, all of which involve those persons who constitute the spokespersons who are entitled to represent their constituencies of interest and communities of practice and sensemaking. The elementary unit of interaction in any multi-level chain of imbrication is, as we have described, B*[A*/B[A–X]], where B represents [A–X], and A* represents B*. (Note that, if you read this expression from left to right, you take a managerial perspective; if from right to left, that of the practitioners.) B's authority is constituted in its speaking for [A–X]: reporting, for example, on the results of an experiment or progress on the garden. This is because B[A is the doer, the agent who does the work of the organization. The authority of A* has a different source, in that he or she represents management, B*. A* can therefore speak in the name of the larger organization, composed of many communities and therefore many domains of enterprise, a larger multi-actor "B/A". These agents take the organizational map, however it has been constituted, as the source of their authority. They are *its* custodian, with responsibility to assure its execution and renewal.

Never a Dyadic but Always a Triadic Game (Caplow 1968)

In an encounter involving two agencies, B and A*, we might be tempted to conceptualize their conversation as the playing out of a dyadic or two-person game (on the model of Goffman's information game). This, however, is to miss the significance of the virtual third party, present only vicariously as it is evoked by the interactants to buttress the authority of their interventions. The third person in the exchange is the organization itself (it is this addition that makes the communication "organizational" and not merely interpersonal). The scientist points to the value that his or her discovery will add to the future welfare of the company; the gardener to how his creation will enhance the value of the owner's property. The administrator cites established corporate strategy, or the budget, as the source of his or her authority.

Each party to the encounter is bound to the other because their roles are explicitly complementary; each is distinct from the other because their basis of authority, speaking for the organization, has different groundings. Both *represent* the organization, voice its rationale, and thereby make it present in their talk. Each is authorized because they do, yet it is not the *same* thirdness that they call on.

Variations on the Game: Crosslinking

Not all imbrication assumes the configuration of a chain. Consider this case:

$$\{A^{**}\} \diagup{\hspace{-0.5em}\diagdown} \begin{array}{l} \{/B^*[A^*/B \ [A–X]]\} \\ \{/B^*[A^*/B \ [A–X]]\} \end{array}$$

Here, two different communities of practice are involved. The three-party dynamic is now complementary, in Bateson's terminology, on the same reasoning as before (both must deal with A**), but also symmetric (each has to deal with each other). The frame games that result now have two possible configurations: (1) a coalition of the two domains of value-adding practice who are thus enabled to resist the imposition of authority by the uplinked agency; and/or (2) complicity between one of the downlinked parties with the uplinked third in order to claim precedence over the other. (These varieties of gaming are illustrated in Chapter 6.)

There is a third possibility: both imbricated parties unite in opposing elements of the new policy, but they do so in a way that is still tinged with competition, since a managerially sanctioned intervention will have a differential impact on their operations. The result is a more complex game, resisting management authority but simultaneously staking out an advantageous position where authority is affirmed (Katambwe & Taylor 2006; Taylor & Robichaud 2007). (Chapter 7 provides an instance of this.)

All of these outcomes illustrate the central role of coalitions in sequences of organizational gamesmanship: all exemplify familiar ploys for anybody who has ever worked for long in a large organization. All are thus vulnerable to schismogenesis (Bateson 1935, 1972), or, to put it less pretentiously, "turf wars."

Problems of Scale

Imbrication also generates another kind of game-playing, one that is the consequence of scale and levels of hierarchy. Consider, for example, this pattern:

{B [A/B[A/]]}{B [A/B[A/]]}{B [A/B [A–X]]}

We have bracketed the extended chain of imbrication that results from scale in order to identify three domains of relatively frequent and concentrated conversation: those of senior management, middle management, and the specialized communities of practice that typically take on the actual work of the organization. Each of these three domains, lower, middle, and upper, privileges conversation internally as the preferred mode of communication: daily, where the work is focused on some concrete object; sporadic but still essential for middle managers, who have their own challenges to face; frequent and sustained for senior management, who spend much of their time in conversation with peers and outsiders.

The problematic connections are at the interstices, where the interaction *between* communities unfolds. Even where there *are* "conversations" linking the three levels, they tend to conform to protocols of "correct" performance that discourage spontaneity: formal meetings or interviews, for example. Another dimension of communication is emphasized: the rules of the game are no longer played uniquely in the kind of conversation Goffman described, but are instead mediated by texts: campaign objectives and parameters, budgets, strategies, software, and regulations (examples drawn from later chapters). And since texts, like maps, are written by someone, an author, who then claims anonymity, these texts lay a special claim to vicarious authority (assuming the text has been naturalized). Except that, as we have pointed out, maps are endlessly being contested and, as they are, re-written.

Why Up–Down Communication Is Problematical

The hazard of up–down communication was identified in a book that is now a classic of the management literature: March and Simon's (1958) book *Organizations*. How people at every junction of the chain of imbrication make sense depends on what frame they privilege. Mary, the president of the company, issues a policy statement that reflects *her* focus and frame, as *she* interprets its purposes. For John, the vice-president, to understand the new policy, he is going to have to translate it so that it conforms to his somewhat different focus and frame. He is going to have to interpolate, to interpret. When he now informs his regional directors, Louise and Fred, of the new policy, they, in turn, are also going to have to re-frame it, first, if they are to understand it and, second, so that each, in their own domain, can apply it. And on it goes at every turn. In the process, the meaning of the policy will have undergone one transformation after another.

Browning, Greene, Sitkin, Sutcliffe, and Obstfeld (2009) offer a telling illustration: two agencies of the U.S. Air Force, technicians and a civilian review board composed of engineers, were both mandated to develop innovations leading to enhanced efficiency ("total quality"). Their sincere efforts to carry out the policy nevertheless led to an outcome that the authors call a "contentious" climate of mutual suspicion. One policy: two very different ways of understanding it, each grounded in practices that were each legitimately located, for the respective communities, in their understanding of new policy, and yet they produced misunderstanding.

That is the hazard of downlinking: transmitting management's intention to its communities of practice. Uplinking is vulnerable as well to the hazards of communicating the reality of daily practice to their hierarchical superiors. March and Simon (1958) identified the phenomenon we allude to in this way: "humans, whether inside or outside administrative organizations, behave rationally, if at all, only relative to some set of 'given' characteristics of the situation" (p. 150). "Rational behavior," they go on, "involves substituting for the complex reality a model of reality that is sufficiently simple to be handled by problem-solving processes" (p. 151). As they explain, "a particular definition of the situations, once it becomes established in an individual or group, maintains itself with great stability and tenacity" (p. 153). The result, where communication is concerned, is that "anything that does not fit the systems of concepts is communicated only with difficulty" (p. 165). There is inevitably, as a result, what they call "uncertainty absorption" (p. 165) at every juncture of the chain of imbrication. "Facts" are really "inferences ... drawn from a body of evidence and the inferences, instead of the evidence itself" (p. 165). It is the inferences that get communicated. Uncertainty absorption thus affects "the influence structure of the organization" (p. 165). As a consequence, "uncertainty absorption is frequently used, consciously and unconsciously, as a technique for acquiring and exercising power" (p. 166). Chapter 5 offers a vivid illustration of this kind of game.

Summing Up

There you have it, succinctly put: imbrication generates ambiguity, because it also generates an ongoing differentiation of interpretations. It is the omnipresence of uncertainty absorption that makes organizational process resemble a game more than a machine. Organization in the large, because of its multiple extensions, necessitates a reconciliation of pressures arising out of differentiation (of specialized practices and their agendas) and thereby a continual preoccupation with their integration (Lawrence & Lorsch 1969). Unless there is differentiation the capacity of the organization to operate in a variety of situations and respond constructively to their challenges is limited. Unless there is integration, on the other hand, the communities that make up the organization fragment and eventually separate.

Doing Field Research in an Imbricated Organization

The study of the negotiation of reciprocity, as we have seen this concept defined by Bateson, is a principal object of organizational communication research. It is here that the lineaments of the underlying structure of imbrication are most clearly revealed, as Chapters 4–8 will illustrate. In this investigation, the researcher is tracking the sensemaking modes and strategies of the communities being observed, looking for the ways members construct accounts to frame events advantageously, to enhance their status and position, much as Goffman described.

Since the topic of research is a triadic game, involving an absent (but rendered present in their talk) third party, the organization, one research strategy consists in observing how people use pronouns to constitute the latter and thus reconstruct its presence in the conversation.

How People Use Pronouns to Define and Give an Account of Their Situation

Suppose that stem cells were self-conscious and could talk. Not only could they act as they do, but they would *know* that they were doing so. They would be able to observe themselves (and others) acting, and they could frame their observations in language. They would no longer, to use a terminology invented by Maturana and Varela (1987, 1994), be *autopoietic* (closed systems), but rather, like we humans are, *allopoietic* (observers, as well as actors). So, when the experiment we imagined earlier had been successfully completed, we imagine the cell saying something like this: "I did it! Those bones are as good as new. And it was all my doing!"

The statement is self-referential: *I, my*. It has been framed as a simple action of an actor on an object, where the "beneficiary" (although we would not normally use that term in such a context) is presumably identical with the actor, the stem cell itself, B = A:

B [A–X]

Now let us suppose that the cell addresses the experimenter this way: "What do you think, boss? Ain't I the best?" The frame has shifted; the stem cell is seen in a different light, to be acting for an experimenter, a you:

B [A/B [A–X]]

What is made salient by this extension, as we saw earlier, is the context of the experiment, where the stem cell A is presented to us as acting for a principal/beneficiary B. A communicative relationship has been highlighted. But we need not stop there. The stem cell goes on, still addressing the experimenter: "You're going to be a super-star in the center, thanks to my efforts, aren't you? Your bosses will be happy. They are going to be very pleased." A new frame has been evoked, including a *they*, where the experimenter is seen to be part of a larger legitimating sphere of activities, and where the experiment figures as one component in a collaborative program of research and the experimenter is now the hero: the researcher who ran the experiment:

B [A/B [A/B [A–X]]]

"I'll bet the center ups its funding as a result of what I've done for you," the stem cell concludes. And, once again, a new frame has been evoked:

B [A/B [A/B [A/B [A–X]]]]

Notice how the stem cell accomplishes the successive re-framings, by using pronouns: *I, my, you, they, its*. At each step, a different relationship is brought to the center of the stage, and, as a result, different facets of the identity of those involved come into focus (the relevance of privileging pronouns in research is illustrated in Chapter 4).

The whole framework of imbricated relationships is inter-connected. Like the nursery rhyme, if the stem cell fails, the experiment fails, the experimenter fails to get recognition in the center, whose funding fails to be renewed, and the entire research program, involving many centers, sees its funding dry up as a consequence. For the want of a nail the shoe was lost, for the want of a shoe the horse was lost, for the want of a horse the rider was lost, for the want of a rider the kingdom was lost. As we wrote earlier, a syncretism is involved: each depends on others for its own security.

The First Step in the Construction of Organization-as-Entity

We have glossed over one facet of the pronoun usage, however: how people refer to themselves as a *collective* agency. We portrayed the stem cell as saying "I." Suppose instead it had used a different point of reference, the collectivity of stem cells: "*We* did it!" Now the actor is no longer an individual, but a community. The relationships that link the different "I's" that make up the "we" are now hidden from sight from the outside: they have been "black-boxed" (Dietz 2003; Latour 1987). We can't tell: perhaps there is competition among stem cells. Maybe they have a hierarchy. They have their own internal sensemaking habits that are disguised from us: *their* "thirdness." Maybe our favorite stem cell evokes, from time to time, the person or goals of the experimenter as a justification for its own actions, thus making the latter an absent (but present) source of authority in the internal dialogue of the stem cell community.

The use of the pronoun "we," in other words, indexes the presentation of an organization with its own internal structures that are occluded by the way they have been framed. The core of all human organization starts here, in the transition from "I" to "we."

Accounts

The "frame game" consists in evoking, by whatever means, those components of the imbricated configuration that make your own role most prominent, and where you are seen to shine because you are the hero. You are accounting for yourself and your actions (a topic we take up in Chapter 3). Making an accounting of one's actions conforms to narrative logic: the cell tells its "story," the researcher his or hers, the administrator as well. For it to be an authentic account, there must be an object, and it is an object because the situation is deemed problematical (think of our earlier discussion of pragmatism). If there is an object, there must be an actor—a "hero." To be a hero also implies that his or her actions in dealing with the object have been legitimated, sanctioned by society, or by a principle grounded in an established collective thirdness. The actor/hero is thus an agent, as we argued in Chapter 1, acting for a principal (the organization) that legitimates his or her actions. There must also be opposition: an unacceptable state of affairs that typically has its source and becomes embodied in a *they*, an antagonist: a rival community, for example, or an incompetent management. The protagonist agent/hero may in turn enlist allies and helpers, each of whom has of course their own perspective and story, and situated point of view. Finally, the accounting must have not only a starting point, but also a conclusion: the experiment, for example, succeeded or failed.

The researcher concentrates on observing and recording the construction of accounts by the respective communities. This is where contrasting accounts rub up against each other, and where an accommodation must be found, if there is to be an achievement of reciprocity. It is at these crossing points that the social space of the organization gets redefined and settled. The "map" of the organization describes, not longitude and latitude, but a composite of situations, each characterized by one or more domains of practice and together defining a common reality that is both differentiated (each with its own thirdness) and integrated (sharing, nevertheless, a common thirdness).

It is the organizational members themselves who play the game, to frame their own actions as plausible and justified, to both stay in the game and do well at it. No matter how "objective" and "authoritative" any policy or directive descending the chain of imbrication is, it will still have to be evaluated from within the frame game.

Authority Again

Whose account (and map) takes precedence over who else's, organizationally speaking, is the issue. Authority—authoring the account—is, by its very nature, distributed. We all confront doubt in our working lives, no matter what role we are called on to play, and, as a consequence, we all become engaged in inquiry in the quest to resolve our doubt and to "attain belief" (to use Peirce's expression). No one is exempt. In resolving our doubt, if we succeed, we too are in effect authoring third-ness, not only singly but collectively. How any organization of some size, given its mélange of communities of practice and modes of sense-making, arrives at a commonality of purpose is determined by its modes of distributing authority: how it writes (and naturalizes) the map. The challenge is to establish, and validate, assumptions of precedence.

Chapter 3

In Chapter 3, we turn to the crucial agency of text in establishing authority. Text not only mediates all human interaction, but has the potential to establish—and to destabilize—people's claims to social identity and authority, including that of the organization. In Chapter 3, we will explicate the basis of the "frame game" in a different way, inspired in part by Wittgenstein's lead: as a construction of language.

Suggested Supplementary Readings

Wikipedia furnishes a succinct outline of classic game theory, quite adequate for understanding the background to this chapter. Also worth checking is the entry on coalitions.

Erving Goffman is his own best introduction. For an appreciation of his ideas on games and gaming, read his chapter on "Expression Games" in *Strategic Interaction* (1969). For an introduction to his ideas on frames, read Chapters 2 and 3 of his book *Frame Analysis* (1974). For a more comprehensive interpretation of the contribution of Erving Goffman's thought, Manning's article in *Organization Studies* (2008) is probably the most authoritative. Also worth reading is Goffman's Chapter 3, on "footing," in his later book, *Forms of Talk* (1981). To see how people position themselves advantageously in a managerial discussion, read Katambwe & Taylor (2006) and Taylor & Robichaud (2007).

For the source of our discussion of maps, see Chapter 9 of our earlier book *The Emergent Organization* (2000). See also Weick (1979).

Nicotera (forthcoming) offers a somewhat different take from ours on the problematic addressed in this chapter: organization as both process and entity.

Language as *both* Meaning *and* Action

Language as an Actant

In Chapters 1 and 2, we proposed a pragmatic framework of understanding for the analysis of how organizations come to exist and how the communication that is their basis both structures and gives meaning to the activities that compose them. In this chapter, we take a further step, to see, through an examination of a literature on language and its uses that has been evolving over the past half-century or so, how its insights can enrich our analysis of these abstract ideas of framing, gaming, and the negotiation of authority.

One central theme will emerge in our exploration: language is more than an inert "medium" for the communication of ideas from one person to another. It is itself an "actant." For one person to address another, he or she must construct a string of language. It is the "string of language" that actually does the acting *for* the person who initiated the communicative sequence. The string, to use Goffman's term, is an *expression*: a text, in essence. What the expression means to its receiver necessitates the formation of an impression: an interpretation of the meaning of the text to fit the circumstances where it is heard or read. In this two-step construction and reconstruction of sense, we communication researchers ignore at our peril the properties of language-in-use: how *it* enters to shape the way people see the world.

When the "text" is embedded in normal conversation (although we do not usually even think of what people say to each other as being a text), understandings are subject to an immediate corrective feedback that limits ambiguity. When, however, those same language constructions serve to bridge communities whose practices and discursive habits are not the same—as they uplink, downlink, and crosslink—the role of text as agent, and not merely mode of transmission, becomes considerably more salient. As we shall see in this chapter, text can hide as well as display. Either way, it constitutes an important part of the environment in which the activities of organizational members unfold.

Language as Meaning

Although earlier authors such as Dewey and Mead in the United States, Tarde in France, and Simmel in Germany had recognized the importance of taking communicative relationships as the starting point for under-standing society, the first systematic attempts to model communication date from the period immediately following World War II, in the second half of the decade of the 1940s. The timing was by no means accidental. The conduct of war on a truly global scale, for the first time in history, had made people acutely aware of the importance of efficient communi-cation. It thus stimulated the invention and application of a whole range of new tools, such as radar and the use of electronic devices to store and analyze information, culminating in the invention of a general-purpose digital computer in 1946. Out of this exploration emerged a fully mathematical theory of communication, in the thinking, most notably, of Norbert Wiener (1948) and Claude Shannon (1948). As we will discover in this chapter, concepts of agency and thirdness were absent in these initial conceptualizations of communication. Those ideas subsequently took shape as theorists, progressively building on the earlier work, eventually incorporated ways of thinking about communication that corresponded more closely to how organizing actually occurs, and how it is rooted in the elemental act of communicating.

Cybernetics, Information Theory, and Noam Chomsky's Linguistics

Wiener and Cybernetics

In the 1940s, as the strategists involved in the war just ended thought of it, communication was conceived as an instrumentality for people to run things: a technology that enables centralized, machine-like systems to react to an environment. One of the founders of the new science of communi-cation, Norbert Wiener, for example, entitled his 1948 book *Cybernetics: Or Control and Communication in the Animal and the Machine*. Wiener (1948) presented cybernetics as a new science of steering, using feedback from the environment one is navigating to stay on course: literally helmsmanship (from the Greek word *kybernetes*). The key to effective coordination of all the components of any complex and adaptive agent, the reasoning went, is accurate information, allowing it to continually update its knowledge of the world around it (and of itself in it) and thus adapt to it—the organization viewed as a system. A systematic, mathe-matical theory of communication was therefore needed to explain in technical detail what these mathematicians meant by "information."

Shannon's Information Theory

In 1948, the same year that Wiener's book was published, Claude Shannon of the Bell Laboratories in New Jersey (he was also associated with the Massachusetts Institute of Technology) published two monographs in a Bell technical journal that offered a full explication of information as the basis of communication (Wiener's book also included a variation on the theory). Their model of communication is better known today as information theory. Through its popularization in a book that appeared the following year (Shannon & Weaver 1949), it was immensely influential in establishing how subsequent generations of social scientists would conceptualize communication. The positive side of this rapid dissemination within the wider intellectual community in which communication studies are located is that it sensitized scholars to the importance of communication. The negative effect was that it did so in a way that limited inquiry into alternative views of what communication is, and how it works.

Information theory assumes that the essence of communication is the transfer of knowledge through the use of a shared code (thus defining language as being itself merely a "code"). In Shannon's treatment, the issue of communication is reduced to the mechanical problem of how to counter various sources of parasitic interference (called "noise") and thus assure reliability of transmission.

Shannon's information theory (he actually named it the "mathematical theory of communication") made two radically reductive assumptions. The first was to ignore the origins of meaningful social activity as grounded in agency, an idea that we began to explore in Chapter 1. In Shannon's theory, communication conforms to elementary cause–effect linearity: A encodes a message and sends it to B who decodes it. As he portrayed the act of communication, there would be a source and a receiver, joined by a channel over which messages would flow and information could be transmitted. The "destination" or receiver was thus where to look for the interpretation of the message; the "transmitter," for the source. Any competing sources—any "C" that was also demanding attention—would simply be treated as "noise."

Shannon's radical simplification largely ignored the complexity of natural language-in-use. He achieved this by translating talk and text into a dry "language" of binary impulses ("encoding" the message): a sequence of *on*s and *off*s (coding was in the air since cracking the enemy code had been one of the wartime achievements). It was this conceptual mapping of language onto an elementary calculus of pluses and minuses that then allowed Shannon to claim that he could measure, objectively, the information content of a message, in bits and bytes: how much knowledge was being exchanged.[4] By "information," however, he meant the ratio of order to disorder, of predetermined pattern to random variation ("signal" versus "noise"). The greater the number of elements in a vocabulary, he noted, the greater the potential for creating complex messages, but also the greater the risk that disorder (*entropy*) would overcome sense, and turn meaningful messages into gibberish as they were transmitted. The technical problem, and the focus of his own work, was how to reduce that danger and, at the same time, to preserve or even enhance the intelligibility of the message.

His findings were of immense importance to those engaged in developing the technology of long-distance telecommunications. They led to dramatic improvements in telephony, and in all of its extensions, such as television and the Internet. Their relevance to the task of explaining ordinary *human* communication was, however, considerably more problematical, because information theory is insensitive to context and its role in enabling communication. Shannon assumed an *unambiguous* code; he thus arbitrarily excluded from consideration the "noise" that is endemic to the use of natural language, which is at best only an approximation to a "code." Natural language is, as we show later in this chapter, *intrinsically* an imperfect carrier of information.

Chomsky's Critique

At one point in his monograph, Shannon ventured an explanation of how language works: how its component letters and words get organized to produce statements capable of conveying information. Here again, he adopted a linear model that assumed one letter or word follows another, purely on the basis of probability. Shannon's notion of how natural language works was simply wrong, as the linguist Chomsky (1957) would shortly afterwards demonstrate. Chomsky did so by pointing out the artificial basis of Shannon's reasoning, since language, like many other kinds of symbolic expression ranging from quilts to fugues, exhibits pattern and is formatted by what linguists call a grammar. Despite this devastating critique, information theory and its vocabulary of "messages" and "transmission" nevertheless continued to have a remarkable influence on the social sciences: psychology, sociology, political science, and mass media studies took up its terminology. Since there *was* no field called organizational communication in the 1940s and 1950s (it only became identified as such in the 1960s; see our prologue), the subsequent adoption

---

4   Shannon's method was the essence of simplicity. It was based on the mathematical principle of the addition of exponents. If $2^3 = 8$ and $2^4 = 16$, then 8×16 can be read as 2^7 (i.e., 2^{3+4}) = 128. Thus the variety of any collection of items, such as a set of messages, can be easily calculated, using bits (binary digits) as the basis of measurement.

of the messaging model by *its* practitioners presumably came about through diffusion from the already established branches of the social sciences.

In spite of information theory's evident inadequacies for the purpose of explaining ordinary communication, you can still find references to "information" and "messaging" in the literature dealing with organizational communication, as if the applicability of Shannon's terms were transparently evident to everyone. Unfortunately, the consequence of privileging only one aspect of communication, the fact that people address their remarks, both written and verbal, to other people, has been to occult its other features: notably the complex relational processes, which we noted in Chapter 2, that are triggered when people actually interact.

Chomsky's subsequent formalization of the mechanisms at the heart of language activity (Chomsky 1957, 1965) attained a level of sophistication that far out-stripped the earlier speculations of Shannon. His work is also limited, however, by another horizon: it was by and large, and has since remained, indifferent to the pragmatics of language: how people actually use language, and how their understanding reflects the situational reality of where it is being used. For enlightenment on that complexity, we must look elsewhere.

Wittgenstein Again

As we saw in Chapter 2, Ludwig Wittgenstein argued that words and gestures do not merely encode knowledge, nor "that language always functions in one way, always serves the same purpose: to convey thoughts" (Wittgenstein 1958: 102). Instead, we recall, he argued that we must first ask what language *does*. Suppose that the gardeners we introduced in Chapter 1 have worked out their firstness and secondness, and one is now assisting (acting as agent for) the other. The gardener says to the assistant (pointing) "pass me that box over there," and the assistant hands it over. It was the gardener's words that acted on the assistant and thereby induced him or her to act on the box. Clearly, the gardener's command would not have worked unless both the gardener and the assistant already possessed in common an understanding of what they were doing—a thirdness, in other words—and their respective roles in doing it.

Wittgenstein dismissed the notion of a "private" language: to even count as a *language*, a sequence of words, he maintained, has to enable communication in a context where people are occupied in doing something. It depends, Wittgenstein wrote, "on the situation in which [the word] is uttered or written" (1958: 24). He thus echoed, although in very different terms, and with no evidence of any explicit historical connection, Peirce's interrogation (Chapter 1), which assumes that the basis of meaning, because it is always grounded in human activity, necessitates the establishment of thirdness (or pragmatic meaning) if there is to be mutual understanding. To return to our illustration in Chapter 1, interpreting the gardener's words to his assistant as a move in a game, the assistant is identified as a firstness (that on which attention is focused), the gardener a secondness (an actor who relates to him or her), and the meaning of the former's command is the thirdness: that which makes the request a *request*.

This shared comprehension of meaning, however, poses a question: What is the special property of language that makes it such an effective tool: to, for example, communicate the gardener's intention to his assistants? It was this issue that another British philosopher of language, John Austin, took up for investigation.

John Austin and "Speech Acts"

Wittgenstein was not the only philosopher of his generation to question the established dogma of the time: language as simply a way of encoding knowledge to be subsequently "transmitted" as "information." At Oxford, Austin (1962) was raising similar concerns. He began his William James Lectures at Harvard University, in 1955 (also published posthumously), by observing that, "it was for too long the assumption of philosophers that the business of a 'statement' can only be to 'describe' some state of affairs, or to 'state some fact', which it must do either truly or falsely" (Austin 1962: 1). He too insisted, like Wittgenstein, that language is how we get on with our practical activities (the title of his book is *How to Do Things With Words*). As he pointed out, by saying "I christen this ship the Empress of France," you are not merely *reporting* a fact, you are *establishing* it (it is made a fact by your act of speaking, since you "gave" the ship a name). You performed an act, as surely as the judge in a court of law who declares the accused to be "guilty as charged."

From this, Austin expanded his view into a thesis: that we are *always* doing something with language, including, but not limited to, making "statements of fact." Statements of fact no longer have the privileged status they had before. They become assertions: *acts* of speech, like any other kind of acting that uses language—baptizing, declaring, requesting, complimenting, dissenting, and so on. Furthermore, like Wittgenstein, Austin (1962) observed that the *force* of an act of speech we are performing—its capacity to move people—is contingent on the circumstances in which the talk is uttered. There must be "an accepted conventional procedure" (like Wittgenstein's rules of the game or Peirce's thirdness). The *right* words have to be spoken, "by certain persons in certain circumstances," and these persons and circumstances must "be appropriate for the invocation of the particular procedure involved" (pp. 14–15). "The procedure," Austin went on, "must be executed by all participants both correctly and completely" (p. 15). The identity of the participants is thus crucial to getting the words to perform correctly. Just like in our garden example. Language is tied to occasion.

The words are spoken *by* someone *to* someone, but note also that the words simultaneously constitute the identities of both speaker and listener, in and by the act of speaking. You know who people are—their identity as social beings—*because* it is they who enunciate certain words—the "right" ones in the ¨right¨ circumstances (Taylor & Cooren 1997). To be officially married, the act of speech, "I now pronounce you joined in matrimony," must be spoken by a recognized authority, but it is the pronouncement also, inversely, that serves to identify him or her as endowed with the authority to perform the ceremony. Similarly, their responses, "I do," commit the couple to being partners in marriage in the future. As we will see shortly, later communication theorists have proposed a term for this reciprocal relationship between speaker and spoken: they call it an instance of *reflexivity*. People speak the words, but the words do not merely identify the speech act; they *constitute* the speakers *as* social beings (Searle 1989), a couple; assign them to categories; or "tax" them (Katambwe 2004; Linde 1988).

The act of speaking creates, and leaves behind it, a set of expectations, moreover, in that the participants are now bound to future obligations: if you make a promise to someone it is a *promise*. A bet is a *bet*. It has consequences, win or lose. There are quasi-contractual expectations that are created by interactive speech. Words, it follows, are the mechanism by which one conversation carries over—is linked—to another: "But you promised!" someone says, and they have evoked a previous interactive sequence. (Of course, making a promise is one thing; holding someone to it is another.)

Austin's philosophical investigation thus focused on those properties of speech that explain its power to convey human action in a social context: to explain how one person acts on another. It is here that the transition from linguistics to communication science is initiated. Linguists commonly recognize two levels of language: syntax (the parts of speech and how they are assembled to make sentences that are grammatically correct) and semantics (the meaning of the sentence). Austin called these already established categories the "locutionary" (purely structural) dimensions of speech, in contradistinction to two other dimensions that he proposed: first, the "illocutionary" (that which lends to an assertion its force in that it is that feature of language which enables speech or writing to act on a hearer or reader). Second, the "perlocutionary" effect (or the state of affairs the utterance actually produces, depending on the response, or "uptake," of the person who is spoken to) then carries us into the domain of pragmatics, but it was never much explored by Austin or successors of his, such as Searle. What Austin did grasp was that language is both constative (says something about the world around us) and yet simultaneously performative (does something in that world).

Austin's understanding that language is performative as well as constative (the topic of Chapter 5) has since been empirically documented and validated by linguists, in many languages, under the heading of *modality*.

Modality

Modality is that feature of spoken language that "expresses a speaker's attitude toward the proposition of an utterance produced in dialogic exchange" (Bybee & Fleischman 1995: 9). This was Austin's insight, although his terminology was different. As Palmer remarks, "the distinction between proposition and modality is very close to that of locutionary and illocutionary act as proposed by Austin" (1986: 14). If words can act ("do things," as Austin put it), it is because they have the property of modality. Modality is how the tokens of speech come to be endowed with "illocutionary force": express an attitude. Say something as banal as "What a beautiful morning!" and you have already committed yourself. The words do it.

The simplest expression of modality, in speech, is the property of verbs called "mood." In this stripped-down sense of the term, we cannot avoid modality, even if we wanted to. As with the other dimensions of a verbal expression, *tense* (past, present, future) and *aspect* (state versus process), the minute we address anyone using language we have committed ourselves modally. It is like the middle-class gentleman in Molière's famous play *Le Bourgeois Gentilhomme*, "Good Heavens! For more than forty years I have been speaking prose without knowing it!" Except that now you can substitute "using modality" for "speaking prose." We all do it, all the time.

Linguists commonly classify mood, in this sense, as declarative or affirmative (asserting something), interrogative (asking someone something), or imperative (requesting something). "It's a delicious pie" (*declarative*). "Did you make the pastry yourself?" (*interrogative*). "Yes." "Oh, please give me the recipe" (*imperative*).

Making a commitment to the truth of something is called *epistemic* modality. *Deontic* modality, on the other hand, "is concerned with the necessity or possibility of acts performed by morally responsible agents" (Bybee & Fleischman 1995: 4, citing Lyons 1977: 823). The pie is delicious and who made it illustrate epistemic modality—matters of fact: what Austin called the *constative* function of language. Asking for the recipe enters into the deontic sphere of who should do what for whom, a feature that Austin called *performative*. There is now an ethical implication of speech: the imposition of a duty or an obligation, on either or both the speaker and the person addressed.

One problem, however, is that in any technical discussion of modality the complexities soon begin to multiply. Just to cite a few, even the simplest manifestation of modality, the mood of a verbal phrase, includes many additional semantic nuances beyond declarative, interrogative, and imperative: *conditional* ("if . . . then . . ."), *optative* ("I wish . . ."), *subjunctive* ("perhaps . . ."), *avolitional* ("I'm afraid that . . ."). Each is a way of expressing speaker orientation to what is said by modifying its potential impact, because, for example, it softens the speaker's commitment to the truth of something, or the force of a request, or establishes a condition.

If you study modality across different languages, the complexity is further magnified. Take the issue of the *subjunctive*, the bugbear of any English speaker trying to master the complexities of a Latin language such as French, Italian, Portuguese, or Spanish. In English, you can say, "I doubt that it will make a real difference." You have used a simple expression that connotes a future tense: "will make." In French, this requires resorting to the subjunctive: "Je doute que cela fasse vraiment une différence." But even in French, usage varies: rather than "fasse" (subjunctive mood), some speakers, in some contexts these days, substitute, like in English, the future tense: "fera." But there is still a difference. In French, both subjunctive mood and future tense involve altering the verb itself—"faire": from "fait" (present tense, affirmative) to "fasse" (subjunctive mood, implying uncertainty) or "fera" (future tense, affirmative). In English, the verb "make" is constant throughout: we say "will make" (where the latter expression serves to indicate both tense and modality). Variations in mood and tense, in English, are typically conveyed by the use of auxiliary verbs such as "will," called *modals*. Latin languages use inflection. Other languages offer a veritable rainbow of alternatives.

There is one consolation for us non-linguists. Modality is more than just a question of language and expression. It is a dimension of pragmatics: language in use, to do things. Even though contemporary linguists may still limit their horizon to the mechanisms language offers for expression, they now realize the importance of taking the interactive context of that expression into account. Guo (1995), for example, argues that, in Mandarin, "the basic function of the modal *néng* is not merely to express notions such as ability, permission and epistemic possibility. Rather, its most important function is an interpersonal one, namely to index the speaker's attempt to challenge the addressee" (p. 205). As Bybee and Fleischman similarly observe:

Modality, as we have discovered, lends itself best to investigation in social, interactive contexts ... many of the functions of modality are inextricably embedded in contexts of social interaction and, consequently, cannot be described adequately apart from their contextual moorings in interactive discourse.

(1995: 3)

To put all this in the perspective of pragmatic research, we briefly review a stream of research that has taken conversation and its dynamic—language-in-use—as *its* topic.

Ethnomethodology and Conversation Analysis

Ethnomethodology

The field known as ethnomethodology emerged in reaction to prevailing ideas about society as a "system," current in the 1940s and 1950 in sociological research. In the macrosociological perspective of Talcott Parsons and his contemporaries, for example, communication is reduced to a "function," and people to components of a social system, whose attitudes and behavior can be scientifically analyzed and predicted. Herbert Garfinkel's (1967) very different ethnomethodological formulation was to propose instead that people inhabit a world of meaning that they have *themselves* constructed. This was truly a new insight, and it changed forever our conception of society and organization: no longer merely the site where people "behave" and communication "takes place," but as products of that very behaving and communicating.

Accounts

A central concept of ethnomethodology is that of an "account." People, as they go about their daily lives, are continually confronted by events and circumstances that they can make sense of and deal with by making them *accountable*, to themselves as well as to others. Accounts come in many forms—justifications, excuses, myths, stories, reports, tallies, financial statements, to name but a few. In his own research, Garfinkel set out to document, through observation of their interactions, how people manipulate their "expressions" to construct an "impression" (to reiterate Goffman's terms, as we saw in Chapter 2): how, for example, a man who had undergone a sex change learned to walk, talk, and convincingly present an accounting of her new self as a woman ("Agnes"). As Wittgenstein had earlier also emphasized, Garfinkel argued that "accounts" are not simply true or false. They are how we make sense of the irreducibly equivocal, ambiguous nature of our circumstances.

"Reality" does not come to us pre-packaged. We have to *make* it real if we are to deal with it intelligently. We construct it singly, as thinking persons, but we also do so socially, as members of a community of people who share a common fate. We use accounts and accounting interactively to sort out what we *collectively* as well as *individually* think. As such, our sensemaking remains a work in progress, something to be interactively negotiated. As Heritage (1984) has observed, "description and concept application are contingent, negotiable and revisable" (p. 147).

Indexicality

Accounts do not so much picture reality (although they do that too) as isolate aspects of it that we want to highlight for each other, bring to our mutual attention: what we called "framing" in Chapters 1 and 2. Out of the flow of stimuli to which we are subjected, accounts bracket certain sequences to be paid attention to. Accounts are therefore what Garfinkel termed *indexical*, in that they "point" to things: delineate a domain of attention, establish a frame. "The mail has not arrived yet" does not simply assert something about the mail. It also focuses our joint attention on a slice of experience, and the need to attend to it: the mail is late today, perhaps. The meaning of words, Wittgenstein had also argued, is not fixed across contexts. Their meaning is in whatever they illuminate, in a given context or frame. Meaning is thus tied to the particular *occasion* or *situation* that frames people's interactive speech (notice here the echoes of our discussion of imbrication in Chapter 1: how accounts select what is to be paid attention to, and thus exclude, as well as include).

The meaningful world that we occupy, including the organizations in which we live, is literally a universe (or congeries of different universes) of our own making, construed through our accounts of it, negotiated in our communicating with each other. Because we make accounts of it—index it—and treat it *as* real, it *is* real. Yet, the converse also holds: the account is only valid if it *is* an account of the real—a "real" that we can never, incidentally, quite control or fully understand. But that reality, let us not forget, is what we have made real for ourselves, by our construction of it as real: that which we have concentrated our attention on and explained to ourselves. As Weick (1979) would later put it, we *enact* it. If we bracket experience differently, it *is* different. Organization, understood in this light, becomes a composition or overlay of enactments or what Vasquez (Chapter 4) calls "stories-so-far": a form of life that is at one and the same time a universe and a multiverse, both integrated and differentiated.

Reflexivity

Ethnomethodologists refer to this reciprocity of accounts and the reality they account for as *reflexivity*. Leiter (1980) expresses the idea this way:

> Because accounts consist of indexical expressions, they depend on the setting for their meaning. At the same time, a feature of any setting is the production of accounts. The setting gives meaning to talk and behavior within it, while at the same time, it exists in and through that very talk and behavior. (p. 139)

An organization is such a setting: it gives meaning to our talk and behavior, and yet it only exists—is "real"—because it *is* that setting, one that we have ourselves constructed. (We'll come back to reflexivity later, in our discussion of the work of M. A. K. Halliday.)

When we have truly grasped the reflexive way of thinking, we have taken a giant step toward comprehending the basis of organization, as seen from a pragmatic perspective, one that is grounded in communication science.

To construct their accounts, people use ready-made explanatory devices based on previous experience, which were themselves grounded in the categories of sense that their language and culture provided them with—these are the "laws" of thirdness. As Leiter (1980) puts it, "objects and events are not unique, but are recognizable as the 'same' thing again and again" (p. 71). There is continuity in experience, beyond the immediate occasion, and its imperatives. Reality is produced, to use Giddens' (1984) expression, *recursively*, through the repeated interpretations that we have learned to make (his recognition of the factor of thirdness). This is how the world of experience is made familiar to us (and why we have so much new to learn when we voyage abroad, to live among other people, in other societies, who have constructed their own version of the "real"). It also explains why changes of social environment are often so hard for people to accept: the new circumstances are discordant with established accounting procedures. They don't "fit."

This is the strength of sensemaking, the continuity it assures, but it is also potentially a prison from which escape may be forbiddingly difficult, since we may all too easily, as an identity that is a component in a self-referential collective entity, become our own jailers. Organization can then become what Morgan (1986, 2006) called a "psychic prison." Except that, organizationally speaking, one person's prison may be another's liberation, and vice versa.

Conversation Analysis

In the 1970s, ethnomethodology spawned a sub-domain of research now known as conversation analysis (CA). As a field, it has accumulated a rich corpus of meticulous analysis of ordinary people's sensemaking practices, as they engage in talk with each other (Drew & Heritage 1992; Sacks 1992; Schegloff 1992; much of the empirical investigation we report on later, incidentally, was broadly modeled on CA principles). What such a disciplined analysis of conversation has revealed is that conversation is itself a complex event: one that requires methodological skills on the part of participants if it is to succeed. It is a subtle language game to be mastered, to use Wittgenstein's analogy. Again, CA serves to illustrate the indexical and reflexive character of all human communication. The "game" is both context and object. When you are caught up in it, it creates a horizon: defines one domain in an imbricated layering of potential kinds of closure, much as Engeström (2000) described in his analysis of the activity system of baseball, where the game the spectators see is a component in the larger "game" that the owners play (or the bettors, or the state that operates the betting enterprise).

Here, we have moved far beyond the reductionist information theory that for so long dominated our thinking about communication. Messaging is no longer simply an instrumentality for the transmission of personal expressions (although it is that too). The situation that the messaging indexes is an essential framework, giving the message a meaning, and yet it must itself be endlessly reconstructed in and by the very activity it enables.

This is reflexivity at work. It is also thirdness, but now conceptualized in a very different framework of apprehension. To see how powerful the constraints imposed by language games are, and how people wrestle with them in the construction of domains of everyday life, we turn now to another literature that developed in parallel with ethnomethodology, a tradition that drew on all these other sources, but is especially illustrative of the importance of treating speech as action.

Labov and Fanshel: Language and Thirdness

In 1977, William Labov and David Fanshel published a book called *Therapeutic Discourse*. It grew out of their collaboration: one, Labov, an ethnographer, the other, Fanshel, a family therapist. Their book reported on a longitudinal study of the relationship between a mother and her anorexic daughter. The nature of this relationship gradually became evident through their family conversations in therapy, which the investigators recorded.

The two began their book by admitting they had come to realize that what seemed like the literal meaning of what their subjects said—what, for example, the daughter told them explicitly, in so many words—was not really what they meant. The "illocutionary force" of a statement turned out to be not nearly as transparently self-evident as Austin (1962) and his interpreter John Searle (1969) had supposed. Words convey both more and less meaning than they explicitly enunciate (Katambwe 2004). If the real "message" is thought of as being in code, it is a "code" that is not even remotely like the reduction Shannon had in mind. You can only begin to understand people's interactive talk, Labov and Fanshel (1977) wrote, when you admit that words convey, not just "facts," but "social and psychological propositions" (p. 29). As they put it, "we have come to understand conversation as a means that people use to deal with one another" (p. 30).

Words are how people construct their situation, and furnish the means by which they both express, and work out, their relationships within it. As the authors explained, "the original sentences are not in any one-to-one relationship with the actions being performed" (p. 40). There is, as Goffman thought, a lot more going on in communication than what the spoken words mean if you merely decode them literally—an insight that both supports and extends Wittgenstein's argument: we are all playing the language game. However, once you start to analyze people's conversations over a longish period of time, you soon realize that certain patterns turn up time and again: a phenomenon Labov and Fanshel (1977) called "recurrent communications." It is only then that you can begin to read the meaning of their talk. This is why the so-called ethnographic approach to the study of organizations, illustrated in later chapters, is so important. Only on close acquaintance over a significant stretch of time can you begin to "read between the lines."

The explanation for the repetitive patterning Labov and Fanshel observed seemed to be the tendency people display to formulate their interventions in a consistent way, which the authors called their "mode of argument" (p. 53). Underlying people's presentation of the situation (their "argument" or account), there always lie a set of assumptions about the proper relationships that *should* hold between them, depending on their identity: a moral code, in effect, or, to use Peirce's expression, a "law" of relationship governing, for example, parent–child interaction. These "assumptions" (the authors' term) amount to tacit ideas about the role relationships involved, the status of each member of the relationship, and the obligations that a given status entails: in their case, those of mother versus those of daughter. The daughter at one point complained that her mother had stayed away too long, and thus implied that the latter had not lived up to her maternal obligations, especially as a mother of a daughter who was having problems coping. In other words, she was questioning the competence of her mother to carry out the role the latter was duty-bound to play, according to her own idea of family obligations.

None of this tacit assumption of roles and their duties, the analysts noted, was ever stated in so many words. It was when the analysts examined the dynamic of the conversation involving the two that the implicit assumption of responsibility became clear. The daughter was not contesting the assumption of her mother as a locus of authority (she even emphasized it). She was, instead, arguing (indirectly) that authority also entails responsibility.

Here, although Labov and Fanshel's ideas are not phrased in this language, we are encountering the phenomenon of thirdness. How people everywhere interpret their experience, and formulate it in their interactive talk, is set against a background of taken-for-granted assumptions of the nature of the "*you*," "*I*," and "*we*"—a "mini-organization" that they jointly constitute and that enables them to identify the situation for what it is.

The crucial dimension of talk, Labov and Fanshel concluded, is not explicit features of speech such as requests and assertions (how speech act theory has often been interpreted), but rather, as our earlier discussion suggested, "challenges, defenses, and retreats, which have to do with the status of the participants, their rights and obligations, and their changing relationships in terms of social organization" (pp. 58–9; we will see several instances of this in Chapter 6). When one person is dealing with another, in the ordinary conversational world where they interact, they continually (and reflexively) match up what they perceive to be the interactive pattern of their exchanges, as they see it from their perspective, informed by a norm, constituting thus a framework of understanding. These tacit, taken-as-given premises that people have about the identity of themselves and others, and the duties that are thereby entailed, are what Labov and Fanshel described as "propositions."

Even more important, from the perspective of understanding the contexts of organizational communication described in later chapters, is the penumbra of ambiguity that is thereby constituted. The mother and daughter that they talked and listened to in their ongoing consultation process may well, in the abstract, have adhered to the same standards of proper behavior, but their interpretation of each other's actions was seldom identical. They each had their own way of framing the relationship, but it was far from the same. Their points of view diverged.

If, in so limited an exchange, there is space for contrasting readings of the meaning of interactions, then we should hardly expect less divergent interpretations when we turn to look at the larger arena of organizational organizing. If you were to extrapolate this finding, grounded in an interpersonal relationship, to a context of organizational communication, the image you would be left with would be considerably at odds with the notion of straightforward "coordination" such as it is often assumed in the organizational literature. Status, rights, responsibilities, obligations take center stage.

M. A. K. Halliday: A Social Semiotic View of Reflexivity

Halliday (2002 [1970]), although, like Chomsky, a linguist, showed himself to be sensitive to the role of context in language behavior in a way that some linguists, Chomsky included, are not. As he has written, "we attempt to relate language primarily to one particular aspect of human experience, namely that of social structure" (Halliday & Hasan 1989). What Halliday adds to our discussion so far, and particularly to our evocation of agency, is an understanding of *text* as a powerful mediator of interaction. *All* communication is mediated by text, he maintains. Whether text is being used to communicate at first hand, or to distantiate interaction more widely over time and space, does not alter its essentiality and its role in the construction of relationships.

Text, as Halliday and his school define it, is any "language that is functional," i.e., "that is doing some job in some context" (Halliday & Hasan 1989: 10). As well as functioning as a presence in the conversational process, it is also "an interactive event, a social exchange of meanings" (p. 11). As Halliday and Hasan remind us, text is "both an object in its own right . . . and . . . an instance of social meaning in a particular context of situation" (p. 11). You exercise *your* agency on text when you focus on it, rephrase it, and work it over. To speak or write a sentence, you have had to learn what a sentence is, how to construct it, and how to use it, like any other technology. Conversely, as an actor in its own right, the text is dictating to you what to do, because *it* sets the criteria for what counts as textual in a context. Once published as a report, for example, a text establishes a set format for the encoding of experience, as we shall see in our Chapter 5 description of how people have had to learn how to prepare a budget statement. As they did so, it in turn began to structure their responses, in a kind of reciprocal, if sometimes uncomfortable, "dance of agency" (Pickering 1995).

Text and Context: Three Uses of Language

Halliday (2002 [1970]) sees textual agency residing in its ability to convey three different kinds of potential for meaning: *ideational, interpersonal,* and *textual* (p. 198). The first is ideational.

The Ideational Role of Language

By "ideational," Halliday is referring to the textual potential for mapping someone's experience (actions, events, states, relations; persons, objects, both animate and inanimate, institutions, abstractions) and circumstances (location, time and space, manner) onto the verbal tokens of language. It is the *forms* that language affords for mapping sentences, for example (like this one), or stories or essays or reports, that he thinks of as its logical basis. Budgets, legal documents, work plans, schedules, company reports also qualify. What he is doing here is to remind us that language is "ideational" in that it is how we express what we experience in its pre-established categories and syntax.

If we were to draw an analogy, it would be with maps, a topic we introduced in Chapter 2. Wittgenstein's point was that language is intrinsic to practice: an instrumentality that people use as they go about their daily business. When we step out of that habitual experience to describe it in language, it is like a passer-by on the street who, when asked for directions, can draw you a "map" of sorts: "Down the street to the stop light, turn left . . ." and so on. What makes it a *map*, however, of the kind we use when we enter unfamiliar territory, is that it has now been inscribed formally as a graphic representation of the streets of the town. It has become a "text" of a special sort in the familiar usage of that word: a convenient shortcut that provides us with the assurance that we can now confidently locate ourselves in unfamiliar circumstances, even though it is in reality no more than a shadow of the complexity that had to be ignored in order to serve as a communication guide for some strangers.

How is this reduction of complexity accomplished? Language has a logical structure of its own, with a vocabulary of terms and ways to organize them into symbolic sequences that, by convention, assume meaning for us. There is, therefore, an inevitable equivocation in the translation of experience into language, because experience is one thing, the categories of language another. Language is inherently an imperfect system for communication, because its structure is, by definition, limited in variety and endowed with a built-in logic of categories and syntax, in a way that experience is not. To cite Schutz (1970: 108), "all expressions . . . have for both user and interpreter, over and above their objective meaning, a meaning that is both subjective and occasional." By "occasional," he meant that, "the added meaning always has in it something of the context in which it is used" (p. 109). Maps simplify experience, and it is this that gives them their power to assume authority in a variety of circumstances.

The Interpersonal Role of Language

By the "interpersonal" potential of text, Halliday meant to refer to the attitudes, evaluations, judgments, expectations, intentions, and demands of the speaker, as they become inscribed in the modal component of the text. "Give me that!" is different from "May I have that, please?", even though they both request or demand (both speech acts) the same action, passing something over. (Here, we need to be cautious. Halliday, a linguist, emphasizes the *speaker's* attitudes, which is Goffman's dimension of *expression*. He does not underline quite so strongly the complementary equivalent: how the person(s) addressed form(s) an *impression* of the speaker's attitude or intention.)

The term "interpersonal" also connotes the role that the author of the text (speaker, writer, artist) "is taking on himself in the communication process, and the role, or rather the role choice, that he is assigning to the hearer" (Halliday 2002 [1970]: 199). Sacks, a former student of Goffman and colleague of Garfinkel, showed that categories count in how people interpret interventions, their own and others', because they place people in roles. (Again, we re-emphasize the need for the communication analyst to take into account the interpretation of what was said by the person to whom it was addressed, as well as the speaker's identification: how he or she reads the attitude of the speaker also conforms to an expected identity, not necessarily that of the speaker.) Categories establish identities (a topic taken up in Chapter 6).

Text and Context

It is the third dimension of Halliday's system of explanation, however, what he calls the "textual," that we want to most strongly emphasize: the relationship of text to its context, because it is here that his work joins up with that of the ethnomethodologists, to explain the continuity of collective organization.

By "textual," Halliday meant the relevance of the text to "some real context" (p. 199). As he puts it,

> Here the semantic system enables the speaker to structure meaning as text, organizing each element as a piece of information and relating it significantly to what has gone before ... The textual component is language as relevance (the speaker as relating to the portion of reality that constitutes the speech situation, the context within which meanings are being exchanged). The textual component provides what in current jargon we might refer to as the ecology of the text. (p. 199)

Any single instance of communication, this implies, is both a continuation of, and an invitation to, a continuing flow of text-mediated interaction, that is to say, a crucial factor in not just how the meaning of the text is assessed but in how the situation is constructed and understood. What something means *now* is also determined by *what went before*, and *what is yet to come*: not just the situation people are in, but how it has already been defined, and how people expect it to evolve in the future. This is in one sense how we have usually thought of text: a full-blown construction in language that we can understand as an imaginative reconstruction of a situation. But the text is also seen in a different way, as that which establishes a context—a *con*-text really, since it is text that frames the continued text-ing that is the essence of conversation.

An Illustration

To grasp the potential of Halliday's system for our purposes, consider briefly a context that we will explore in Chapter 5: accounting practices in a large construction firm. A formal financial account is something to be constructed and continually updated: a text that links the many activities making up the enterprise, administratively. The account has thus first an *ideational* dimension: how that which is actually happening on a certain building site comes to be understood by its translation into the language of the budget—whether the project is on target, for example. Constructing a budget statement imposes a formal or *logical* syntax: a set of categories to be used in recording events. The site manager's *experiential* account of the everyday reality in the workplace, therefore, must be encoded into those categories, however artificial they may seem to him or her.

As considered from the *interpersonal* perspective, next, the budget is a tool by means of which site managers can be interrogated and, when they deviate from standard procedure, may be disciplined. Roles, each accompanied by powers and responsibilities, are implied: those of a site manager, a regional director, a comptroller, people in head office.

There is, finally, the *textual* dimension. As we will see, when the people who are responsible locally for finalizing a budget statement get down to work, perhaps in the comptroller's office, they may refer back to earlier budget reports, and forward to projections that predict states that they might have to deal with. The outcome they are looking for is a well-constructed, fully justified, convincing account. The account will then, presumably, be amalgamated with other accounts, interpreted and re-interpreted by analysts, to build an image of the state of affairs of the company as a whole: a way to grasp what the company is about, and where it stands.

To summarize, there is a real context here: the material sites where developments are occurring, for example, or alternatively the situation of a meeting between the site manager and regional authorities, and it must be described in the language of the account (this is the ideational dimension). What the text of the budget accomplishes is to transform the state of the site into an account that can be shared by everyone in the organization (as well as by others outside it) to thus become *their* joint point of reference and thus their context (a textual dimension)—a "map." That same text will be read in very different ways, however, by the various communities making up the organization, and yet it will nevertheless supply a common environment (or, as Halliday puts it, an "ecology") that establishes the organization *as* an organization (the interpersonal dimension). It is also, however, a component in an ongoing flow of documentation, the lifeblood of the organization. It creates a context. It is how people in a situation materialize their organization for themselves, and thus create an ongoing reality where they can locate themselves and establish the meaning of what they are doing.

The Text in Multiple Contexts

Halliday recognized that "every act of meaning has a context of situation, an environment within which it is performed and interpreted" (p. 201). What he does not address is how text works in an *organizational* environment, when there are *many* contexts, *many* environments, and distance separates the performance from the interpretation: the "expression" at one time and place, the "impression" at another. The role of text may be the same, in principle, but the supplementary mechanisms that come into play are very different. People, as Halliday puts it (and here he is arguing like an ethnomethodologist), have to make "intelligent and informed guesses about what kinds of meaning are likely to be exchanged. They do this on the basis of their interpretation of the significance—the semiotic structure—of the situation " (p. 201). They must read the text in the light of "(i) what is going on, (ii) who are involved, and (iii) what part the text is playing—whether written or spoken, in what rhetorical mode and so on" (p. 201). That principle still holds as true in organizational communication as in any other context. All we add is that the reading is made more problematic whenever what is going on and who is involved occur in different places and at different times, embedded in very different experiences of practice and adaptation.

Conclusion

Summary of Chapter

The purpose of this chapter has been to review what we know about language, conceived, not as a system of logic or a code, but as an instrumentality that is activated in practices that are directed to the enactment of a both materially and socially grounded world of experience. This was Wittgenstein's profound insight. It was he who, for the first time, taught us to understand that language is a technology to be mastered and used in dealing with concrete situations, such as ordering a meal in a restaurant, or buying a new pair of shoes. Austin identified and named that property of language that makes it an effective tool for dealing with other people. His rather strange terminology, "locutionary, illocutionary, perlocutionary," has not stuck, but the insight has. People *do* use "words" to "do" things. He was right. The sub-field of linguistics that deals with modality as a property of speech has verified his insight beyond doubt.

The communication scholars who followed, Goffman, Garfinkel, Sacks, Bateson, Labov, and Fanshel, built on this earlier work and extended its insights. Goffman taught us the importance of situation: to understand it as an interactive game of framing and reframing, where the stake is establishing identities and maintaining "face" (a topic we return to explore in Chapter 6). Labov, with Fanshel, translated notions of frame, and how frame works, to show how they are grounded in deep-down understandings of the rights and obligations that accompany, and establish, identity. This understanding, we have argued, is the thirdness that supplies a sense of meaning to people's experience, because it identifies their current embedding in interaction as an instance of a more general (and already socially sanctioned) pattern. Bateson and his disciples explored the implications of this intuition, but with emphasis on the devastating effects that ensue when identity is denied. Garfinkel rejected the dominant conventional wisdom of his time, of society as a "system," to make us look at how we individually and collectively infuse meaning into the mundane, everyday world of our own experience. He built further on Wittgenstein's view of language to see meaning, not like a dictionary definition, but as how its words and phrases serve "indexically" as tools to construct the elements of our experience. Words have meanings, not in the abstract, but *in context*. Sacks and his collaborators pursued this insight into the special world of conversation, to display graphically the complex set of mechanisms that people had to have learned in order to play the "language game." Finally, the linguist and social semiotician Halliday presented us with a systemic understanding of how language as text works to (a) encode experience and thus make it available to others, (b) enable the essential mechanism of any imbrication, namely the communication of agency, and (c) reflexively infuse the current situation with meaning by supplying a *con*-text, or layer of inherited experience and understandings that now informs, recursively, our present experience.

These are tools of the trade whose utility we will be exploring in the five empirical chapters that follow.

What These Authors Did Not Address

None of the authors we have cited, however, addressed the questions we have posed, namely what an organization is, and what the mechanism is that holds it together. Certainly, all of them turned away from an analysis of language as some special, privileged domain of its own, a "house of knowledge," to emphasize instead its mundane, everyday role in how people deal with a practical world. Yet every one remained focused on the situated domains of interactive talk occurring in a single place and time. None of them delved very far into the use of text to integrate the communities of a large organization. What they left us, instead, is an enriched understanding of language, and how it enters seamlessly into the daily reconstruction of a hybrid world of materiality and the symbolic. This is what we take to be the essence of the pragmatic method: understand the link between sensemaking and situation.

There is still work to be done, however, once we try to use these tools of understanding in the analysis of the organizational experience. The chapters that follow are thus not so much exemplifications of established theory and practice, as they are original investigations into how the ideas we have been developing can be construed to shed a different and more constructive light on how organization works.

The Challenge

To take communication as the point of departure in the study of organization is, historically, new. The original formulations of Shannon, Wiener, and Chomsky were all sited in a set of premises about human knowledge that have, for centuries, dominated European thought, with roots in the classic tradition of ancient Greece. That tradition assumed that knowledge emerges in the experience of individuals and, once formalized as experience and now encoded in language, can be progressively elaborated and improved on, like any technology. In this way, objective knowledge can be accumulated, criticized, improved, exchanged, and stored. Communication, you may have noticed, figures nowhere in this conceptualization, other than as a means of transmission that people use to share their individual understandings. Against such a historical background, it is not difficult to understand communication formulations such as those of Shannon, nor why they proved to be so appealing to a wider audience than that formed by telecommunication engineers.

Communication science, as we are thinking of it in this book, starts from a different premise. We see relationship as primary. People, as George Herbert Mead understood, are born into a web of relationships. They grow up and learn to use language there. Communication both engenders and mirrors patterns of relationship. People's knowledge is continually shaped by the mixed social and material environment where they learn to be "individuals" in the full sense of that word, not merely as recognizable bodies, but as individuals with a "personality": an identity. That is why "organization as a person" has meaning for us: language use supplies it with an identity.

Clearly, no two social and material trajectories are quite the same, not even where identical twins are concerned. Each of us enters the relational web of social life from a perspective. This means that, when even as few as two people interact, they do so from ideational and interpersonal positions (to use Halliday's terms) that must be reconciled—cutting a path, metaphorically, through the thicket of language—if they are to be effective cooperating actors in their world. Instances of this kind of collaboration are everywhere: you can hardly even make it through breakfast without coordinating your actions with those of someone else. So, it follows that the issue is not to transmit your knowledge (although that is part of the equation) but, as we argued in Chapters 1 and 2, to establish a tissue of precedence, in and through a negotiated joint understanding of what your program of activities is. Unless you arrive at an amicable understanding about precedence, a reciprocity of perspectives, your two different readings of the situation will remain opposed to each other (a source of conflict), or one of the two must cede to the other by remaining mute, or in other ways giving in (dominance). Both are "schismogenetic." Neither route is likely to produce a harmonious basis of organization. How people attempt to sort out, in their transactions with each other, their common fate is the topic that future chapters address. Our purpose in this chapter has been to lay the conceptual foundation for understanding how they do so, in relating to each other by communicating, using language, and the agency of text.

The chapters that follow illustrate how these principles work out in the crucible of organizational practice.

Suggested Supplementary Readings

For an understanding of our use of speech act theory in this chapter, see Taylor and Cooren's article on the subject in the *Journal of Pragmatics* (1997).

Drew and Heritage's *Talk at Work* (1992) offers an accessible introduction to the practices of CA. See in particular their opening chapter, but also Chapter 3, contributed by Schegloff, the acknowledged "dean" of the field. Also recommended: Llewelyn's (2008) analysis of the contribution of Harvey Sacks.

Heritage's *Garfinkel and Ethnomethodology* (1984) is still one of the best introductions to the work of Garfinkel and ethnomethodology. See also Rawls (2008) for an insightful analysis of the approach developed by Garfinkel.

Halliday's work is somewhat daunting without a prior background in linguistics, but his early essay on "Language Structure and Language Function" is quite understandable. It is reproduced in Volume 1 of *The Collected Works of M. A. K. Halliday* (Halliday 2002 [1970]). Dip also into Chapter 8, which is the source of the tripartite analysis of the functionality of language developed in this chapter. See also Halliday and Webster (2006).

For background on our interpretation of the relationship between text and conversation, see Taylor, Cooren, Giroux, and Robichaud (1996). See also Taylor (2004) on parallels between the approach developed in this chapter and the work of Bakhtin.

Part Two

Research

Chapter 4

Text as the Constitutive Basis of Organization

The Organization as a Circulation of Artifacts

Recent work by Anderson (2004), Kirsch and Neff (2008), Piette (forthcoming), and Sergi (forthcoming) sheds a new light on the communicational basis of organization, as emerging *out* of conversation but inscribed *in* text. Anderson, for example, writes that,

> in the translation from oral discussion to written text, individual experiences are converted into public and permanent representations of organizational reality. Writing and the dispersal of writing are actions by which members define the organization and ways in which they sometimes change that definition. (p. 142)

Kuhn (2008) similarly sees communication as "a process in which contextualized actors use symbols and make interpretations to coordinate, and control both their own and others' activity and knowledge, which are simultaneously mediated by, and productive of, texts" (p. 1232). Writing the text, for Kuhn, now takes on strategic importance. As we did in Chapter 2, Kuhn depicts the construction of the organizational reality as "textual coorientation systems through which actors engage in 'games' that serve a variety of purposes" (p. 1228). The ultimate goal, the crucial outcome of the "game," is, however, control (p. 1234). Authority is at stake: whoever gets to *write* the map of the organization, or to authorize its writing—"map" it—is the one who can claim to define its purposes and articulate its attitudes.

The parallel with the concept of textuality that Halliday has bequeathed to us is striking, in that Anderson and Kuhn see text to not only constitute the matter of conversation but also to construct its context in a loop that ethnomethodologists think of as reflexive. Anderson, however, goes further to emphasize how text serves not merely to transcend the interpersonal dynamic of any given exchange, to thereby serve as a framework for future conversations, but, in addition, how it also serves to materialize the organization: to make it physically as well as conceptually present to the people who enter into a relationship with it. "Texts," he writes, "are not simply windows into organizational behavior but are, as Smith (2001) noted, essential to the objectification of organizations and institutions and to how they exist as such" (p. 145).

There is, of course, a long-standing tradition of research that focuses on plans, reports, minutes, documents, and the like, but such artifacts are usually portrayed as derivative processes, something going on *in* the organization, rather than as themselves *constitutive of* the latter. Anderson argues for an approach where "communication is not seen as a method for information transmission but instead is seen as the means by which organizational reality is constructed" (p. 143).

Texts as "Flow"

Is there empirical evidence that text does indeed play such a crucial role in establishing the reality of organization: that in effect it is the text that constitutes the organization as both a spiritual and a material entity? It is here that Kirsch and Neff's (2008) research takes on special significance, because, in their investigation, they confronted the physical remains of organization when the spirit had already fled. There were still texts, but no longer conversations. In 2003, a well-established American law firm, Brobeck, Phleger & Harrison, founded in 1926, with offices in New York, San Diego, San Francisco, and Los Angeles, declared bankruptcy, a victim of the high-tech boom/bust of the late 1990s and the beginning of the 2000s. Because of the prominence of the firm, it was one of the most visible failures in the entire history of American legal practice. Kirsch and Neff (2008) set out to preserve what they could of the materials that still remained in the vacated offices, traces of the written records of the company's business when it had been in full flower. They visited each of its four locations and collected a voluminous body of materials left behind when the individual partners decamped in search of a niche in other law firms. They interviewed former employees, filmed the abandoned premises, made field notes on their observations, and, above all, packed up the remaining documents and hauled them away for prolonged examination.

The processes that materialized the organization as a corporate actor, one that had made it present in many people's daily affairs as long as it was alive, had ceased. The offices had been vacated. What they discovered was the residue: the embodiment of the former organization, in its texts, the machinery that produced them, and the offices that housed them. A shell of its former self, perhaps, but still a substantial "self."

This research points up (and in doing so reinforces Anderson's point), not merely the crucial role that text plays in mediating the interaction that links up the multiple, diverse communities that go to compose a large organization, but also how it and other concrete signs of the organization *materialize* it as an entity in its own right by doing so. As Kirsch and Neff observe, you could even describe the functioning organization as essentially "managing, curating, and circulating artifacts within its boundaries" (p. 3). It is the material routines, they write, that "help define the organization" (p. 7): establish it *as* an organization. Documents, like blood in the circulatory system of mammals, exhibit flow, mobility. As the authors remark, the collapse of the organization entailed a progressive deceleration, or a slowing of the traffic through the "normal circuits" of the organization until it stopped altogether (p. 10). The organization was in its death throes.

It is, they comment, precisely in the process of document circulation that a live organization normally "enacts its existence" (p. 12). The flow of documents and other such artifacts necessitates the existence of those communicative circuits for the process to continue. Inversely, that same ongoing traffic, in its materiality, is also the lifeblood that sustains the circuits and thus turns the organization into a functioning entity. The flow constitutes "the artifactual embodiment of the legal, economic, and social boundaries" (p. 15) that serve to separate segments of the organization (externally), while simultaneously unifying its communities of practice (internally). As they remark,

> If organizations consolidate multiple interests into what appears as a coherent culture, then organizational failure brings those distinctions into sharp relief . . . In the process of failure, the artifacts that are most specific to the formerly functioning organization and that most embody its routines and processes are precisely those that are the most likely to be abandoned. (p. 23)

Uplinked Versus Downlinked

In any healthy organization, they intimate, there is one flow that sustains the relative autonomy of the constituent communities that make up the organization (perhaps limited to one office, for example), and another that binds those same communities together into an at least partial commonality of purpose. The first flow is an instance of what we have called "downlinking," preoccupied with the value-adding primary activities of corporate litigation and the paperwork it requires. The second flow illustrates "uplinking," since it consists of communicative activities that connect up the disparate domains of legal work to the management of the firm. The combined organization-wide flow is therefore not seamless, but punctuated. When breakup occurs, the downlinked—the community-specific—are the first to decamp: the lawyers at Brobeck, Phleger & Harrison packed up their active files and vacated their offices, leaving behind them only those artifactual traces that had once stitched them all together into a firm with a definable identity. Kirsch and Neff were left to study the remainders.

Taking the Next Step

The challenge Kirsch and Neff now face, like good archaeologists, is how to decipher from this unique corpus of documentary artifacts what their organizational meaning was when the company was going strong. What were the modes of organizing that gave the company its life, as well as its considerable success (until the roof fell in, that is)? When an archaeologist comes upon a cache of old pottery, or a pile of ancient weapons, or is able to trace the foundations of a long-lost village, he or she wants to discover something previously unknown about how people then lived, and what their society was like. Archaeologists can do this because they know that the artifacts they have stumbled upon once played an active role in shaping and constituting the daily life of people there. From pottery, they learn something about family life, from tools what the economy was like, from weapons where the demographic and political divisions lay, from symbols something about the belief system of the community. But what functions do *documents* play in a contemporary organization? What do they do in an organizational context? How do they shape the activities of people who use them to do things—give *them* meaning and, by doing so, lend a meaning to the actions of the actors *themselves*? As communication researchers, we have to ask ourselves, if we are to develop our own "archaeology" of organization, how *do* texts integrate—and incidentally also divide? What is their mode of existence? How do they indexically and reflexively constitute the reality of a working law practice by entering into its conversations and thus tying its many components together?

The Text in the Conversation

This is the question that we address in the five chapters that follow. The approach we adopt, however, is different in one important respect from that followed by Kirsch and Neff. We focus our attention, not on characteristics of the text as such, but on the manner in which it operates by playing a role in the conversations of organizational members. We understand text, i.e., documents, to be usually understood as something that is acted on: an object to which people address their attention, and which they may modify as they do so. But we will be looking, as the next chapters unfold, at the corollary: how the text acts on *them*—a perlocutionary and not merely an illocutionary dimension, texts as actors. To do this, we make what might seem at first to be a radical move: we take all linguistic expressions, including those that go to compose a conversation, as varieties of text.

This is the logic that has been advanced by Halliday and his associates: text is not merely that which links conversations *to* each other by creating a common point of reference. It is also the material basis *of* those same conversations: that which they are composed of to begin with. As we have already seen (Chapter 3), text is any "language that is functional ... doing some job in some context ... playing some part in a context of situation" (Halliday & Hasan 1989: 10). That is our topic: how *does* text "do the job," when the "job" is stitching together the multiple threads of all the communities of practice that compose a large, complex organization?

Organizational, Not Merely Interpersonal, Communication

Social semiotics supplies a crucial step to an answer to our question. Halliday, we recall, proposed three dimensions of textuality: (1) text serves to translate people's experience into language, (2) language enables interaction, and (3) the texts that are thus generated cumulatively construct a common context for everyone who participates in the conversations. The authors we cited at the start of this chapter saw text as the "glue" that holds organization together and gives it coherence. Halliday's work carries us even further, however, because it prompts us to examine how text enters into the conversations that are the vital organs of any organization, and how they in turn reflexively construct a text/context. Halliday's tripartite perspective can thus be translated into an agenda for the communication researcher: an empirical guide to analyzing the constitution of organizational reality in the stuff of conversation.

Structuring a Research Agenda

First, we might ask ourselves, do the texts that circulate to form the common property of those who identify with the organization actually reflect *their* experience? When people are confronted with a document produced somewhere else, we should ask, as researchers, how do they evaluate its relevance to their *own* context? Does it enable them to get on with what they are doing, make sense of it? Does the matter inscribed in the formal syntax of the document match up with their own experience? Is it seen to be an authentic representation of the reality they daily live?

Second, assuming there to be differences in interpretation, how is the meaning of a text reconstructed in the interpersonal channels of talk and interaction where, because it is here that differences of perception are expressed and defended, authority is also being negotiated? What are not only the interpersonal but also the inter-group implications of the differences? Is the task of authoring the purposes of the organization distributed in a way that supports people, by enabling them to act in their own contexts, or does it reduce their ability to respond constructively to the challenges they face? How are authority relations understood, and what these relations say about people's sense of identity? Are they comfortable with the relationship the text serves to mediate?

Third, does the text serve to construct a convincing context, by portraying the purposes of the organization in the imagination of people such that they understand it and so that it legitimates their own activities? Does the text correspond to, or fit with, their vision of what their organization is really about: what *its* identity is, and how it relates to theirs?

All of these questions have a similar aim: to answer the question, does the text unite or divide? Is the organization being sustained? Is the "flow" that Kirsch and Neff described working?

In this chapter, we report on ethnographic research, with implications for understanding the agency of text, conducted in Chile by Consuelo Vasquez for her doctoral dissertation at the Université de Montréal in Canada (she is now Assistant Professor of Communication at the Université du Québec à Montréal). In doing so, we pursue our introductory theoretical interrogations by following her traces as she conducts her research in a mixed voluntary and governmental body where everything depends on collaboration, since many communities of practice must be stitched together if the purposes of the organization are to be even minimally realized. It is thus an ideal vehicle for pursuing our own questioning of how text works.

"Espacer L'Organisation: Trajectoires d'un Projet de Diffusion de la Science et de la Technologie au Chili"[5]

Chile is a fascinating country. With the towering Andes to the east and the mighty Pacific Ocean to the west, it is squeezed into an elongated band of territory stretched out over some 6,500 kilometers (roughly 4,000 miles) from north to south: "from Arica to Punta-Arenas," Chileans like to say. It is one of the longest countries in the world, if not the longest. At its Peruvian extension to the north, it turns into a

---

5 "Spacing Organization: Trajectories of a Chilean Science and Technology Diffusion Project." See also Vasquez (forthcoming).

blistering desert. At its other extremity, it is the last stop before the South Pole. Punta-Arenas, for example, is located near the Straits of Magellan, where, in the age of sail, many a sailor once allowed himself to breath again after rounding Cape Horn.

Chile has a population of some 16 million Spanish-speaking inhabitants, including about 5 percent of people whose ancestors were native to the country before the arrival of Europeans, as well as 65 percent *mestizos*, that is to say people who can claim at least one indigenous ancestor as well. Most people live more or less in the middle of the country (the north is too dry to be habitable, the far south too barren). As much as 40 percent of the population, for example, lives in the area surrounding the capital, Santiago, a bit to the north of the geographical center of the country.

The country has a long history of independence, dating back to 1818, when it declared itself a republic. With some notable exceptions (the Pinochet régime for two decades, in the 1970s and 1980s, for example), Chile has generally enjoyed a stable democracy. It has now established itself as one of the most prosperous countries in Latin America, with a strong economy, a good, if uneven, education system, and a comparative lack of corruption in government.

Most of Consuelo Vasquez' research was conducted in a central region of the country, to the south of the capital, Santiago. It includes a large urban area with a busy port city having a population of about 300,000, a surrounding urban agglomeration with about a million and a half inhabitants, and a major university, as well as other institutions of higher learning. Consuelo herself comes from this region and she knows it well. For her fieldwork, she chose an organization where she had once worked, called *Explora,* an imaginative venture in popular education.

Explora

Chileans place a high value on education. Explora is a governmental organization whose mandate is to promote science and technology to young Chileans in every part of the country, when they are still deciding on what they want to do with their lives. Its head office is located in Santiago. Many of its activities, however, are organized by regional offices, in places such as Coquimbo, Valparaíso, O'Higgins, Concepción, Maule, and Biobío. All of Explora's activities assume contributions by individuals in the field of education, teachers, and researchers. These resource people, other than a small permanent staff in the regional offices, are not remunerated for their time. All but a few full-time employees are volunteers.

Activities include the organization of field trips, visits to laboratories, conversations with scientists, a regional conference where students present their projects, an exhibition, guided tours, and a news bulletin. The showpiece event of the year is what is called the National Science and

Technology Week (*Semana Nacional de la Ciencia y la Tecnología*, or SNCYT), which unfolds in October (the southern hemisphere equivalent of a northern April). Its most ambitious component (although there are many others) is called *1000 Scientists, 1000 Classrooms*. The idea is to marshal visits by practicing scientists to at least 1,000 schoolrooms. All of the scientists contribute to the success of the week on a voluntary basis.

Explora's regional offices outside of Santiago are typically located in universities. The character of the organization is thus unusual, since, although it is governmental in name and mission, it incorporates many of the features (and challenges) of a non-governmental organization: how to assure personal commitment on the part of its resource persons, the teachers and practitioners of science. The region Consuelo studied, for example, Sur, is headed up by Mariana, whose office is located at a major university, where she not only teaches on a part-time basis, and thus has academic status, but also assures the continuing administration of ongoing activities making up the regional program of Explora.

Mariana

Probably the best way to describe Mariana is to say that she has *presence*. So much so, indeed, that she has problems delegating, since her instinct is to be everywhere at the same time. Her commitment to her mission is, however, contagious, and she inspires loyalty in her staff, even when they occasionally find her polyvalence frustrating. She is an idealist, but with a realist's humor and conviviality. The gap between public and private education in Chile is striking, and she is one of those who finds such inequality of opportunity unacceptable. Now graying, but full of energy, she radiates warmth, intelligence, and confidence. She is not someone you want to cross lightly, if only because of her integrity, her down-to-earth humor, and single-minded determination. She is no by-the-book bureaucrat. She is a committed public servant. It is not quite the same thing.

By its nature, a regional office of Explora is modest in size. Mariana, for example, counts on the assistance of a permanent secretary, Claudia (all names are pseudonyms). In addition, she can call on the services of a designer, Lorena. The third permanent member of the team is a journalist, Javiera, who handles public relations, takes care of the Website and contacting the press, as well as contributing to building a network of ongoing links with some 50 schoolteachers who participate in the various programs. Others join the team on a contractual basis, part-time. One of her unpaid mainstays is her husband, Gerardo, a professor of journalism at the university but always an enthusiastic presence at Explora (the boundary between family and work is more porous in Chile that in North America or Europe).

The highlight of the year, as we have said, is the SNCYT. It takes a great deal of advance planning in order to mobilize the scientists, publicize the main event (*1000 Scientists, 1000 Classrooms*), and make arrangements with all the schools where the Explora-sponsored activities actually take place. It is an operation that Mariana knows well, since she has been there since the beginning of Explora, in 1994.

Vasquez' field research took place during the 12th year of Explora's existence, in 2006. She spent from July to October of that year doing fieldwork using a methodology known as *shadowing* (Meunier & Vasquez 2008). Shadowing consists of literally following people around as they conduct their daily work, recording them in their context using an unobtrusive video camera (acting like their "shadow," in other words). Vasquez filmed ordinary activities such as meetings and telephone calls, as well as special events such as a children's scientific "congress," a technology exhibition, and a youth conference. In addition, she collected work documents such as e-mails, design materials, and organizational charts. Finally, she interviewed both local members of the project team, as well as representatives of the central committee who oversee the national organization.

From this rich corpus, we have selected only a few incidents that serve to illustrate the crucial role that texts play in the life of an organization such as Explora. We concentrate on two events. The first, which concerns the "form," illustrates how the regional office sets about lining up volunteer scientists by getting their commitment to participate: downlinking, in other words. The second focuses on the confusion of purposes that may arise as a result of a regional office's communication with its head office in Santiago. This latter, from Mariana's perspective, is uplinking, since now it is her office that is acting as the organization's regional agent. Both illustrate, but in very different ways, how text performs: how it maps experience to logical categories; how it serves to establish precedence and authority, locally and globally; and how it constructs a meaningful interpretation of the organization, its mission, and its image.

Downlinking: Building a Local Program by Enlisting Scientists

The "Form"

We are about two months before Tuesday, October 2, when the 1-week long *1000 Scientists, 1000 Classrooms* set of visits will kick off. It is August (deep winter in Chile). We are in Mariana's office, peering vicariously through Consuelo's camera at the interaction as it unfolds there. We are watching Mariana brief Fernanda, an assistant who has been hired to help out in recruiting the support of the scientists (she is also, incidentally, Mariana's daughter). Mariana sits behind her desk, which is strewn with piles of documents. At one end of the desk sits a computer. A number of preliminary planning meetings have already been held by Mariana and her staff. The atmosphere in this one is relaxed and friendly, but also business-like. We pick up the conversation at the point where Fernanda is being instructed on how to circulate a form to potential contributors, soliciting their willingness to participate (the extracts from the conversation have been translated by the researcher herself from the original Spanish into English).

Fernanda: I need you to explain it to me, I have to get going.
Mariana: Okay, okay. Let's see. Here is the form for the *1000 Scientists*; I'll send it to you by e-mail.
Fernanda: Okay.

In Chapter 2, we explained what we called a "frame game." The principle that motivated our use of the phrase is well known to visual artists: any object or event takes on meaning only when it has been framed. Framing is thus consequential—and strategically loaded. People's actions and interactions are always framed: by drawing an imaginary boundary around any sequence of talk involving more than one person, the situation thus delimited constitutes a frame that allows people to perform intelligibly within it. But constructing the framework also establishes, by the principle of reflexivity, the authority of its authors.

People accomplish this boundary delineation in conversation by using the resource of language, as they construct their interventions in, to follow Halliday, text. Building a text—even if it is just plain talking—means marshaling certain components. For it to be an intelligible text, for example, an object or objects must be established, often expressed verbally by using a noun or a pronoun: *it*, for example, in Fernanda's words. We, the readers, do not know, as we drop in on their conversation from the outside, what "it" is, but Mariana and Fernanda do. We learn right away from Mariana's response: "the form," she says. One component of the frame is established: what their attention is focused on. In their talk, they are building, using language, a common point of reference on a shared experience.

Second, if there is an object, there must also be someone or something to act on it (remember Peirce's distinction between firstness and second-ness: acting on is a precondition for the establishment of any meaning at all). An *acting-on* implies in turn an *actor-on*: a subject who has an obligation to act on an object. "Okay, okay ... I'll send it ..." says Mariana, thus establishing herself as the responsible agent, simultaneously conceding, modally, Fernanda's right to ask her for "it." "Sending it" constitutes, linguistically speaking, *transitivity*: an actor-on ("I") linked to an acted-on ("it") through an action, "sending" it to someone (again, we reiterate this was Peirce's basic condition for meaning to even exist). Mariana is, for the moment, framed as Fernanda's agent. That is Halliday's second, interpersonal, dimension. Its effect is to embed the interaction in a framework where, to echo Austin, one person acts *on* another or, inversely, one person acts *for* another. This communicative framing is indexed, in the instance we are considering, by Mariana continuing ". . . to you." Now we have two actors, Mariana and Fernanda, linked by a common object, the form that Mariana will e-mail to Fernanda. Fernanda has told Mariana to do something: *actor–(speech) act–virtual agent*. Mariana will then, she promises in response, send "it" to Fernanda.

Linguistically, reciprocity of agency is known as *ditransitivity* (Taylor & Van Every 2000). Ditransitivity is the *sine qua non* for the construction of a communicative relationship in that it establishes, via the text, someone who will act on an object for the benefit of the other. When they do so act, they confirm the framing.

Ditransitivity also implies firstness/secondness. "*I* need *you* to explain *it* to *me*," says Fernanda, "I have to get going." In other words, *I* Fernanda am acting on *you* Mariana so that *you* will act on *it* by sending it to *me*. One act, Mariana's text addressed to Fernanda, embeds, by implication, another: an instance of imbrication. It is the initial and indispensable component of all organization, no matter how complex the latter. The ditransitive is the basic component of story construction (for discussion, see Taylor and Van Every's (2000) treatment of Greimas' theory of narrative). Text, in other words, simultaneously *enables* and *interprets* interaction and, in doing so, constructs a web of meaningful relationships (Giddens 1984).

Back to Fernanda and Mariana

Mariana understands. She first clarifies the nature of the object: "the form for the *1000 Scientists*," she adds, and then she makes her commitment: "I am going to send it to you." She has been acted on. She may be the official principal, the "boss," in her relationship to Fernanda, since she has employed the latter to act as an assistant, but she also recognizes her own responsibilities in the resulting conjunction of agencies. As Bateson argued and Labov and Fanshel found, all meaningful human relationships are characterized by reciprocal obligations, and it is in this reciprocity that social action is differentiated from physical action, as Goffman (1974: 22) also reiterated by his distinction between *natural* and *social* frameworks.

The pronouns are the tip-off. Fernanda acts *on* Mariana (as Austin told us language makes possible) by her formulation of a text that conveys the modal force of an instruction, or a request, or a command: "*I need you* [to explain *it* to *me*]." Mariana recognizes the deontic implications of the phrase (a duty has been laid on her), and she responds by making a promise.

This interaction does not, however, occur in a social and material vacuum. As we argued in Chapter 2, the modal force conveyed by Fernanda's intervention depends indexically on the already-established context. We, as observers, people from the outside, can only infer the modal implication of Fernanda's words from the circumstance, as Consuelo has explained to us, that Mariana has employed Fernanda, her daughter, to perform a certain task. That enables us to make an informed guess as to the modal force of each of their interventions. But our interpretation should also be based on the text itself. Fernanda uses the phrase "I need you to . . . ," which is a mode of speech that serves to soften the implication of the command "explain it to me." She evokes her mission, "I have to get going," and, since it was Mariana who had delegated her to be her agent in the first place, Fernanda's "command" (*explain!*) is thus both a reiteration of her proactive role as agent-actor, and also a confirmation of her acceptance of Mariana's commission. It is the taken-for-granted *mission* they are both embarked on that constitutes their joint thirdness, with the result that, while Mariana is Fernanda's principal in *their* interpersonal frame, both are conjointly subject to the rule of the mission, organizationally—a different frame. It is what supplies a context. There is both precedence and equality, depending on the framing. Fernanda, consequently, is asserting a certain autonomy: in her frame *she* will be the effective agent, as she meets the eventual contributors to the *1000 Scientists, 1000 Classrooms* week: "I have to get going!" she says. The talk of the two manifests both complementarity and symmetry, never tipping toward schismogenesis.

We have been establishing in our analysis the basis of what Goffman (1974: 21) called a "primary framework" or "one that is seen as rendering what would otherwise be a meaningless aspect of the scene into something that is meaningful." A primary framework, Goffman wrote, "allows its users to locate, perceive, identify, and label a seemingly infinite number of concrete occurrences defined in its terms." Seen in this light, it is we, the readers of Consuelo's transcription, who have, without any sense of artificiality, supplied a framework. Fernanda is working for Mariana, and the latter briefs her on her task: a primary framework, in our society. Fernanda, however, is also Mariana's daughter. That suggests a second primary framework. Once we understand that both those frameworks apply here, we automatically build in interpretive assumptions that are grounded in our understanding, part of what we inherit from the culture we grew up in. As Goffman wrote, "each primary framework allows its user to locate, perceive, identify, and label a seemingly infinite number of concrete occurrences defined in its terms" (p. 21). We *know* about contractual relationships, including those of a family (Labov & Fanshel 1977). There is a thirdness of family, as with any stable organization.

But if *we* do this, without effort, we also expect Mariana and Fernanda to be doing it as well, and pretty much like we do. That is what makes a framework "primary." It is also presumably why Peirce chose to use the word "law" to describe thirdness. As Goffman (1974: 27) put it: "the primary frameworks of a particular social group constitute a central element of its culture." Like gardening, or experiments, we understand the framework. And, reasonably enough, we assume that Chileans do too. There is an Explora thirdness, it would seem, at least in what we have seen so far.

Projecting Beyond the Initial Framework

With this in mind, let us return to our analysis. As we do, focus again on the pronouns. As we argued in Chapter 2, pronouns are one powerful tool in delineating which frameworks the speaker wants to establish. In the sequence we have just been considering, the terms used were "I," "you," and "it": the framework was *inter*personal Watch now to see what gets added.

[In the following dialogue, the = sign indicates that no time has elapsed between two utterances.]

Mariana: This is the form that the scientists fill out. You must have seen it before.
Fernanda: No, never. I hadn't seen it before.
Mariana: No? Okay, hum, but I'll send it by e-mail and uh in filling out that form *they* put =
Fernanda: = The topics that *they* want to speak about.

There it is: the shift from *inter*-active to *trans*-active: from one conversation, inside, to one that is linked to others, outside. "*They*" are not physically present in this arena of talk, situated in Mariana's office, but in other imagined future encounters that are evoked textually:

Mariana: In fact, *they* give a title for *their* talk; *they* indicate if *they* have any preferences. This is something that *we* try to avoid because if *they* say: "ah, *I* want, ah, *I* studied in the F550 school of, *I* don't know where, *I* want to go there" =
Fernanda: = Okay.
Mariana: And, what really happens is that in that school =
Fernanda: = Nobody cares.

Mariana: Exactly. And for *us* it is suddenly like more complicated. Now, anyway, if *somebody* insists on it, and everything, *we* do it. But *we* trust that, hopefully, *they* will be open and available and in-in-in the letter that *I*—because this form is accompanied by a letter signed by *me*. In that letter it says that, "please be open to going to any place in the Region."

To reiterate, the function of third person pronouns, singular or plural, is to project *beyond* the interpersonal framework of interaction involving people who are co-present, physically, in the same conversational space. Conversations, as interpersonal forms of organizing, occur in a here-and-now: a physically and temporally delimited space–time. To qualify as an organization that transcends individual conversations, however, it must exist differently, in a there as well as a here and a then as well as a now. It is a universe composed *of* conversations, never limited to only one.

What Mariana is doing is using the constructive power of text to portray activities in a different space–time than the one she is currently in: Fernanda will be interviewing the professors who will constitute the resource base of the *1000 Scientists, 1000 Classrooms* week-long activities, in *their* offices. By doing this, she will effectively be trying to embed one context of conversations, that of the scientists, within another, that of Explora. This is downlinking: one set of activities, the visits to the schools, that enables another by constituting a component of it, in this instance Explora. Like the stem cells that made the experiment a success, and thus empowered the scientist who planned and ran it, the professors' collaboration in the week is the indispensable performance that will realize the purpose of the organizers. We have transcended the limits of the interpersonal to enter the domain of the organizational. This is the whole point of organization: how it becomes extended, downlinked, to do things that far exceed what any individual could expect to accomplish. The linking, however, also establishes *conditionalities*, as Mariana emphasizes in her description of the professors' likely responses. Mariana's success depends on Fernanda's success in signing up students and professors. The success of Explora nationally depends on the multiplication of this accomplishment everywhere in the country. And there are others as well, it turns out, who must also be committed: the teachers, and their school administrators, in the larger area.

Fernanda: If this scientist is ready, do you have a list (*she means of potential places to visit*)?
Mariana: The list is here. That's the one you had to ask Panchi, it's in a—in a file.
Fernanda: Yes, in a file.

(*Panchi's file, incidentally, includes correspondence with the schools they will eventually be working with.*)

Constructing Organization

This conversation is thus not simply about Mariana telling Fernanda what to do. It is, rather, how they collaboratively establish an agenda, a context where Fernanda's mandate originates with Mariana, but both are committing themselves to a course of action: in effect writing the narrative of the next step to take, a plan of action, mapping out what has to be done, when, and how. They thereby construct, by inscribing it in *text*, a campaign of interviews: a map of events, where, and when they are to occur. The "text" they "write" in their conversation is at one and the same time ideational (it maps experience into verbal form), interpersonal (it establishes responsibility and authority), and textual (it is part of the symbolic construction of an event, *1000 Scientists, 1000 Classrooms*).

It is, however, more than "text": it is the organization itself in construction. It is an event, in an office, but it is also a component in an extended network of actors who must be imbricated for there to *be* a program. The teachers, for example, will have to fill out a form to indicate which topics they are especially interested in; how many students they teach; what level they are at; the facilities they can provide; the rooms and equipment that will have to be mobilized. And then there is the publicity: posters to be mailed out, newspapers to be contacted. It all has to be tied together through texting, verbally and by circulating documents, but it is simultaneously material—not merely enabled *by* text but, as Kirsch and Neff found, a composition *of* texts: a real and tangible world, grounded in materiality—the materiality of text, to start with, but eventually of buses, cars, lecture rooms and their projectors, laboratory equipment, and computer programs.

And if it Doesn't Work?

Imbrication, however, is something to be accomplished, not a given. Fernanda executed her commission faithfully, but the outcome was disappointing (Consuelo also "shadowed" Fernanda as she made some of her visits to professors' offices, filming the interaction with the skeptical target). The previous year, 2005, some 120 scientists had signed up for the week. This year, Mariana had hoped to at least equal or even to top that record, and, since some volunteers are always prepared to give two talks, she thought she might be able to count on as many as 150 separate talks taking place. That was the expectation when Fernanda's and Mariana's initial meeting took place. A month later, the situation looked less rosy. Consuelo was there with her camera for another encounter between Mariana and Fernanda.

[In the following dialogue, (. . .) indicates a very short pause, a fraction of a second.]

Fernanda: (*She opens a folder in which she has archived the subscriber forms received at the moment for the planned activity.*) I have received twelve =

Mariana: = Twelve!!! (*She stops rearranging the mass of papers on her desk and looks Fernanda straight in the eyes.*)

Fernanda: Forms at this moment.

Mariana: You must now begin to call by telephone.

Fernanda: To call by . . . I telephone, yes.

Mariana: Yes, that is question one. Second, a reminder by e-mail.

Fernanda: Okay.

Mariana: Okay. To all the people, to all the people that you sent to, send them a second mail that says that you have extended the deadline because the deadline is . . . has passed.

Fernanda: No, no, no, it's until next Friday, the deadline.
(. . .)

Mariana: Okay . . . Fernanda, this is urgent.

They never did manage to sign up the 100 they had hoped to. They got 80 to commit from the university. Rather than present this as a failure, however, they engaged in some creative re-framing of their own in how they described the week's events to the press and in the final report they submitted to their Head Office. In the report, for example, they listed 123 scientists, but not all these had been recruited by Explora (sometimes it was a local teacher who had drawn on other university faculties). In the newspaper reports, the term used was "about a hundred" (*un centenar*, in Spanish, or "roughly a hundred"). The number of schools reached, as reported in the press, was also vague: 45 in one report, 40 in another. These reports, however, played a major role in the subsequent evaluation of the success of the week's activities. They became *its* text.

Within the organizing team itself, however, Mariana recognized that, the following year, recruitment should start earlier, and the person responsible should be committed full-time to the job, as opposed to taking on a variety of tasks. The other side of the coin, however, was their grievance with the professors who were too often forgetful, or failed to live up to their commitments. Mariana was heard to remark ironically "1,000 professors, 1,000 problems!" She decided that, next year, the answer would be to institutionalize the activity by making it a mandatory requirement, authorized by the university, and coordinated by the various faculties.

Uplinking: The Other Dimension of Organizational Coherence

We have seen in the Explora example how Halliday's three textual dimensions generate organization in conversation. We now turn to look at how text works in the larger extended network of the multi-site organization.

The Center Versus the Regions, Act I: "The Poster"

For the first ten years of its existence, the director general of Explora was Haydée Domic. When Michelle Bachelet was elected President of Chile, she replaced Domic with Alejandra Villarzu, who entered office with a different vision of where Explora should fix its priorities from that of her predecessor. For one thing, she was preoccupied with the need to develop a more powerful corporate image. There was a rationale for this: Explora can be seen as having two missions, to educate children by inspiring in them a scientific curiosity, but also to sensitize the general population and awaken them to the importance of education and science. The new director general focused on this second priority and set about upgrading the strategic role of an improved public awareness. (Of course, new administrations almost always see their role as authoring the purposes of their organization in a new way.)

The poster advertising *National Science and Technology Week* became an ideal target. She thought the previous ones had lacked impact. She therefore hired an advertising agency to design a new and more striking announcement of activities. We are in Mariana's office quarters when the new posters are delivered, about a month prior to the special week in October. Others present are her secretary Claudia, Gerardo (Mariana's husband, a journalism professor), the designer Lorena, and of course Consuelo herself. The sequence begins with the arrival of a deliveryman, bearing hefty boxes.

[In the following dialogue, the [sign indicates that the following portions of the utterances are produced simultaneously. [XXXX indicates that her words are unintelligible.]

Claudia:	Señora Mariana, more posters are coming.
Mariana:	What?
Claudia:	More posters are coming?
Mariana:	They're here? [XXXX
Claudia:	[Now

Gerardo's voice can be heard in the background as they all, except Mariana, walk down the corridor to the front office. The deliveryman brings in the box filled with posters and gets Claudia to sign a form confirming their receipt. Claudia signs the form. Claudia goes to the kitchen and gets a pair of scissors. Gerardo is approaching through the corridor.

Gerardo: There are thousands!—But these are the posters from here? The ones you made? (*He is addressing Lorena, the designer, who has just walked in.*)
Claudia: No, from Santiago.
Lorena: Are these the thematic ones?
Claudia: Mmm. (*She takes a poster out of one box and hands it to Lorena.*) Take it, Lorena. (*Lorena opens it and looks at it, as does Gerardo.*)
Claudia: And the other one must be the same one we saw before. (*She is referring to another poster that had arrived earlier from Santiago.*)

This new poster is horizontal in shape. On the left side, it states in bold, colorful letters the slogan of this year's campaign: "New Materials: The Play of the Atoms." Its main colors are black and orange, quite dramatic. Explora's usual logo, however, is missing. The poster now instead announces in large letters: Explora–Conicyt. On the right side of the image, there is a white space, where details about particular activities are presented, as well as contact information. It is this zone that will become a crucial identity issue, because it implicitly pits Explora's central committee, located in Santiago, against the regional coordination units: all the information written there refers to the Santiago region, and there is no space left over to advertise local activities.

Consuelo: Comments?
Claudia: What does Lorena say? [Lorena, we recall, is the regional designer.]
Gerardo: (*Before Lorena can reply*) That it's a shame that they are making a poster for Santiago. (*Lorena smiles. She puts the poster on the desk near the window where the light is better.*)
Claudia: They keep on getting better at spending money for horrible things.
Gerardo: (*He approaches the table to see the poster better.*) By the way, look. (*He points out the right area of the poster where the contact information and activities are presented, all taking place in the Santiago metropolitan area.*)
Lorena: What use is this for us?
Claudia: It looks like a curtain. (*She means the horizontal printing in the area to the right.*)
(*0.3 seconds pass.*)

(*Lorena moves her hand over the poster as if to say, "I don't know."*)

Lorena: If we put here another little paper hiding this (*she is pointing to the area on the right where the printed information is bunched*). Is that the idea? (*She looks at Professor Gerardo, presumably trying to make sense of what this area might be useful for.*)

Gerardo: But look at the extension they've put there (*He points to the URL address: www.explora.cl/sncyt2006/regiones/actividades. html.*) Aren't they stupid! (*He walks away, fuming*)

Lorena is still looking at the poster. She doesn't talk. She smiles ironically, takes the poster and displays it for the camera to see.

Claudia: We'll have to put here a paper so it'll have our activities, our contact information.

Lorena: (*Looking at the poster she is holding*) Information with Claudia. (*She laughs. She puts the poster on the table again, looks at it, and scratches her head.*)

Claudia: There's no way, hunh?

There was, they collectively decided, "no way." The image itself was powerful, and guaranteed to catch the attention of the public. But, because it left no space for them to publicize their activities, for their regional public, its utility was drastically reduced. So they made a radical move:

Claudia: We are going to have to do what they did in Journalism and cut. They did cut . . . (*She laughs.*)

Claudia is referring to a previous situation, in the Journalism Department, when they had cut another of Explora's posters, retaining only the information they found useful for the department. The part they envisioned shaving off highlighted the official sponsors of the event: Explora, the government of Chile. This is why they all laughed.

Not everybody hated the new poster, however. Javiera, the press relations specialist, for example, found it inspirational:

Javiera: It's nice. I like it a lot. Let's see. (*She holds it upon a wall.*) "New Materials" (*she reads*).

Lorena: The bad thing is that it only has the information for the Santiago region. I thought it would be different.

Javiera: Well, you are dreaming if you think they are going someday to send one more regional. But it's nice, this one. Ok, I would even put it up there. "New Materials" (*She reads the title again.*) It inspires me. (*She laughs.*) Up there.

But the consensus was that the offending right side, with its exclusive focus on the central metropolitan region and its neglect of contacts in the other regions, had to go. And there were also objections to the omission of the standard Explora logo. Mariana agreed:

Mariana: Yes, they designed it with that purpose. But, you know that I don't think it's so bad if we cut it. (*She laughs.*) Of course, the Conicyt [the National Commission on Science and Technology] is going to disappear. But, but, you know, I would cut it. (*She makes the gesture of cutting the right area of the poster.*) And I would paste a logo of Explora here. (*She shows it on the poster.*) A sticker.
Claudia: But don't they want to get rid of the logo?
Mariana: (*She looks at the camera smiling.*) This year =
Claudia: = We put on the logo.
Mariana: Gonzalez's style. Claudia, let's use Gonzalez's methodology. The methodology of the knife. (*She laughs.*) (*Both laugh.*)

The reference was again to a previous, similar situation, where the professor in the Journalism Department shaved off another poster, for an earlier Science Week whose theme was communication. "Gonzalez's method" meant to cut. And that is what they did. They cut. The part on the right where the contact information was written disappeared.

Comment

Earlier in the chapter, we outlined an agenda of research based on three questions: Does a text accurately represent the experience of those who are its recipients? Does it effectively mediate interpersonal relationships? Is it coherent with its pre-established context?

The incident we have been considering reveals a translation from experience to linguistic representation that was, from the perspective of those in the regional office, infelicitous: the poster listed information about Santiago's local campaign, not theirs. They then reacted in a way that suggested that the interpersonal relation between themselves and Santiago was less than trusting: "Aren't they stupid!" And, finally, Mariana in particular focused on the absence of the usual logo, thus questioning whether the context she had previously taken for granted was any longer the same. The "text," in the form of the poster, still operated as a crucial organizational link (once "cut" it was put to good use), but it left a residue of schismogenetic tension, and led to a sequel. The book was not yet closed on the incident.

Act II: "In Santiago"

Shortly after, on September 8, the biennial meeting of Explora regional coordinators was scheduled to take place in Santiago to discuss national policy and practice. One of those present at the meeting was the director of the advertising firm that had been awarded the contract to develop a new corporate image for Explora, Fernando. It was his firm that had produced the offending poster to which Mariana's group was reacting. All the regional directors were there as well. Mariana, with her usual directness, but also her customary vivacity and expressiveness, found an occasion to quiz the head of the design company.

Mariana: Let's turn to the other side (*She points towards Fernando, sitting across the table from her, on the other side of the big table where all are seated.*) Now, with respect to the redesign of the program image, I am worried that the criteria for this redesign, in one way or another, are going to exclude us. And when I say exclude us, I mean all of us who are not Santiago.

She points to everyone around the table who fits her description. The regional directors are all sitting together along the sides, while Explora's central committee is located at the head. The tables are placed in a U, seminar fashion.

Mariana: We have just heard a conclusive discussion about the Program in its graphic proposal—just look at the Website. A national program, where the regions get a mention only after three Web pages, as if they do not even exist. And they don't exist in the contents, they don't exist practically anywhere. Just look at (*she turns her head looking for something*). Where is the poster? This one, please, the long one. (*She makes a dismissive gesture with her hand.*) No, the long one. (*There is a sound of people shuffling papers, whispering. Someone hands the poster to Fernando.*) This one. I think that, in fact, and I am very sorry (*she looks around the table*), it's a joke.
Fernando: Why? =
Mariana: = A joke. Look what it says about the regions. Please, look. In the last line. (*She points out from where she is sitting towards the poster that Fernando has in his hands.*) There, the last line on the right-hand side (*whispers and comments from the audience*).
Fernando: Ah!
Mariana: It's a joke, sincerely.

Mariana, as we said earlier, has presence. When she talks, she gestures, and, while what she says has a bite, her manner of saying it is so interactive that it would be hard to take offence. Her fellow regional directors, sitting each side of her, are laughing as she expostulates, but they also cheer her on. She *is* speaking for them, and they say so.

Francisca: It's not useful. [Francisca is the Regional Coordinator for another province of Chile.]

Mariana: This, even someone with a pen and a paper ready wouldn't be able, he would not even want to write down the Web page. (*She moves her hand as if she was writing something down. In fact, she gestures freely with her hand while she talks.*) As a reference, it would be better if it weren't even there. It doesn't make any difference if it's there or not. Sincerely. I think that you'd have to agree with me?

The person sitting next to her, Amanda, smiles ironically. Amanda is a member of the central committee, a hold-over from the previous administration, and shortly to be excused from the management of Explora. Unlike other members of the executive, she is seated with the regional delegates. Fernando, for his part, is not without his own interactive skills. He refuses to argue with Mariana, or to downgrade what she is asserting.

Fernando: Absolutely.

Mariana: OK.

(*Laughs all around from people on both sides.*)

Paz: If not. (*She pats Mariana's shoulder.*) [Paz is regional director for another province.]

Mariana: That's what I mean when I say that there is a vision that is very centralized. And we feel excluded. When I get 1,000 posters like these =

Again, Mariana finds support from her fellow regional directors, who laugh and nod vigorously, and so she goes on:

Mariana: Go to the printer and decapitate this part. (*She makes the gesture with her hand.*) It's much more economical, and I can use the piece, because if not, in reality, it's just plain noise (*whispers and comments*). It makes a tremendous noise because it doesn't give me anything. So, when I say this, this is a concrete and clear example. A piece recently done, for which you have responsibility, I ask when you are designing the logo, and you are thinking image, how is the regional imagery incorporated in the image? I am telling you that because, because I think that the proposals that we have received correspond to young people, let's say, from ages,

I mean for urban kids who are very different than for rural children.

Fernando is quick to seize on the opening she has just offered him: she has raised the issue of what population Explora is seeking to energize:

Fernando: And if you take into consideration even more the age difference, kids from 15 years old to 4.
Mariana: Very complex. Now [I understand . . .
Fernando: [The 15 year old kid is stimulate and auto-stimulated visually by images and by a world, an imaginary world completely different than for an [11–12 year old child . . .
Mariana: [and furthermore urban and rural children . . .
Fernando: And they are also very different. Now, I, look, I have, let's see. There are two things that I should take into account here. One, with respect to this (he points out the posters), we are in a phase of the process of image identity construction for Explora that goes along in parallel with this. In this case I cannot answer for visions that are more administrative or that are consequences of a part of the Web system that existed before. But for me, this meeting here is a clear demonstration of the contrary. Precisely the point of me coming here today and not simply resolving this in the office in Santiago was to make you participate in a debate that would probably occur when I was probably not present. And then, that's why I think it is important what you say. And second, I think, that we don't have to overvalue the differences between urban and rural children, not even between Chilean and Russian children, because . . .

They are now both talking at the same time:

Mariana: = Excuse me, but I forgot the last part of my intervention. I know that a good image is able to be [involving and to cover
Fernando: [It's more than that. Another thing, every time and more and more, [I have been 20 years in
Mariana: [What worries me
Fernando: [And I realise more and more that we consume the same images in spaces that are completely different. See that a, it's very probable =
Mariana: = globalization is here, I understand it clearly
Fernando: Ah?

Mariana: Globalization is here, I understand that clearly, I . . .
Fernando: Exactly, exactly.
Mariana: But independently . . .

Fernando drives his point home.

Fernando: Then what we have to do is to balance the local identities
            with universal languages. And I think we are in this topic, in
            this debate with respect to the Web page.
Mariana: I completely agree with you. The point is that we don't feel,
            because you are presenting it with respect to what our
            perception is, that we do not want to feel excluded. When
            you send me a poster like this . . .
Fernando: I think you have to be included.
Mariana: When you send me a poster like this =
Fernando: = You feel excluded.
Mariana: I feel excluded.

Summary of Analysis

This chapter has illustrated how people use text to frame what it is that
they do: to make their actions intelligible, not only to themselves, but
also, they hope, to others. In Santiago, Mariana used the pretext of the
new poster to display a frame she knew well: getting information about
Science Week out to the public she and her associates aimed to interest.
The malaise she expressed in Santiago illustrates all three of Halliday's
dimensions: the poster did not accurately map her reality; the interpersonal
dynamic was faulty because there had been no consultation; and the
image of Explora projected by the poster was "wrong"—even, as she
noted, Explora's established logo was missing.

Fernando accepted the validity of her complaint that a crucial
component, the activities of the regions, had been short-changed. But then
he did something else: he re-framed the poster by placing the activities of
Explora in a *global* context, where not only Chilean but also Russian (!)
children have educational needs, and where the most salient question is
one of "identity construction": that of the national project. He was, in
effect, concretizing, at the new director-general's behest, a changed vision
of the purpose of the organization, he implied: reinterpreting its thirdness.
Mariana's story had as its heroes the conscientious stewards of the
program who labored away in the vineyards of the regions. *His* story
was all about the identity of Explora itself, and how it must project an
image to a diverse population that includes both rural and urban children,
of many ages, all of whom live in an increasingly globalized world:
balancing "local identities with universal languages," as he put it. His text

meant to recognize the validity of hers, he insisted, but it also transcended it. He was, in effect, constructing a *meta*-text (Robichaud, Giroux, & Taylor 2004). He offered a "larger" vision, he intimated, without ever meaning, he implied, to downgrade the validity of hers.

The discussion in Santiago cleared the air in some respects, but there was still a residue of ambiguity. This is not an untypical fact of organizational life. Multiple frameworks are always in collision with each other, downlinked, crosslinked, and uplinked, and their reconciliation is seldom altogether complete.

Vasquez' Singular View of Organization

Vasquez' research breaks new ground. It does so methodologically in her use of a video camera to record interactions, but more radically in how she conceptualizes the interaction her camera portrays. Her research was informed by an assumption that breaks with conventional views of communication, and that thereby obliges us look at organization in a new way—what it is and how it is constituted. She set out, she explains in her dissertation, to explore the empirical implications of seeing organization as an overlay of different spatial/temporal realities that may be manifested in and through people, but that also become that which defines them and their situation.

When people interact, she argues, contrary to what we usually think, they do so not *in* a certain place and time. Instead, it is their embeddedness in a materially situated practice characterized by typical modes of sensemaking that actually *constitutes* that time and place to begin with. The product of their interactions simultaneously configures the organization, to the extent that it is *also* spatially and temporally emergent, as they are. To cite Suchman in this context (1996: 35), "work activities and workspaces are mutually constituted . . . Place is constituted by, rather than the container for, culturally, historically, and locally meaningful forms of lived activity." But the same principle applies to time: the workday is not a homogeneous flow but a configuring of successive phases and events. It is that configuring that enables people to deal coherently with their world and each other's: Monday, for example, is when Science Week starts, Friday when it draws to a close.

The emphasis shifts from a conventional view of people as autonomous units of action: individuals motivated by attitude, interacting *with* each other *in* a context of time and place. Instead, people and their preoccupations are *where time and space even come to exist at all*. The perspective alters from psychological to communicational: it is no longer people who, by interacting with each other, construct a conversation. Instead, it is the conversation that constructs people and their preoccupations: a configuration of times and places, in a context that is both material and symbolic, manifested in their realization as persons who deal with it. It is not people *in* a circumstance or situation or context, but people as the indispensable medium *enabling*, constituting, and yet also *a product of*, an emergent circumstantially defined situation/context.

Relativity and Organization

It is now more than a century (1905) since Einstein published his historic paper on the special relativity of time: "On the Electrodynamics of Moving Bodies", to be followed 10 years later by his paper on general relativity, "The Foundations of Physics." To conceive of each of us as living in a four-dimensional (and therefore dynamic and ever-unfolding) space/time manifold, where *our* position and time can only be defined as a relationship to *other* positions and times, is now a commonplace of physics, a law of nature long since verified empirically. Even a century later, however, the social sciences still have difficulty reconciling themselves to the loss of an objective Newtonian three-dimensional space: a framework that we can count on because it is just *there*, for everyone the same, a parameter that serves to form a boundary to our activities, not a component of them. Newton made space seem static, uniform, something to be mapped. It pinpointed locations, because we could identify them as coordinates of a frozen spatial image, the map. We also tend to cling to an image of an objective and homogeneous time, measured by the clock: another parameter that is everywhere and always homogeneous, transparent, merely a yardstick that applies to all experience.

We're out of date.

Vasquez chose the more adventurous route of examining the organization as it would appear were we to think of it as an intersection of temporal/spatial trajectories that constitute its different actors, each of whom thus sees the world through a different lens, like the passenger in a train versus the spectator on the platform who watches it fly past. Each, passenger and onlooker, is enacting a world—a configuring of time/space from a perspective. It is the passing of the train that establishes the relativity of their respective spaces and times. Identity becomes itself part of a configured reality: something constituted in the ongoing experience of people in their interactions with others, human and non-human, as George Herbert Mead understood. "Selves," he wrote, "can only exist in definite relationships to other selves" (Mead 1967 [1934]: 164).

The organization, like the individual, is also an ongoing construction of a time and a place. That is how *it* becomes a "self": an actor continually evoked in the worlds of talk and action of its members. An Explora, for example. A key actor in *their* spacing and timing: an "other-ness" indispensable to the identification of their own "us-ness."

"Stories-So-Far"

Rather than conceive of organizational actors as all sharing a single framework defined by constant parameters of space and time, Vasquez therefore opts for what she calls "a performative view" (Vasquez forthcoming). It assumes that both space and time must be constituted in and by the actions of people—neither space nor time is a given—and this can only be done by fixing one's own time and space *relative to* that of others with whom we interact: Mariana and Fernanda versus the professors; the local office versus "Santiago." As Vasquez writes, "Space can then be imagined as the coexistence of multiplicity, of heterogeneity, what Massey (2005) terms a *'simultaneity of stories-so-far'*" (Vasquez forthcoming). Massey (2005: 4), a geographer, describes space as itself a "meeting-up of histories"—a crossing of space/times—rather than as a "surface." Relativity, in other words: how can I know who *I* am other than in a context of *you* and *they*?

The same logic applies, of course, to time. To cite Lindley (2007: 213), writing on Heisenberg's uncertainty principle, relativity theory is grounded in the notion "that what you see varies according to what you are looking for, that the story depends on who is listening and watching as well as who is acting and talking."

The phrase "stories-so-far" is evocative. The assumption of a world still in creation, rather than a fixed environment, follows logically from the geographer Massey's main thesis, "that we recognize space as the product of interrelations; as constituted through interactions, from the immensity of the global to the intimately tiny" (p. 9). In the same vein she describes space as "the sphere . . . of coexisting heterogeneity . . . a product of relations-between, relations which are necessarily embedded material practices which have to be carried out . . . always in the process of being made" (p. 9).

It is the "stories" part of Massey's expression that might give us pause, especially since she herself makes little attempt to explain her use of the term, beyond acknowledging that its connotations are "ambiguous" (p. 197). Mariana and Fernanda's meetings, for example, as encounters of "stories-so-far"? That is surely not the usual way of thinking of a conversation. Fernanda's interviews with the professors in the university? The reaction to the posters? Mariana and Fernando in Santiago? Aren't these just people talking to one another, conversing, explaining, arguing, whatever? Why "stories"?

The answer is located in the camera Consuelo carried around with her to record the interactions she witnessed at Explora. What does a camera do? It *includes*, to start with: Mariana behind her messy desk, Fernanda sitting in front of her; the excited talk in the office when the posters arrived; Mariana in Santiago confronting Fernando. But it also *excludes*: by focusing on one set of actors, in one context, it leaves others out. Consuelo herself, for example. She was a part of what she observed, and people sometimes turned to address her directly, but we never see her, because the story her camera is constructing is from the privileged perspective of an observer, who directs the camera but is invisible to it.

Weick (1979: 179–184) observed that experience is equivocal, not because it has no meaning, nor because its meaning is obscured by "noise," but because it affords the potential of many simultaneous meanings: an embarrassment of riches. We would, consequently, be unable to see at all unless we bracketed things: framed them by including some things and excluding others. As Weick argued, to enact a world we must first select those patterns that have meaning for us. A camera constricts our view and in doing so constitutes it *as* a view. But that is exactly what a story does as well: it frames the components of a scene so that we can enact them, make sense of them.

A story recreates an event, in retrospect and in prospect, but it also reflexively constitutes an event *in and through its telling*, as Garfinkel and Halliday, coming from very different disciplines and traditions, both nevertheless emphasized. All that Vasquez adds, following Massey's lead, is that any human interaction is an encounter of *two or more* story lines, in their actuality as well as their reconstruction of events: their convergence *is* the event. Had Consuelo asked both Mariana and Fernanda afterwards what had occurred in their meeting, she would have ended up with two accounts, not one, because it was the encounter of their enactments—*their* "stories-so-far"—that constituted the event they were living. Text is not merely a discursive reconstruction of organization, in a context. On the contrary, the context is itself the product of texting: an ongoing reconstruction of the materiality of space and time.

Conclusion

Text as the Cement of Organization

We began this chapter, citing the work of Kirsch and Neff, by asking how an organization comes to be constituted in its texts. We argued that text is not merely the support system that links the parts of an organization and the participants in a conversation but is the actual bonding agent that holds them all together. How text works to link the conversations, however, is not the same as how it works in a conversation. The immediacy of situated talk favors the development of coincident modes of formulating experience in a shared linguistic representation. And it is often easier to work out the kinks of misunderstanding that inevitably arise when the feedback is immediate. In the extended network of an organization, however, the experiential worlds are different. Text is no longer, as Halliday conceived it, merely an enabler of conversational interaction. What gives text its power to bind together communities of practice that have otherwise little in common, beyond their joint affiliation with the organization, is what the ethnomethodologists (Chapter 2) think of as the indexicality of language. The "form" that professors must fill out may look the same as that which Mariana and Fernanda will read, but it plays a different role in their respective life-worlds. The "poster" that arrived from Santiago may have been the "same," but that is not what Consuelo's camera told us. The final report submitted by Mariana will be read and interpreted differently in Santiago than where she, its author, has lived.

The text is, in other words, a "boundary object" (Star & Griesemer 1989). It is the binding agent that cements the parts of the organization together, precisely because it can become a constituent within the many communities—part of their conversation, read in their way—even though the "spin" they give it is so different. It is not that the different communities now understand each other's perspectives, as enthusiasts of the uses of dialogue suppose, but rather that it can be understood differently to become, through its agency, a simultaneity of *integration* (a singularity of the organizational text) and of *differentiation* (understood by each component of organization in its own way).

To Come

In the chapters that follow, we continue to look at how text works, as it interfaces with the multiple communities of practice that make up the organization. One manifestation of text, for example, is an account. "Giving an account" is a conversational event. But, in the extended network of the organization, linked by written texts, the mode changes to that of a formal account, mediated by documentation. In Chapter 5, we look closely at the intersection of informal and formal accounting. Text, as we have defined it, is the mediator in both the immediate circumstances of the conversation and the larger arena of discourse that constitutes the reality of the organization. As we will see in the chapter, that "fit" is far from seamless.

Suggested Supplementary Readings

For background on the technique described as "shadowing," see Meunier and Vasquez (2008). Chapter 1 of Massey (2005) is short, and in it she explains her idea of space as fluid and mobile: a construction of experience or "stories-so-far." Also worth a look is Anderson's (2004) article.

Chapter 5

The Accounts of a Business—or Perhaps the Business of Accounts?

In this chapter we continue our exploration of the active role of text and texting in organization. We do so, however, in a different kind of organization from Explora. This time, the site of research was a for-profit French private enterprise, a construction firm whose current operations span that entire country. And the "texts" we focus on—the documents generated by formal accounting procedures—also differ from those we have just been considering in Chapter 4, where they were, essentially, personal expressions of people's "stories-so-far." In both cases, nonetheless, making an accounting of what you are doing, however constituted, becomes the source of the "flow" of documents that Kirsch and Neff (2008) perceived to be the basis of all organizing in the large: how up-, down-, and cross-linking are accomplished.

Accounts and the Establishment of Authority

In spite of the contrasting modalities of organizing that these two contexts illustrate, one public and the other private, one in South America and one in Europe, there is a common thread that characterizes both, namely a latent preoccupation with authority. Authority, we argued in Chapter 2, is not a property of any individual per se. It is instead the authoring of thirdness through the production of a legitimated text or map that gives a shared meaning to everybody's activities—lends them a thirdness. Authorizing activities is a way to imbricate them: frame them in such a way that they conform to shared perceptions of how members collectively see their organizational world, what it *is* and where it should *be*: its objects, its practices, and its relationships, human and material.

The authority that sustains organization is therefore distributed. It is, we argue, not an inherent attribute of some privileged person or persons, because, if the authenticity of the author's text fails to be generally acknowledged and translated into practice, then the basis of organizing is eroded, since there is no longer the commonality of purpose that is necessary to hold the parts together. The "map" only works, as we argued in Chapter 2, if it becomes "naturalized": what *everybody* knows.

The problem that frequently confronts complex organization, therefore, is not the *absence* of authority but, as the previous chapter illustrated, a confused *proliferation* of interpretations of the thirdness of organization: *too much* authoring rather than not enough. Authority may—indeed must be—distributed; otherwise it is ineffectual. But, since we are all sensemakers grounded in our own practices, we tend to construct the bases of organizational authority differently, to fit with the exigencies of our own context. The consequence is a recurring risk of mismatches of perspectives—and misunderstandings that may engender confusion and conflict.

The theme we develop in this chapter is how organizations attempt to brake and homogenize such diversity by imposing a single modality for the production of accounts. Organizational members are required to conform to a protocol to account for what they are doing. We explore, to be more explicit, some of the implications of implementing a formal accounting system in a large and diverse company.

Accounting as the "Glue" of Organization

The dictionary offers alternative readings of the words "account" and "accounting." On the one hand, an account is defined as the computing of some quantity (the German term for account, for example, is *Rechnung*, or reckoning). It records the details of a transaction inscribed in a formal written statement of money spent and received, in the same language as a budget. Alternatively, an account can also be a description of an event: a report on who did what, when, to or with whom, for what reason, and with what consequence. This interpretation implies a narrative, and we usually think of it as being expressed orally. In French, for example, *compte* is translated both as a recording in figures or statistics and, alternatively, as a report or an explanation (*compte rendu*). One interpretation leads us to imagine dry-as-dust statements of numbers (things bought or sold, payments or receipts). It all appears to be very objective, merely factual. The second interpretation is visibly infected with subjectivity. As Garfinkel described it, an account, in this second sense of a narrative, is indexical and highlights certain aspects of a social context. To reiterate a point we made in the previous chapter, ask three people who attended a meeting what went on and why, and you are inviting very different reports, or "accounts," to the point where you sometimes wonder whether they had even been sitting in on the same event!

Historically, every society has developed its own mode of accounting. Some went on to invent a way of keeping written records, as texts. The Sumerians, millennia before Christ, were already registering commercial transactions in cuneiform characters on clay tablets. They also left us a written narrative of the heroic and semi-mythical figure, the king Gilgamesh, who may in fact have ruled the great city of Ur at one point in its history but is transmuted, in the story of his exploits, into a demigod. The Egyptian civilization used papyrus for similar purposes. The mystics known as Essenes, a branch of Judaism, bequeathed us the Dead Sea Scrolls, again discovered centuries after they were written. Nothing could better illustrate our impulse to record for posterity economic exchanges or to account for our experience, by inscribing it in an enduring medium. Freezing the account in text is how we create for ourselves a North Star of constancy, a guidepost to navigate through the otherwise uncharted seas of our own current activities. It is also how societies out-live their own actual existence, as Kirsch and Neff discovered in their investigation into the traces left behind by a failed legal firm.

Making, offering, and exchanging accounts is, Garfinkel found, a normal feature of all discourse. Ordinary conversation and dialogue are, however, evanescent. More to the point, what you say in them is deniable. Make a verbal promise, and then a day later regret that you did (or, more charitably, forget that you had), so you say, "Well, no, that's not quite what I said. I never promised *that* even though it may have seemed I did. What I really meant was this . . . ," and now you feel free to re-interpret what you had said earlier. How many times have we heard politicians or business leaders protest that they had been "misquoted" or "quoted out of context"?

The indigenous peoples of North America found a way around this slipperiness of talk by using wampum belt records to tie down verbal understandings (Foster 1985). When two tribes had come to council together, with the intention to sign a treaty of peace or cement an alliance, each tribal leader arrived with a wampum belt that was a token of his tribe's intention. Then, when the powwow concluded, a new wampum belt was designed to record symbolically the reconciliation of the parties and the terms of their agreement. The European peace treaties of the same era used a different recording mode, but the effect was the same: concretize in text that which had been decided in talk.

The inscription of an account in text also has organizational consequences, since it is a way of stitching together conversations that are separated from each other in space and time. Texts, once generated, can migrate from one conversation to another, even if, physically speaking, the people who produced them do not. The obligation to communicate textually, moreover, imposes a discipline: it is a means, for example, to require both managers and employees to give an accounting of what they are about, following certain rules. It is, moreover, uniquely in the authoring and dissemination of an account made material in a text that the authority of the organization can *itself* be established.

How else would we know what the organization thinks or wants if its intention were not authored and published as its "account"? It has, after all, no voice of its own. But the same logic applies to its members: making an account and inscribing it in text are how all organizational identities, both individual and collective, get to be recognized in the wider context of the organizational network, once the boundaries of a concretely situated local conversation, and a practice, have been crossed over.

Constative Versus Performative

This chapter is about the activity of preparing a budgetary report in a large firm. In it, we pursue a theme that we have been exploring from the beginning, how people frame their own activities and, as they do, contribute to the imbrication that is, we have proposed, the building block of any organization that transcends the bounds of local practice. Imbrication, however, may be construed differently in people's spontaneous accounts, depending on their image of the organization, as we saw in the previous chapter. If, as we suggested in the prologue, the organization is conceived of as a "machine," then communication is looked at one way: as the assembling of the information that leads to a well-designed, integrated structure of activities grounded in logic. Here, imbrication is conceived as infrastructure. If we think of imbrication differently, following the lead of Goffman or Garfinkel, then imbrication is negotiable: a frame game where boundaries are established interactively, and sensemaking is the medium. It is no longer *a* machine, but a *concourse* of differentiated local domains of practice.

To translate these contrasting visions of organization into communication terms, we borrow Austin's distinction between the constative and performative dimensions of talk: language as merely information versus language as the modality enabling the establishment of relationships. The chapter uses his concepts as the basis for questioning the validity of drawing a distinction between objective versus subjective interpretations of accounting. Isn't accounting instead, we will be asking, always *both* objective *and* subjective, whether spoken or inscribed in a permanent medium? And what are the consequences of that bi-dimensionality? Is accounting merely a way of transcribing the reality of organizational practice? Or is it not, perhaps, rather a constituent of practice: how it is realized—made *real* to people?

We will be looking for answers to these questions through the eyes of a researcher who undertook an ethnographically inspired investigation of communicative practices necessitated by accounting in a large enterprise in France: Bertrand Fauré (Fauré, Brummans, Giroux, & Taylor 2010).

"Les Activités de Production de l'Information Budgetaire: Communications Organisationnelles et Régulations, le Cas d'une Entreprise de BTP"[6]

The research discussed in this chapter was the work of a scholar who was, at the time, a doctoral student at the Université de Toulouse III (Le Mirail), Bertrand Fauré (2006), now Assistant Professor at the Technical University of Tarbes, France. With a training that included instruction in both economic analysis and discourse studies, Fauré set out in his dissertation research to explore how accounting takes place in a context where people are engaged in running the day-to-day operations of a large and successful construction firm (more than 500 employees in his region alone, not counting the personnel who are furnished by sub-contractors). His intention was to observe employee interactions, particularly during the period when the informal accounting that is a normal part of any practical activity was expressly translated and inscribed into a formal document or text and became the official record of the current state of affairs of this phase of the company's operations. Such translation is the indispensable first step in what Vollmer (2007), borrowing a term from Goffman (1974), calls a chain of "up-keying" activities. Upkeying, as Goffman defined it, is "a shift from a given distance from literal activity to a greater distance" (Goffman 1974: 366, cited in Vollmer 2007: 587). Goffman called such a shift "an unauthorized increase in lamination of the frame" (p. 366): a translation from one imbricational level to another, in other words, that involves a layering of successive interpretations in order to conform to the frame imposed by the translator.

Distantiation—"Spacing and Timing" the Organization

Inscribing an account in a permanent medium is where the initial phase of what Ricoeur (1991) named *distantiation* is accomplished: the opening and closing of a distance between source and destination that will be bridged by the migration of a text (Taylor, Cooren, Giroux, & Robichaud 1996; Nicotera forthcoming). Distantiation, for this reason, is the *sine qua non*, the indispensable basis, of all organization-in-the-large, even though, as we shall see, the text is not simply passed on from hand to hand; it is re-written as it is filtered through the respective frames of interpretation. This is how the integration of the *here-and-there* and the *now-and-then* of a large organization is made possible: we see it as the

---

6   "The activities of producing budget information: Organizational communication and regulation, the case of an enterprise, BTP."

construction of a heterogeneous "spacetime" constituted, and occupied, by a large organization and supported by a quilt-work of text.

Professional accounting practice thus involves a sequence of translations at the boundaries separating communities of practice as a result of which, at each phase of the process, a new set of numbers is produced, increasingly distanced from the source and ever more abstracted from it as they take on added complexity. But the upkeying has to start somewhere. Fauré chose to focus on that initial point, where what Goffman called the "literal activity" of (in this instance) a construction site was being inscribed in an account in accordance with the company's requirements for regular project updates and conformity with the overall budget estimates.

Focusing on Language Activities

Fauré's account of what he found is of special interest to us because its inspiration was an explicitly communicational view of organizing. Bertrand wanted, he wrote in the introduction to his dissertation, to focus on the *language activities* that contextualize accounting, as the *making*—the actual fabrication—of sense (Weick 1995). He was determined to do so in the concrete circumstances of the production of the company account, where it is initiated, at only one remove from the actual work site itself.

The ostensible or stated goal of accounting as a core managerial activity, Bertrand knew, is to produce as objective an account of the facts of current activities as their transcription into numbers allows. In Austin's formulation, as we saw in Chapter 3, this is what he called the *constative* function of language, whether the "language" be numerical or not. But what of Austin's other dimension, the *performative*, Bertrand asked himself?

It is far from news in the extensive and highly sophisticated social scientific literature on accounting that the process of making, circulating, and interpreting accounts is a construction, not a mere transcription, of reality (Mattesich 1995). The word "performative" is used often enough in this literature (Armour 1997; Case 1995; Catasús 2007; Lowe 2004, to cite only a few examples), but not, Bertrand discovered, in quite the same way its inventor, Austin, had in mind. The inspiration for the currently dominant usage in this literature is based on a view of organization as a product of discourse rather than a process of communicative interaction: how reality gets portrayed, discursively, in the accounts. The frequently cited article by Morgan (1988), for example, has this to say about the profession and its activities: "Accountants often see themselves as engaged in an objective, value-free, technical enterprise, representing reality 'as is.' But in fact, they are subjective 'constructors of reality':

presenting and representing the situations in limited and one-sided ways" (p. 477). Morgan's emphasis here is on constatively oriented discourse ("presenting and representing the situations"), not on communication—or at least not communication in the way we define it in this book, as a constitution of relationships that add up to the organization.

Morgan's view is now shared, with variations, by many of those who write about accounting. Nevertheless, Fauré noted, there is still a dearth of empirically based field research, centered on the local dynamic of constructing an account (although see Lowe & Jones 2004). What are largely missing in the mainstream literature are observations that zoom in tightly, in close-up, on the actual communicative exchanges, especially at the point the account is first being authored and where, presumably, the "reality" is initially *being* "constructed." Or, he asked himself, perhaps the better term would be "performed"?

Austin (1962), in his introduction to the distinction between *constative* and *performative*, chose to leave the terms somewhat loosely defined, beyond observing that "performative" "indicates that the issuing of the utterance is the performing of an action—it is not normally thought of as just saying something" (pp. 6–7). His disciple Searle has since attempted to clarify the insight by establishing four conditions that define a performance (Searle 1989: 548):

- an extra-linguistic institution;
- a special position by the speaker, and sometimes by the hearer, within the institution;
- a special convention that certain literal sentences of natural languages count as the performances of certain declarations within the institution;
- the intention by the speaker in the utterance of those sentences that his utterance has a declarational status, that it creates a fact corresponding to the propositional content.

With due allowance for the shift from "natural language" to the artificial conventions of a budget update, the relevance of Austin's/Searle's idea of performative is here made transparent: accounting is institutionally justified, position is crucial (there must be an accounter, an accountee whose accounting relationship is in turn mediated by an accountant who sets the rules). Accounting conventions establish how to make a declaration. What is inscribed in the budget report thus creates a fact, and does not merely report on it: a performance, and not merely a statement. The budget update is, however, performative in still another sense in that the performance *constitutes* a time–place—and a "story-so-far"—and does not merely occur in it.

Mapping a New Territory

The young researcher thus set out to map this relatively uncharted territory. He would sit in on, and as far as practically possible be literally present, when and where the "construction of reality" was taking place, at ground zero. The observational perspective from which he was observing what occurred would allow him to concentrate less on whether the resulting account was constatively accurate than on how it was performatively accomplished in the to-and-from of interactive talk.

For Austin, as we recall from Chapter 2, a "happy" or felicitous performance meant that the circumstances had to be right, that the appropriate people took part, and that they performed their roles correctly and responsibly. The ethnomethodologists' additions to this formulation were the principles of indexicality and reflexivity. Not only does the meaning of what people do and say depend, performatively, on the appropriateness of the occasion, but the occasion is indexically a crucial determinant in how those participating understand what is being said and done. By "framing" the interaction (Goffman 1974), the context becomes crucial to the establishment of the meaning of what is occurring there. Even more to the point, the circumstances and the identities of those same people are being simultaneously and reflexively reconstructed in, and by, the very act of performing them in the exchanges. This is to study accounting not merely as an activity that occurs *within* an organization, but rather as a continuing *reconstruction of the organization itself* in the ongoing activities of its members (Taylor & Van Every 2000).

The Organizational Context of Fauré's Research

The organization where Fauré conducted his research is the fourth largest in the construction sector in France, with a growth rate at that time of about 5 percent a year. By the nature of their sphere of activity, construction firms operate on the principle of local projects, in this case scattered over the length and breadth of the whole country. They thus respond to a variety of different challenges, depending on whether their object is a new airport, a shopping center, a highrise apartment, a new road, or whatever. BTP.SA (a fictional name; the "SA" part stands for *Société Anonyme* or "Company Limited") reflects this dispersal of fields of activity in the way its administration is structured. The architecture of the firm consists of a consortium of subsidiaries, each specialized in its geographic sector. The affiliates, in turn, split up their operations into regions, each with its own managerial cadre, in undertaking projects that correspond to development sites.

The delegation of accounting operations produces four layers, from head office down to site manager, with, at each level except the site itself, a regional director (to whom site managers in the area report), seconded by a financial comptroller who reports to the director. The comptrollers, in turn, have their own hierarchical reporting relationship, although official authority remains the prerogative of the directors at each level of operations other than the site, where the manager is his or her own accountant.

At the site level, responsibility is split between two functions, that of local manager and that of crew chief. The site manager, typically an engineer by training, is responsible for the supervision of technical activities and coordination with sub-contractors. His or her duty (in all cases studied, his) is essentially administrative, bringing into play the skills of a professional engineer delegated to look after relations with sub-contractors, prepare and update the budget, and assure an adequate level of quality and safety. On-site crew chiefs, on the other hand, focus on the immediate supervision of on-the-ground activities, notably the daily coordination of the workers, including those supplied by sub-contractors. The site chief is hands-on; the manager is the one who relates to the superior levels of the company. Normally, the site manager is the recognized superior of the crew chief, but how this works out in practice also depends on their respective qualities of expertise and experience. Some crew chiefs also become skilled in management, and this affects the distribution of authority on the site. It is the site manager, however, who must prepare, track, and defend the budget to his or her superiors. Concretely, this means responding to both the regional supervisor on operational matters and reporting on financial matters to the regional comptroller: the classical division between line and staff. The relationship is thus triadic: site manager, regional director of operations, and comptroller (the communicative significance of this division of responsibility will become clear later in the chapter).

Projects are organized at BTP as follows. The process is initiated in the business-planning group at head office. They are continually on the lookout for development opportunities—new construction projects with a potential for profit for the company. Once identified, a project is the object of a strategic analysis that evaluates the eventual advantages and risks. From the start, financial analysts as well as technical specialists are involved. The proposal they come up with includes an estimate of standard cost ratios applied to each component of the project. If the analysis leads to a positive recommendation, a sales plan and a preliminary budget are finalized, and these become the basis of negotiation with the client.

The project parameters, once fixed, are then transmitted to the site engineer, who must produce an operational plan in greater detail, including the tasks involved, their cost, and timing. This becomes the basis of the operational control of the project. Budgetary oversight is negotiated in regular meetings between the regional operational chiefs, their comptrollers, and the site manager for the duration of the project, under the aegis of the commercial division of the company. Revisions to the budget may well, by necessity, occur, depending on progress on-site, but the goal is to keep these to a minimum. Once the project has been completed, wrapping up the paperwork becomes the responsibility of post-production services at head office.

The Organizational Challenge

BTP, like many large enterprises, is constantly pushed and pulled in opposite directions. The construction industry would seem, on the one hand, to be ideally suited to reliance on economies of scale, based on advanced technology, such as prefabrication, uniformity of practice, specialization of services—the ideal at one time of the promoters of total quality such as Deming, Crosby, Juran, and others, part of the post-World War II drive to advanced industrialization (Giroux & Taylor 2002). On the other hand, there is no way to escape the imperative to constantly adapt to the uncertainties of a local situation: material that arrives late, or the wrong material, or material that is delivered but is defective or not what was required. Workers fall sick, or unexpectedly threaten to go on strike. Managers leave in the middle of a project. Clients change their mind. The site itself proves to have hidden problems, necessitating a quick change of strategy: a foundation needs to be dug deeper than expected, for example. If the managers on the actual scene have not been delegated enough authority to react quickly, the whole project goes on hold while head office catches up. Decisions take longer, after all, if they have to go up and down the chain of command, and that also costs money.

Over the years, therefore, the company administrators came to a realization that their kind of enterprise needs to develop the type of local management that favors initiative and encourages a strong local culture of cooperation. And, in fact, their results seemed to have borne that assumption out. By delegating authority, not only had the company flourished, but it had achieved enhanced productivity as it did so. Building networks of project-centered collaboration locally was leading to prosperity nationally. As Fauré (2006) puts it, "a certain fluidity in the administrative rules allows for evolution, adaptation to changing circumstances, taking account of multiple constraints" (p. 16, our translation).

Staying Ahead of the Wave

A diversification of activities and a recognition of the necessity of continual adaptation, however, generated a new kind of challenge: how is head office to keep itself informed in the face of this fluidity at the local level? The necessity, after all, to remain abreast of contingencies and the imperative to innovate are far from restricted to the local sites. The company as a whole is continually called on to react to issues having to do with the larger economy, its financial institutions, and its regulators. It is responsible for the overall budget. If that is not handled well, the repercussions will soon be felt locally. Furthermore, negotiating sizeable contracts, especially if they involve more than one site, is not something the local manager can take care of. So management continually faces the need to know where its own operations stand and how they are faring operationally and financially. That means collecting and disseminating up-to-date information.

A Technological Solution

In many enterprises as big as BTP, the answer to the challenge posed by the conflicting pressures of integration versus diversification has typically been to implement a computer-based and fully integrated communication technology that is supposed to stitch together the whole organization by offering a single mode of information capture and display, typically known as an ERP (Enterprise Resource Planning). Fauré (2006: 87) describes how such a model of the organization ties the threads together, as if they were indeed the parts of a machine:

> The organization is constructed as far as possible as a composite of integrated practices, effected by this circulation of managerial documents, which allows for activities of measuring, categorizing, compiling and finally the linking up of diverse practices, dispersed in time and space, whose coherence may be reified after the fact in a final document.

Not only does the technology become a facility for exchanging documents, it now becomes evident that it is, in fact, "molding social reality by coordinating and structuring the activities and anticipations of the actors who make up the company" (p. 86, citing Eyraud 2003).

Like most companies, BTP had previously, over the years, implemented a mixture of specialized systems, often not mutually compatible in that they were designed for a particular unit's needs (sales, for example, or warehousing). The resulting fragmentation made it hard to piece the whole picture together, because the logics of the systems were different. BTP had actually implemented and tried out a variant on the integrative technology model now known as ERP some 15 years or so before Fauré's study. This earlier one was initiated by the company's accountants and top management and was therefore oriented to the objective of furnishing financial tools for management, rather than to local needs for tracking the projects under their responsibility. Typically, those most affected, the people who had to supply the data, were not consulted on its design or application. It was simply imposed.

Adapting to a New System

Comptrollers and site managers nonetheless perceived certain advantages, because the new system enabled them to do work such as checking up on outstanding orders, invoices, and deliveries, in real time. They discovered that the system could also be used as a tool for tracking and balancing their local budget. They could now break the latter down, evaluate the potential of alternative purchase strategies, and keep abreast of possible overruns. It also, on the other hand, proved to be a temptation for accountants to translate smart ideas into new facilities. One innovation was a "CyberCatalogue." With this particular add-on, it was no longer the operational units, but the company as a corporate whole, that now negotiated with suppliers. The rationale supporting this increase in scale was that it would open the door to more advantageous deals and better prices. The disadvantage was that, once an arrangement with a supplier was concluded, the product in question appeared in the CyberCatalogue as the preferred and *only* choice, even if a local manager might have come up with a better alternative. It was as though the contractual supplier now became a virtual department within the company. When they needed a certain material, site managers had to consult the catalogue to establish availability and price. Although the subsequent paperwork of issuing an invoice, submitting and paying a bill, and so on, was now handled by the system, thus "liberating" the local manager from this duty, mostly, it meant that the latter must accept the catalogue service.

Up to a point! As Fauré pursued his investigations, he discovered that, in reality, each affiliate had over time developed its own modes of adapting the central technology to its purposes. Furthermore, the researcher soon realized, each manager had figured out his or her own way of preparing and presenting the budget. He or she used the centralized modules to do so *only in part*. Even so, one consequence was clear: the local manager was impelled to spend more and more time doing the paperwork demanded by the system and less and less time supervising the integration of activities on the site. That side effect may not have even been evident to the senior managers who had initially authorized the implementation. It imposes the kind of supplementary effort that Suchman (1995) characterized as "invisible work": the "workarounds" (Sachs 1995) that people do to make the system fit their own need to fulfill their tasks —needs that the people at the top never know, nor are even interested to learn about. Once again, it revealed the limitation of any idea of a system being conceived as mere "technology." Such a facility needs to be understood in its performative side effects, as well as its constative or "functional" use to store, forward, and access information (Taylor & Virgili 2008). This is Fauré's point.

The Performative Dimension of an ERP-Type System

It is what happens, organizationally, as a result of this ever-increasing interference in their work (from the site managers' perspective) that was interesting to Fauré. Over a period of 10 years, the personnel of the company had doubled in size. On the opposite side of the ledger, the number of accountants had stayed as it was to start with: a group now proud of its efficiency, and forming a tight-knit culture of its own. In the past, they had been the ones with the boring job of data capture and verification, having to update and verify the books themselves. With the increasing systemization, that had changed. The dog work that used to consume two days can now be done in two hours or less. Most billing has now become routine, with no more than 1 in 50 cases presenting any problem to speak of. Computerization, in other words, did not result in more accountants. It merely gave them more scope.

Neither computer technology nor accounting practices, however, are stagnant. On the contrary, as the technology becomes almost daily more complex and elaborate, pushed by the demands of the marketplace (as we will see in Chapter 6), the specialists in the financial sector now find themselves the masters of an increasingly rich array of powerful tools for the sophisticated manipulation of data. Why not, for example, play with new presentation formats: "sexier," and easier for a non-statistician such as a site manager to interpret? Here is where your project stands, right up to date, you can show the people in the field. All well and good, except that, as Fauré found, the managers prefer their own modes of reminding themselves where they are. They are lukewarm to the "Flash" innovation (the brainchild of one of the financial people in the company, offering an animated picture of project progress). As Fauré (2006) puts it, "It's not the managers who propose new tables, but the financial people. It is part of their function and it is in their interest to do it" (p. 98). Apart from any other consideration, it is a good career move: it might get them a promotion.

Collectively, the site managers, he observed, are resistant to the trend to ever more fancy statistical manipulations. From their perspective, it is all very well for the accountants who reserve to themselves the "noble" work of system conception and manipulation to experiment with the figures. It is the operational people, on the other hand, the engineers, who are stuck with the lowly job of inputting ever more detailed data for their clever opposites to play with. The more the company organization becomes "textualized" as a result of computing, the more the textualizers (the accountants) appear to the operations people to be rubbing *their* noses in the indignity of status differences. Furthermore, they pointed out to Fauré, there is a tangible negative consequence. The more time the managers have to spend in their office feeding the computer, the less time they have to give to running the project, which is what they thought they were hired to do in the first place. Computerization is trumpeted as the road to productivity. But, if they no longer have the time to manage the sites, won't that itself be a threat to productivity, they ask?

Their resistance, Fauré noted, was not expressed uniquely in individual grumbling. He discovered that texts outlining their grievances periodically circulated among the managers. One document, for example, on "improving performance processes" (p. 104) was based on a survey conducted to evaluate managerial views on the topic of computerization (unlike the accountants, it is hard for the managers to be physically present together, so they have to rely on surveys). The survey found that the managers spent about 70 percent of their time in administration and only about 30 percent managing operations on-site, whereas they estimated that a more healthy division of their time would be 50–50. The survey, however, it turned out, dated from 1998, some six or more years earlier! Because it had never been widely circulated, local managerial resistance tended to, as Fauré puts it, "reinvent the wheel" (p. 105) many times over, year after year. They produce documents, but they seem not to have much cumulative effect, and certainly less so, the managers sense, than those of their opposite numbers, the accounting experts, with their sophisticated running of the numbers.

Speech Acts and Precedence

Such was the climate that greeted Fauré as he conducted the preliminary phase of his field research. His findings will allow us to extend observations we made in Chapter 3 on the performative dimension of speech. When Austin and his interpreter Searle presented their ideas, for example, they construed that which embeds the constative function of speech in a performative relationship as being confined to *interpersonal* interaction. There is a speaker and a spoken-to, both persons. What Fauré's work will allow us to do is generalize from the immediacy of conversation to the mediated domain of organizational communication. Inputting data on a computer screen conforms to a constative view of the organizational relationship: a report on objective facts of what has been spent, and where the project is in its trajectory. The engineers in the field, however, perceived the performative implication of a greater reliance on computing (although "performative" is not the term they would have used). What they saw was a constitution of authority where the autonomy that they needed to perform their primary task, the construction project itself, was being invaded by the imposition of a framework where they were treated as the object and not as actors, to whom agency had been delegated. It was, to them, a device to instantiate a status difference where, as we noted above, one party, the accountants, sets the rules and claims the "noble" work of design and interpretation, while the other party, the developers, does the actual work. An outside observer might find this a considerably distorted view of the actual situation: the parties are objectively mutually interdependent, after all. But feelings are feelings.

In the next section, we sit down with Bertrand Fauré, vicariously, in a room where the two parties to the relationship actually meet and interact. This is where translating site activities into a report of them occurs, in conformity with the strictures of a pre-established budget.

Updating the Budget: The Organization in the Conversation

The inspiration for Fauré's approach to research was ethnomethodological: go, look, ask, listen, record. Try to understand from the inside out, not from the outside in. Fauré's field research consisted of three phases (in addition to the extensive pre-research phase of documentation and reading in order to inform himself on the infrastructure of the industry and history of the company). An initial phase of field studies took the form of interviews with company financial officers and observations of the latter's day-to-day operations (in one region, southwest France). The second phase concentrated on tracking the activities of one financial comptroller, meeting with site managers working in his region. It was during this same phase that the researcher sat in on some 30 meetings in a dozen locations, where, typically, comptroller and site manager, and, less often, the regional director, discussed and finalized the latest budgetary update. Although the company did not authorize audio recording of those meetings, he was frequently able to accurately capture verbatim conversations in writing, simply because the talk was continually being interspersed with silent periods while the numbers were being looked up. The third phase of field work coincided with the final phase of data analysis, as the researcher used this time to feed back to his informants his emerging analyses and interpretations, inviting them to correct him whenever he struck what they perceived to be a false note. For the most part, the feedback was confirmatory, and, where it was not, Fauré used it as an opening to clarify and occasionally correct his earlier impressions. Overall, the research, including pre-research and fieldwork, extended over more than a year.

Focus On Managing at the Level of Local Work

Fauré spent three months, as we have noted, observing the interactions that occur when the local manager presents his report on how operations are proceeding on the site to his regional supervisors. It is here, he remarks, that the "two worlds of reality [operational and administrative] meet and where the figures are interpreted through a confrontation of different logics" (Fauré 2006: 139). What he means by "worlds of reality" is this:

> The figures can measure very different realities. It could be a float, a stock, at such-and-such time rather than another, a final value or an intermediate value, a definite value or a provisional value, a value you keep to yourself or a value you communicate. The document offers an image, necessarily partial [in both senses of that word, although strictly speaking the meaning of the French word *partielle* is that of "incomplete"] of the financial evolution of works in progress. Furthermore, its validity is restricted to the moment when it is authored (p. 140).

The irony, he learned, is that,

> In a context where the written and its appearance of objectivity is supposed to predominate, it is the verbal that takes the spotlight: people have to explain, justify, argue . . . but also suggest, promise, express a preference . . . It is that expression in language that allows for the production of accounts that, in the end, amount to persuasive figures ["*chiffres parlants*," in the original text, or, literally, "figures that speak"], that is to say, that will make sense to the people involved in the meeting and that can be argued for where other parties are involved (p. 140).

Here, the ambiguity of that word "account," which we noted at the beginning of the chapter, is made salient to us. It is this that we understand Fauré to mean by his idea of "different logics." The site manager confronts a material world of sand and concrete and steel; he deals directly with employees, contractors, and consultants. Comptrollers and planners operate in a symbolic environment where the objective realities of the building site have become names with mathematical figures attached. That which joins the two is accounting. But managers do not merely write the account, they also negotiate it, discuss it, work it over. As we will see in the meeting we sit in on with Fauré, both senses of the word "accounting" are present: making a periodic update written in figures, but also explaining, questioning, justifying, interpreting, voicing an opinion.

Selecting a Communicative Event for Analysis

From among the 30 or so sites he studied, Fauré has selected an excerpt for us from one where the successful outcome of the project is singularly problematical. In July, the site manager had quit mid-project to take a position with another company (not an infrequent phenomenon in this sector, apparently). A new manager took over the site in November. He is the one who must turn up at the meeting, now 2 months later in January, with an updated budgetary estimate. The project is not especially complicated: two rectangular buildings, each three floors, destined for military training. The budget, however, is very tight. There is no slack, no room to maneuver. In the months following the previous manager's departure, deviations from the estimates have begun to accumulate, with the result that the company now expects to take a loss on the project of between 150,000 and 170,000 euros. Each month the problem has been growing worse. Although the new site head was hardly responsible for the situation when he arrived, the company has now set an outside limit of eventual loss at 150,000 euros.

This is the context in which the meeting occurred. Fauré chose it as an example of a communicative event because it was both typical and exceptional. It was typical in that the unfolding of the conversation was like other meetings he attended, where the site manager was delivering a report to his supervisors. It was exceptional because the situation was *not* routine: things were not going the way they should have. The effect of this at-one-and-the-same-time routine report and crisis situation was that the configuration of roles and identities is highlighted for us: made visible because, although it is one more instance of the usual practice, it is now charged with tension. The customarily played-down, unstated hierarchical assumptions of precedence that underpin all these occasions are, in consequence, made more evident, easier to read, as if the crisis-charged conversation functioned like a photographic development process, revealing to us the real picture—one that would otherwise be less visible.

Imagine the scene. It takes place in the office of the regional comptroller, Alain, an accountant (not his real name). He is seated behind his desk, with his computer in front of him. At his side, behind the desk, sits Georges, the regional director of operations and his immediate superior. The site manager, Jacques, enters and sits across from them (Fauré sits discreetly off to the side). The manager has a thick folder of documents that he has prepared, including a summary report on progress on the site replete with categories that furnish updated estimates of expenditures for labor, concrete, and so on. Everyone present also has the budget that had been finalized at the previous meeting in December. After the minimal opening pleasantries, the site manager, Jacques, hands the others a copy of his prepared one-page summary financial statement, with the updated figures broken down by function: an abstract giving the salient highlights of the current situation. First discovery: a slippage in the overall deficit amounting to 91,000 euros! From a maximum estimated loss of 170,000 euros on the project, they are now staring at a cumulative loss of no less than 260,000 euros on the project as a whole. It is, to put it mildly, an unpleasant surprise.

The conversation unfolds between Alain the comptroller and Jacques the site manager as follows:

Alain: I hadn't seen the figure at the bottom of the page before. What is it?
Jacques: It's the figure.
Alain: What happened?
Jacques: Some things were forgotten.
Alain: What?
Jacques: ... (*Silence.*)

As Fauré notes, not all meetings display quite so starkly the underlying performative character of the relationship between comptroller and site manager. Firstness and secondness as exemplified in the interpersonal relationship are confirmed as the comptroller asks the questions, the manager furnishes the replies: "What is it?" ["It's the figure"], "What happened?" ["Some things were forgotten"], "What?" [no answer]. The comptroller literally exacts an account: an assumed right of precedence on his part. The *interrogative* mood of the utterance of the comptroller (or its "illocutionary force," to use Austin's term) is a thin disguise for what it really is: an order, an imperative, however indirect, that demands a reply. The manager, Jacques, begins by offering an account, although in ambiguous language ("Some things were forgotten"), thus bowing to the accountant's right of precedence. When he then fails to expand, however, a breach of the presumed relationship of authority has potentially occurred.

That breach, in and of itself, would normally itself need an accounting-for: it has occurred *in* a communicative situation, but now, meta-communicatively, it *becomes* the situation. To cite Labov and Fanshel (1977: 87–8): "In ordinary, face-to-face interaction, the only way in which a request may be refused with reasonable politeness is to give an accounting: an unaccounted refusal can lead to a break in social relations (a 'huff' in Goffman's terms)." Is Jacques merely unable to frame a reply? Or is he subtly contesting the authority of the comptroller? If the latter, this would be setting a dangerous precedent. The manager, by his silence, is in effect challenging the right of the comptroller to act as interrogator, whether that was his intention or not. Nobody needs this, least of all the immediate boss of both men, the regional operational manager, Georges, who, given the pattern of that company's imbricated frames of responsibility, will himself be on the mat in his dealings with his superiors if the project is in bad trouble.

Recall that the direct hierarchical superior of the site manager is the regional director of operations, *not* the comptroller. He is the one endowed with official authority. Unsurprisingly, therefore, it is this operational manager who now intervenes, possibly to forestall a more serious breach.

Georges:	I hope there are mistakes? Is it all in the main budget [he means the component that was not sub-contracted out]?
Jacques:	There was a bit of over-run on labor costs.
Alain:	What about the 35,000 euros on concrete?
Georges:	With 29,000 euros of expected further costs [he is still pursuing the issue of labor costs]!?
Jacques:	Yeah that must be the problem.
Georges:	There was no adjustment?
Jacques:	The 29, it's on two budget items, and they haven't been updated.
Alain:	Yes they have, they're at 100 percent.
Jacques:	No, that's where your problem is, they haven't been updated.
Alain:	Oh right, there was a problem with the budget module.
Georges:	On the item "Other categories" we go from minus 21 in December to minus 26 in January. That adds up though to 35,000 francs. Plus the 13,000 euros of labor, that comes to 100,000 francs. If you are thinking in francs, that's a big amount. On labor, you have 13,700 euros in there still to be spent. With an average hour wage of 24, that leaves you 570 hours still to do. Do you really need so many hours of work to finish?
Jacques:	No. In fact I need 287 hours.
Georges:	287 x 24, that comes to 7,000 euros, that's better than 13,000.

Georges, the regional director of operations, thus pursues the interrogation initiated by the comptroller, but in the way he does so he shifts the performative mode of interaction from aggressive questioning to an invitation: "I hope there are mistakes?" If the comptroller comes on like a bad cop, his superior acts more like the good cop, in effect inviting the site manager to collaborate in tracking down the source of the problem. In this respect, his mode of intervention could be connoted as implying a solidarity among those who identify with the operational wing of the enterprise, and who confront a distant administration. Whatever happens to the project is, after all, his responsibility too. He will have to answer to *his* superiors.

However we interpret the motivation for Jacques' initial absence of an answer to Alain's question, the tone of the exchange becomes less overtly interrogatory (although both Georges and Alain continue to press by, for example, calling attention to the neglected detail of concrete). But it is Georges who identifies a factor that may alleviate the anxiety somewhat: he gets the site manager to alter his estimate on remaining labor costs and thus considerably reduce (although not eliminate) the apparent discrepancy between the projected budget cost provisions and the actual need. This is the item that was not updated on the sheet they are looking at, with the result that it had skewed the perception of the real situation.

Fauré notes a curious disconnect here, incidentally. Throughout the entire course of the meeting, those present were focused on getting the budget report right. At no time was there any discussion of the operational realities of the project itself. The regional director and his comptroller both accepted without question the right of the site manager to run his own shop where details such as labor were concerned. The regional director, Georges, relied instead on his acquired experience of how projects generally unfold to ask Jacques shrewd questions, such as, "Do you really need that much for labor?" But he accepted without any evident reservation the manager's estimate, as soon as it was forthcoming. The crucial thing was to get the budget *statement* right. To accomplish this, Georges made a number of mental computations. He broke down the total estimated for future costs by the average wage of workers, for example, and compared this with the written estimate on the document before him, noting the anomaly. On this basis, the absolutely crucial "Remaining To Be Spent," which was the item that raised an alarm to begin with, is reduced from minus 26 to minus 21, which corresponds to 35,000 euros.

The discussion continues.

Georges: The framework, it's the same RAD as December ["*Reste à dépenser*" or "RAD" means literally "Remaining to be spent"]. You'd said you would finish in January, but it's going to be February.

Alain: That's what he'd said.

Georges: The minus 13 on materials?

Jacques: It's a combination. There is the mini-shovel, the 3,000 euros for roadways, the 2,000 euros for fencing, 1,500 euros for sand, and then I built in a little reserve. And then there are the site shacks and the generator plant that I have to keep and that was not planned for.

Georges: Okay, then we don't have to do everything over. What you need to do is readjust the RAD on labor, diverse, and framework. I don't understand the divergence from the month before. I understand that it's not all your responsibility, but you can't leave yourself so exposed when you produce a figure like that. Especially on the summary sheet. That's what everybody looks at. In the end, it is the only really important figure. If someday the boss wants to look at the budgets to get an idea of where they are at and he happens on this, it's going to have to be justified. You can't just say: "No, but there it were just a few mistakes in calculation." Minus 91,000 euros in one month, you just can't say that. OK, so there is 30 that is going to disappear on concrete. On labor, you're going to go from minus 600 to minus 182. On materials, if you stick with minus 13 on supplies, then perhaps there is no need for the RAD. On equipment, we break and in addition we increase the RAD, there's perhaps a doubling.

Jacques: That's right, I had just kept the RAD of the previous site head.

Georges: Don't leave yourself exposed but try to be more accurate. The 90, well they're there. You are going to have to re-do the evaluation. I prefer that you take your time but that you get it right. I know you have other demands on you. We can wait.

They had basically arrived at a basis for future negotiation. Authority had been re-established.

How People Use Pronouns (Picking Up From Our Discussion In Chapter 4)

Fauré points here to something that we have been emphasizing, namely how language is continually recreating a social context that frames that same language. One way this occurs, as we have seen in previous chapters, is in how people use pronouns in their conversations. Consider once again the words of the regional director of operations, this time with the pronouns highlighted:

Georges: Well, *we* are not going to do it all over again. *You* have to make some corrections. *I* don't understand the gaps as compared to last month. *I* know it's not all *your* responsibility but *you* have to be careful when *you* put down a figure like that. Especially on the first page. This is where *everyone* looks. If one day headquarters zeroes in on *your* budget to verify the figures and *they* find this figure, *we* will have to justify it. *We* can't say "Oh, it was only a mistake in calculation."

Note who is physically present among those he evokes by *We* (the three persons, with, by implication, the regional director speaking for two of them, the comptroller as well as himself, thus reinforcing the subsidiary relationship of the site manager); *I* (which establishes, by implication, the regional director both as someone who must be made to "understand," to be convinced, and as someone who "knows"); *You* (the person to whom responsibility to act has been assigned, and whose performance may be judged); and *They* ("everyone," "headquarters," or what we might call the third virtual person in a two-person exchange: "present" only in Georges' evocation of "them"). Fauré also notes a further implication. By the invocation of the third (corporate) person, the regional director Georges is, by indirection, implying his own obligation to render an account for *his* performance (as well as those who report to him and he is duty bound to represent, or "re-present"), to *them*. This is an evocation of different frames: imbrication.

The silent organization, the virtual "third person" in the conversation, is literally being reconstructed, or at least evoked, before our very eyes. And because every such *re*construction is conditional on the circumstances in which it takes place, as Fauré's example illustrates, it is never *quite* an exact recreation. In this instance, there is a crisis, and it demands an accounting that is exceptional. The organization has changed, simply as a result of the over-run on this budget. To cite Fauré (2006),

> The internal social order (in this instance the hierarchical structure) has acted in giving to the director the legitimacy to take this line, discursively. But it is also because the director acts discursively in the way he does, and because the site manager does not offer any opposition, that the social order is reproduced. The laconic response of the manager is in effect acquiescence. It counts as acceptance. (p. 158)

It is what Cooren (forthcoming), citing Garfinkel (2002), calls "another next first time." Given a different situation, and other people, it might well have come out differently.

Georges: When do you [he used the familiar second person singular "*tu*" to indicate he was addressing the site manager, not the comptroller as well] want to meet again?

Jacques: No, no, it's okay, I can do everything in a week. Friday, for example?

Alain: As for me, any day other than tomorrow (Wednesday) I'm free.

Georges: Alright, Friday at 3 p.m.?

Alain: OK.

Jacques: OK.

Georges: (*Handing the document back*) Fine, take this back, we'll pick it up then, and it will be as if we had never seen anything.

So the meeting came to an end. The site manager having been given his marching orders, he gathers up his papers and leaves the room, and the regional director and comptroller continue on to other business. The potential for an outright impasse has been avoided. The site manager has shown he knows where he is as far as the work is concerned (how much work remains, knowledge of the state of machinery and materials, how much labor he needs). He has also demonstrated his willingness to correct his mistakes on the budget. But he has been disciplined, and the budget was the instrument. The regional director, for his part, has shown some sympathy for the difficult position of his subordinate by recognizing that it originated with the previous administration of the project. And he has, in fairly direct and colorful language, warned him not to be so naïve: he should always present an attractive picture to the higher-ups ("*ne te mets pas à poil*" translates literally as "don't leave yourself exposed down to the hide," but it is probably better rendered in English by the colloquial expression "cover your ass!").

This is the kind of advice that usually does not pass unnoticed. We'll come back later to consider its collective effects, generalized to the whole network of hierarchical relationships that characterize the organization.

A final word on this extract from Fauré's field research. As he warns us, it was not typical, because the circumstances—taking over a project in mid-stream—were themselves exceptional. Nevertheless, neither was it untypical, in the configuration of identities of those involved, and their respective rights and responsibilities. It is in this respect that it sheds an illumination on the control processes of the organization, both in this context and elsewhere.

Analysis

In interpreting Fauré's research results, we need recall what it was that he set out to do. Although he appears to have focused on an interpersonal encounter, his objective was not primarily to probe *its* dynamic, but rather to use it as a stepping stone to understand the communicational workings of the organization and the role that accounting plays there. Classical CA offers an intensive examination of the mechanisms and modes characteristic of face-to-face talk—the *here-and-now*—in contexts such as the encounter Fauré describes. Organizational communication researchers, as they pursue their research, are also inevitably located in a *here-and-now*. The organization they study is not, however, so limited. Its existence transcends the boundary of any single occasion, because it exists within a larger space–time arena, as we have argued. It is both here *and* there, and now *and* then. BTP, for example, operates in multiple sites scattered over the whole face of France. It has a company history that goes all the way back to 1850, even though its character and mission have evolved more than once since, and continue to do so. Its existence transcends that of any single person, place, or time.

The regional director knows this. He understands that the conversation he is engaged in is linked to a larger *there* and *then*: "If one day *headquarters* zeroes in on your budget to verify the figures and *they* find this figure, we will have to justify it," he says. Those people in the head office are not physically present in this conversation, but they may be in the future, and their emissary already *is*: the budget statement. It originated *there-and-then* (in the past), and the update they are preparing to submit will end up *then-and-there* (in the future). Its *here-and-now*-ness is no more than that of a mute document that they are working to produce: a passive object. But it is also a link to all those other *there*s and *then*s that make up the company. The rules of budgeting were originally formulated in head office, and, when the project is concluded, the report will be evaluated there. Its reach transcends that of any single occasion, even when it is being made physically present in an actual here-and-now: the office where the conversation took place. It directs the people there, modally, because they have to answer it, even as they produce it, materially. The document thus becomes a communicative bridge linking all of the *here*s and *there*s, *then*s and *now*s that constitute the organization. It fragments into the many site budgets of the enterprise, but they in turn add up to it, the financial account of the company.

Our way of capturing imaginatively this mechanism of organizational communication is thus to see the thirdness of organization as being rendered at once *absent* (physically) and yet, paradoxically, *present* (discursively), by its texts. As we saw in Chapter 4, Santiago became present to people in the local regional office when the posters arrived. The budget report in the office where Fauré was sitting linked them, vicariously, to other communities whose members may well have been unknown to them, and whom they will never meet.

As a "law" of enterprise—its thirdness, in its legitimization of a standard practice, embodied in a text—the logic of accounting is established by precedent: grounded in a historically legitimated principle, the practice of double-entry bookkeeping. Any transaction may be read in two ways: *qua* transaction, or alternatively in its impact on the profit and loss balance sheet of the company. When you work for a firm such as BTP that is a "law," you buy into: make a profit. It is a way of establishing the meaning of what people do. But, as the regional director is quick to point out, that same thirdness could find a human voice. "The boss" will start "asking questions" if he sees a major cost over-run.

But we can go further: the budget, in demanding repeated updates, is *already* acting as an agent of the organization. By *its* acting, the budget makes the organization virtually present in office conversations such as the one Fauré was observing: where the organization becomes an insistent virtual thirdness. The budget is the glue that holds together a congeries of widely varying contexts, actors, objects, and practices. Its role is not merely constative, but performative: it interrogates the local representatives of the organization. It continually reminds people that they live and work in an imbricated set of transaction-based relationships.

Imbrication Reexamined: The Role of the Third Party

Consider again the identities and functions of the actors in the conversation we have been looking at. The local project manager is in charge of a site. That is his object, both in the sense of being responsible for it, but also as where his attention is directed, and the focus of his day-to-day activities. The object is to get the building up in a way that conforms to the terms of the contract, and at the lowest possible cost. Suppose, therefore, that we call the manager "A" and the site "X." Then we could describe the sphere of action that he represents, [A–X]. He acts on the site project, but it in turn also preoccupies him, and he has to react to how it progresses. It is his baby: he is authorized by his company to take responsibility for the site and to direct its activities. If it goes well, he gets credit for its success. He will become a beneficiary, as well as an actor, perhaps get a promotion:

B [A–X]

That is the site manager in his context: one possible framework. Of course, if we were to open up the parentheses, to concentrate on the daily dynamic of the site itself, we would discover other delegations and emergent spheres of action. But, in the context of the conversation we have been considering, those remain unexamined. As we have seen, the director of regional operations takes A's word for the state of the site's activities.

The meeting Fauré attended, however, was not on the site, but in the comptroller's office, with the regional director present. The local site manager now finds himself in the position of someone who must account to his superiors for progress on the site: he will be its spokesperson in a different context, that of regional operations. From being the person acting on, and in charge of, a project, he is re-framed as the person who is being acted on, quizzed: "What is the figure at the bottom of the page, what happened?" This new framework, following our earlier discussion in Chapters 1 and 2, is thus:

    B [A/B [A–X]]

The relocation of the brackets indexes the change of framework. This new exchange comes with different communicational rules and practices from those the manager follows on the site, with his helpers, his work chief, contractors, and employees. The object has changed as well, in this new context, nor is the protocol of procedure the same. The site manager must now learn different rules, consistent with the change in his identity. The initial sequence described above suggests this site manager had some difficulty adapting to these altered exigencies. We could even read the situation as a regional director who is giving his subordinate a lesson in how to respond to the need to submit a "clean" report on the progress of the project: to "smooth" it, in Fauré's interpretation, so that it will not attract unwanted attention. To do this, he introduces a third way of framing the meeting, by evoking the virtual presence of head-quarters: "the boss" who may demand an explanation. This framing of the conversation looks like this:

    B [A/B [A/B [A–X]]]

The regional director warns the site manager not to leave himself exposed, to protect himself, to present a better picture. But, of course, the head of the region would also be "exposed" if he let sloppy reporting slide by, thus awakening the sleeping lion.

Three parties, not two: site manager and his team, regional director seconded by an accountant, and head office to whom the account is being rendered. That third party is both a reason (the project must be profitable) and also its materialization in actual managers.

Frame Games

In Chapter 2, we introduced the idea of a "frame game." What we meant is well illustrated by the sequence we have been describing. You play *in* a game when the game furnishes a clear framework, where certain kinds of move are permitted, and others are not. The site manager, we might surmise based on his reactions, was uncomfortable, even awkward, playing in the accounting game where he now found himself, seemingly needing to be coached by his superior. Perhaps engineering school had not prepared him very well for the protocols of accounting, however well it inculcated skills in site management. We have no way of knowing, beyond idle speculation. Whatever the reason, he found himself "out of his league." He didn't understand the imperatives of this kind of three-person game.

Every conversational context, as the analysts in the field teach us, comes with its own implicit understandings about how to ask a question, how to make an account, how to criticize and praise (Chapter 3). That is playing *in* the game. The comptroller, for example, asks *questions* and thus initiates an *interrogation*. The director's modal range is larger: he *encourages* ("perhaps there are mistakes?"), *calculates* (and thus provides a model of how to proceed for the manager), *sympathizes* ("I know it's not all your responsibility"). But he too *asserts* his authority, in his choice of speech act: he *corrects*, *advises*, *warns*. An order of precedence is both established and reconfirmed: the regional chief and his colleague ask the questions, the site manager replies; the regional chief explains what he wants, the site manager undertakes to satisfy his requirements.

The regional director, however, did something that is even more sophisticated: he shifted frame, and by doing so he was no longer merely playing in the game. He was also illustrating what it means to play *on* it—metacommunicate. This is the topic we take up in the next chapter: how people use their capacity to re-frame in order to gain a strategic advantage. In Fauré's case, playing on the game is no more than a sidelight that reveals the regional director's greater understanding of the enveloping organizational "game" than that of his subordinate. Playing on the game, we will discover in the chapter that follows, becomes a great deal more salient when inter-group conversation is involved, because there, one side's win is the other's loss.

A Word on the Limitations of Formal Accounting

The manager's account of the site activities he supervises, obviously enough, is no longer the activities themselves. Fauré's thesis is that accounts, because they are a form of language, are *both* constative *and* performative. Constatively, the site's activities are inscribed in the cold language of a budget statement. Performatively, the manager was obliged to offer an interpretation, using the usual verbal medium of conversation, to explain this and that. The text—the budget update the site manager has arrived with—enters the conversation as a text. Inversely, the conversation will in turn generate another text—a revised budget update, to be reviewed at the following meeting on Friday, after corrections. The reality at the site will not have changed much, but the budget report on its progress will have.

The accountancy chain is thus in part an instrument for the establishment of precedence and the legitimization of authority. It is where organizational reality is collectively constructed, interpersonally and textually. The process occurs as an imbrication of iterations of accounting. Organizationally, there is not—*there cannot be*—a single, transcendent, agreed-upon-by-all, authoritative, definitive account of reality. This is because accounting is imbricated, with the consequence that meaning must be reconstructed at every juncture, depending on the relevant framework. The site chief makes sense in one frame, [A–X]. The regional director makes sense in a different frame, B [A/B [A–X]], where it is now he who is the actor and the site manager the one who is acted on. He does so by interpreting what is happening in the light of his own "thirdness," generalizing on his considerable experience.

The two individuals, however, do not make the *same* sense even though each conforms to a shared logic of sensemaking. Their sensemaking activities are imbricated. As the frame changes, so does the logic of making sense. To again cite Maturana (1997), the resulting knowledge is *constitutive*, not *transcendental*. Site manager, regional director, comptroller: each has their own preoccupation. It would be a miracle if their interpretive frameworks were quite the same. They look at the same object, but what they see is not quite the same.

"Slippage" and its Constative Effects

It would, however, be an error in thus privileging the performative dimension of organizational communication, Fauré argues, to overlook the other dimension of speech: the constative. The accounts of the company are expected, in principle, to offer a relatively transparent and faithful picture of how things stand, financially. What Fauré points out, however, is that performative and constative interact. First, there is an "esthetic" of accounting (Goody 1999): as anyone knows who has ever read an accountant's report, it should *look* right. Second, there is an issue of economy of expression. The whole must be reduced to its barest essentials. One effect of this concern for simplicity is what is known in the profession as "smoothing" (*lissage*, in French; see Fauré 2006). Statisticians do this all the time. In the place of some original distribution of observations, they substitute what is called a "central tendency" such as a median, a mode, or a mean and standard deviation. Something that is, by its very nature, unpredictable is made to take on a look of solid certainty.

The logic, however, is not only statistical. For example, when the director quizzes the manager on the number of hours he needs to finish the project, the latter says without hesitation "287" (the figure on the budget is 570). Why 287? Why did he not say, "Oh, let's say roughly between 270 or so and 280. I think I can squeeze by under 280." Or something like that. The chances that the final figure will come out as 287, rather than say 285 or 290, given the contingencies of any such project, are probably minuscule. But the regional director happily seizes on the figure, without reservation. Why? If we follow Fauré's reasoning, it is because it will make the budget look better. And, at this point, the constative and performative are so closely intertwined that there is no prising them apart.

Cumulative Effects of Smoothing

If the intermingling of the two dimensions of speech is, however, a feature of organizational communication at every juncture in the extended network of interactions that characterize an organization such as BTP, then we should expect cumulative effects. When the logic of smoothing the account to fit a superior's expectation is generalized, the danger is that, cumulatively, the consequence will ultimately be a distorted image of the reality of company affairs. There will be information *gain* as well as *loss*. What we saw through Fauré's eyes was, however, only the first step in a process. The repeated smoothing, characteristic of the budgeting activity as a whole, was not part of Fauré's focused research (although he was aware of it), but there is already evidence in the literature on accounting for it. Vollmer (2007) describes, for example, the transcription of figures as upkeying, such as we have been considering: using the information at hand to make a new and more spare version to conform to the imposed standard of reporting. Information is lost because the details are left out. But, he observed, there is also downkeying, as people make interpretations of cumulative reports to draw conclusions that fit into *their* particular framework of activity: turning, for example, a compilation of site reports into a trend, represented on a chart.

Extrapolating from an accumulation of figures to draw a broad conclusion, or a special interpretation, means *adding* information—interpreting, generalizing, expanding. The information that is gained, however, reflects, not the original context, but that where the translation occurs. Upkeying and downkeying are thus a consequence of uplinking and downlinking, but they are not the same thing because one is constative, establishing an account, the other performative, establishing a relationship.

Shannon (1948) had terms for these different versions of rekeying: *noise* and *equivocation*. Noise results in a loss of distinctions: the reality of a site reduced to figures in a budgetary update. When there is *noise*, less is received than was sent: there is smoothing. *Equivocation* is when the receiver's set of distinctions exceeds what was sent: goes beyond the message. This is what Vollmer (2007: 583) calls, "eclectically combining signs of different types and sources, re-embedding them in novel forms of expressive behavior."

Everybody, Vollmer goes on to argue, knows that this is happening and that it is biased by strategic motives: a way to advance personal agendas. The extrapolations based on a special reading of the numbers put a face on a reality that reflects favorably on the interest group that made the interpretation. It supports their concerns. And yet, as Vollmer writes,

> The regulatory framing of activity is often kept up *despite* common knowledge of backstage collusion and *despite* substantial distrust

between the parties, because the participants of regulatory drama—regulators and regulated alike—have a *common interest in keeping up appearances*. (p. 591; emphasis in the original)

He calls it a "regulatory drama"; we call it a *game*.

Text as the Basis of Organization

Fauré's research and analysis point to an even more fundamental finding. The configuration of identities of the three individuals involved in the conversation he sat in on was mediated by, and revealed in, the modal configurations of their interventions: questions, clarifications, warnings, counsels. Yet if we step back a pace, we confront the question of what it was that drove them to engage in the conversation as they did. The answer has to be the budget. It was the budget that set their agenda, interrogated them, oversaw their performances, judged them. In its guise as a text, it entered the conversation performatively. It oriented and structured the same conversation because they focused on *it*. But this, in turn, implies that it is texts such as budgets and the texting they stimulate that stitch together the many fragmented conversations that constitute the organization in its relationship to the world. It, unlike the individuals who treated it as an object, is not just *here* and *now*, but simultaneously *there* and *then*.

The true importance of Bertrand Fauré's work is in his careful delineation of the corporate background against which the accounting is taking place. Accounting—and its empowerment by a technology such as an ERP—is initiated on the rationale that it will furnish a more accurate constative picture of the operations of the organization. Once we accept the performative implications of communication, however, we understand that the budget is itself a corporate actor, fully as much as any human agent. Fauré discovered how this is experienced by one of the company's communities, the local site managers. They have watched their own reality of work being gradually transformed from that of hands-on managers to, as they see it, glorified file clerks, who spend, they claim, 70 percent of their time punching in the numbers. The result is no longer solely interpersonal: one comptroller, for example, quizzing one site manager. Now the relationship is translated into an issue of class: the numbers people versus the nuts-and-bolts managers. Each party sees itself as protagonist, and the other as antagonist. What is harder to get one's head around is that both are being manipulated by what they think of as merely an object they have to deal with: the account.

In Chapter 6, we pick up the thread of the role of text in stimulating frame games, only now we consider a different kind of text: a strategic plan.

Suggested Supplementary Readings

Vollmer's (2007) article is a good introduction to the critical view of accounts. Varey (2006) takes a quite different view of accounts and accounting, by seeing them from the perspective of a managerial conversation. Chapter 6 of Heritage's (1984) study of the work of Garfinkel is a superb introduction to the ethnomethodological version of accounts. Also worth looking at is Chapter 6 of Boden's (1994) *The Business of Talk*; she focuses in particular on what she calls "doing reports."

Playing *on* the Game While Playing *in* the Game

Frames, Identities, and the "Fall Plan"

In recent years, currents of thought known as the "linguistic turn" (Thatchenkery 2001: 113) and the "discursive turn" (Grant, Hardy, Oswick, & Putnam 2004; Oswick et al. 2007) have rejected earlier views of the role of language in organizing—"viewed naively and simply as the medium of communication" (Westwood & Linstead 2001: 1). The new approach is to "consider organizations as texts" (p. 3). Organization, these latter authors write, "exists in the text"; it has "no autonomous, stable or structural status outside of the text that constitutes it" (p. 4).

An unstated premise of this literature, however, seems to be that there is a single, unique organization to be constituted by a text (rather than a concourse of texts). The investigations we have been delving into in the last two chapters do not so much refute this idea of unity as qualify it by their recognition that an organization can also be envisaged as a variegated geography of different texts and the organizational contexts that they reflexively constitute.

True, the accounting procedures of the company described by Fauré were aimed at presenting the firm as a single corporate text, materialized in a formal account. But Fauré also documented how the tension generated by this imposition of a standard accounting mode masked a gulf between the people involved in the nitty-gritty of local, on-site construction work, on the one hand, and the accountants who reigned in head office, on the other. The result was a "slippage" that was due to reiterated translations from one mode of accounting, and one text, to another.

Similarly, Vasquez described an initiative of the government of Chile to mount an innovative, text-mediated campaign to sensitize students to the potential of a career in science, an organizational image materialized, among other ways, in a poster. But she also uncovered the tensions that lie just below the surface, triggered by an omission of the regions' perspective in the national poster. *Their* texts were not receiving the attention Mariana and her colleagues, like those in other regional offices, thought was their due. *Their* organizations were in effect being neglected by the official text—a poster that did indeed "speak for" the organization, nationally. But not, they complained, regionally. Vasquez therefore invited us to think of organization differently, as a topographically differentiated configuring of *alternative* time–spaces—of "stories-so-far," each generating its own texts. In their disparate constructions of the organization-as-texts, they at one and the same time include *and* exclude, unify *and* separate.

Piette (forthcoming) writes that the organization is "a social construction built by 'everyday life' interactions, knowledge process and situations." It is, she continues, "created out of interactions, interpretations, mechanisms of power, texts and discourses." It is continuous and, as we will show in this chapter, often intense. It aims, she observes, at *the* definitive organizational text, but it never quite arrives there.

How to Constitute the Organization in a Text

The process of constituting organization as a text, Anderson (2004: 146) observes occurs in two phases. First, there must be a "translation of conversation into spoken narratives." This is what we understand by Vasquez' evocations of "stories-so-far": the vision and history of Explora itself as an agent of change. Second, Anderson (2004) posits another step, the "translation of conversation into writing" to produce an actual *text*. The final report submitted by Mariana, for example, bearing the title *"XII Semana Nacional de la Ciencia y la Tecnología y Ferias Regionales Explora 2006, Rendición Tecnica"* was a retrospective, narrative account of the week's success in her region, now materialized (and idealized) in a formal text. Fauré's site manager submitted a budget report that was, in its own way, a narrative that recounted progress on the site, but now made real, concretized, in a text. Identities are at stake, but not *only* those of the mother organization. Its specialized components have their own story to tell.

What Anderson does not elaborate on is the third step, namely the legitimization of the text by its translation into the practices and understandings of those to whom it is directed. This is what we called in Chapter 2, in our discussion of maps, its *naturalization*. In this chapter, we turn to look at a hi-tech commercial firm, to discover how text works and how its authority is eventually recognized, after intense debate, to establish a basis of commonality of purpose in an organization that is quite different in style and substance from those we have been considering until now.

Earlier, we drew a distinction between the organization as machine and the organization as game. To the extent that we can identify a single text of the organization as its faithful representation, we would be entitled to compare it to a machine. Its parts fit together to make what Chomsky (1965) called "well-formed strings": machine-like in their orderly concatenation, such as a strategic plan that explicitly lays out the steps a manufacturing company envisages in the development of future products. If, however, organization is a patchwork of communities, each with its own story-so-far distinct from the others, with the consequence that the text is treated as negotiable, then we should see it rather as a game. Different narratives confront each other—and different *texts* that struggle to claim precedence. Because it is a game there are rules, but, as in many games, there is also competition, and sometimes people subtly bend—even re-write—the rules if it will help them to win.

Bear this in mind as you read Senem Güney's account of her research that earned her a Ph.D. at the University of Texas (she now teaches at the State University of New York, in Albany) (Güney 2004; see also Güney 2006).

"An Ethnographic Case Study of 'Building the Box'"

Senem Güney's study was undertaken within a large technology development corporation, with extensive research and development facilities spanning the globe, to which she has given a fictional name: "Deep Purple." Her attention became focused, while she was there (about 3 years in all), on the collaborative development of an innovative high-end server to position the company in the rapidly expanding UNIX market of the 1990s (servers are the powerful workhorses of any system, since every subsequent application depends on them).

Senem began her internship in mid-April, 2001. She is remarkably candid about how she experienced the transition from classroom, as a doctoral candidate in the field of organizational communication at a major university, into the complex social reality of a very large hi-tech enterprise. No matter how many courses you have taken, nothing quite prepares you for the messy complexity of a multinational enterprise, with its mixture of esoteric domains of specialized skills and scientific/technical knowledge, its many divisions, and its intricate human dynamic. How do you proceed to assure your eventual integration into the life of the firm?

Getting In

First, obviously enough, you have to get *in*. You begin, in Güney's account, by consolidating whatever conversational bridges are available to you, initially with the people who have been delegated to look after you as a summer intern. Lydia and her assistant Rosa, for example, both "welcomed me very warmly." Lydia, it turns out, was just "getting back to work after a two-week visit with her family in Puerto Rico." The door to conversation opens. Senem grew up in Istanbul, Turkey, so she can chat on with Lydia about non-North American food. Lydia has arranged a meeting that afternoon with Richard, Senem's designated sponsor and a senior manager in the area of technology development. Richard is cordial, informed, and supportive, but also very preoccupied with his responsibilities, meaning, among other things, that he is almost continually on the road. Senem can only keep in touch with him by e-mail or in short interviews. Frustrating. So, some time later, Richard's assistant Joanna suggests she meet Anthony, "a manager in Richard's organization and . . . the program manager in charge of developing Royal Fleet PT+, the next generation of Royal Fleet PT—the server system that was soon to come out as a breakthrough in the UNIX market." Anthony, a 22-year veteran of the company, turns out to be accessible, and in effect it is he who becomes her mentor. He introduces her to the world of technology development, as he lives it:

> In the development lab, Anthony led me down aisles of "test servers," which looked like big black metal cabinets with drawers that were stuffed with strange metal objects. Cables stuck out from these drawers and hung loose, making me think of eerie medical pictures showing complicated surgeries. Anthony must have figured out that his lab tutorial would be more challenging than he expected when I said I did not know what a "mother board" was. He still seemed determined to teach me how a server worked. I was, however, clueless about how to put together what he was saying . . . After the first ten minutes, I stopped listening to what he was describing and tried to concentrate on how he was doing the describing. He used comparisons to "[my] computer at home" to give me a sense of the power and capabilities of these machines and quoted what sounded like impressive numbers. When we left the lab, after a twenty-minute tutorial, I had learned one thing about building servers—that developers took a significant amount of pride in what they did.

"A server system is an extremely complicated machine," she goes on:

> When I saw a "box" for the first time, I immediately wondered how on earth so many different groups of people could work together to build one. Anthony told me that no one person in the company would know how the whole thing worked. He said, "But it works! It is a miracle."

Senem was a visibly enthusiastic novice, even though she was "clueless about how to put together what he was saying." Since she had introduced herself as an "ethnographer" (*not*, he said he had feared, an

MBA student), he seemed to accept her as legitimate. Ethnography of organization was a category he could relate to, it seemed. At least it was not overtly managerial. The door had opened.

To all effect, Güney was now "in." As she notes:

> Anthony's willingness to guide "the anthropologist who came to study the tribe," as he told everyone in his introductions of me, was a bonus that came with that opportunity, especially after the frustration of failing to get on Richard's calendar. My struggles to gain full entry into the organizational life of the Hotville program management organization were definitely over when I began shadowing Anthony in mid summer.

She could not have known in advance the full significance of this patronage, however. Anthony, it would transpire, was to become a key figure in the drama that was shortly going to unfold and that would become the central theme of Güney's dissertation: what she terms in retrospect the "NuevoHyp episode."

The Organizational Communication Research Challenge

Güney's personal account illustrates a challenge that confronts any organizational researcher. What could be described as the paradox of organization, its simultaneous one-ness and many-ness, can also be translated into a law of research. *There is no panoptic position from which to view an organization—no "neutral" point of observation where the whole landscape of the organization opens itself up to you.* You, like every member of the organization, can only observe it *from a perspective.* An *angle,* a *view,* a *focus,* a *frame.* Güney's privileged relationship with Anthony and, over time, with the entire community in which he worked ("Hotville"), means that her account has the authenticity that derives from seeing events through the eyes of participants, even at second-hand. All ethnographically inspired researchers strive to do this: learn how the people they study themselves understand events. But this advantage also implies a limitation. If organization is ultimately a composite of A and B in their relationships to X, then one cannot simultaneously enter intuitively, with equal validity, into the life-worlds of both A and B. The danger of a privileged point of entry to the organization is the flip side of the authenticity coin: one risks being "captured," a prisoner of a single perspective associated with a particular interest, rather than an objective observer of the whole process. You know one story very well. But there are other stories you can only guess at.

Formulated in the terms of our introduction, an organization is understood as an environment for the purposive activities of its several members: a context that comes with its grounded meanings, or thirdnesses. Their reading of the organization, at this level, is manifested, as Labov and Fanshel concluded, in how it informs their own separate activities with meaning. This is thinking *indexically*: things mean what they mean, not in the abstract but *in a context*. Anthony's visible pride in the machines he was showing to Senem cannot be understood unless we grasp the central role that the server played in the success of the company, and the prestige this in turn conferred on them, as a team, and on him, as its leader.

The enveloping organization whose existence gives meaning to Anthony's work is, however, not objective in the way the machines are. It is, in fact, fabricated out of the accounts that give *it* life and meaning: those of its members, of its customers, of its competitors, of its regulators, of marketing, of the press. In Anthony's laboratory, there are real, objective constraints that are operative: the properties of materials and the nature of electronics, for example. But the reality of Deep Purple is not that—or at least not merely that. *It* is a composite of accounting and accounts, formal and informal, all jostling up against each other in the continuing quest for legitimacy. The constitutive accounts may, to be sure, be separately grounded in materiality because they are each the product of a hybrid constellation of agents, human and ultimately also material. The account of the organization is not so tied to the world of grounded practice, however, except vicariously, at second hand. It is fabricated out of human relationships: a greatly scaled-up A–B, addressing a multi-faceted X.

The researcher, accordingly, is obliged to try to grasp the immediacy of the situated life-worlds of the informants without losing sight of the complexity of the enfolding process. The way to do that, Güney concluded, is to focus on how the organization constructs an account of itself and its purposes. It is in the dynamic of accounting that the lineaments of the organization reveal themselves. In Deep Purple, one such organizing account was called the Fall Plan. We will come back to it after some additional clarification of the context of technological development. (Note the very different connotation of the words account and accounting as they are used here, compared with the preceding chapter. What these respective uses have in common is that both recognize accounting to be a process—performative—as well as a content—constative.)

Some Background

Technology development has a built-in contradiction. It is innovation that allows the company to establish its position in the first place: new products that sweep aside the old because they claim to perform the tasks of customers much better than those they are replacing. To benefit from the advantage offered by innovation, however, the enterprise must establish economies of scale of production to assure that it can meet the voracious demands (it hopes!) of its customers. It is in sales that profit emerges. This means building an expensive infrastructure to develop, produce, and market the goods. Investment in infrastructure, however, is a sunk cost: the pay-off comes only with time and the economies of scale that continuity enables. Infrastructure, furthermore, needs to be understood as not merely the machines that turn out the goods, but also all the human activities that are needed to run them. Assembling that hybrid infrastructure takes time. It also represents an investment that is justified only by continuity of production. Infrastructure may thus become the enemy of innovation, because innovation, by definition, threatens to make the older, established modes of production, the people who sustain them, and how they collaborate with each other, obsolete.

In the decade of the 1990s, a corner was turned in the area of information technology. As the computing business had developed before then, companies marketed specialized products, targeted for a particular entrepreneurial function. The product destined to support the accounts department, for example, might be quite different from that developed for purchasing or advertising. The result was that a user firm might end up with as many as a dozen or more systems, mutually incompatible in that they used non-communicating servers. The hot new innovation of the 1990s, which has since become associated with the market dominance of companies such as SAP, Oracle, and IBM, was integrated systems: "one-stop shopping" that promised a single information and communication infrastructure to support *all* the functions of the buyer's enterprise and link them up. In Chapter 7, we investigate the processes, formal and informal, that are triggered by the *implementation* of such integrated technology (now called an ERP) into a company. Güney's research, however, focused on the processes inside the firm that *develops* the technology in the first place. What this meant for developers, she discovered, was that, whereas, previously, system development had involved a diversity of relatively autonomous production centers, each with its own specialized product, the company was now being impelled toward a merger of the distinct product lines these centers had specialized in.

A Compulsion to Innovate

This is the context in which Güney found herself when she joined Deep Purple. For years the company had been remarkably successful merchandizing its specialized products. Now, as "integration" became the new gold ring, the company confronted a challenge of rapid techno-logical innovation, both in hardware and software. This meant, notably, developing a single server that would support all its systems. The new server technology of the 1990s was called UNIX. Thus, in 1996, the company division responsible for server development faced a decision: how to proceed? Which would be best, they asked themselves: "buy or build" the new UNIX-based technology? Corporate headquarters in the east appointed a task force to recommend a strategy. When the task force proposed building the new microprocessor in-house, top priority was then given to pulling together a development program.

The company gave the proposed new system a code name (again fictional): Royal Fleet PT. Its development would become the baby, it was decided, of two existing Deep Purple development sites. One, Hotville (fictitious name), was located in a southwestern city in the US that had grown into a hub of the 1990s high-tech boom. The center's current product line, which Güney calls Hot-Boxes, was known in the marketplace for its sophisticated, very expensive hardware—a product that already enjoyed third place in the competitive UNIX market and whose priority clients were the US Defense Department and the international scientific research community. The other center was located in a small, midwestern town, Snowfield (the name is also fictitious), where the major sources of employment, other than computer development, were dairy farming and a medical center. Its product line (also successful) was "Cool-Boxes." It featured flexible, multifunctional software applications that appealed to a customer base of small to mid-size businesses. Royal Fleet PT would, in theory, build on these two strengths by consolidating them into a single system. It would, however, be a first collaborative venture link-ing the two divisions: one very much hardware-oriented, one definitely software-oriented (although a server, of course, integrates hardware, "firmware,"and software).[7] Royal Fleet PT was just entering its second generation of development (Royal Fleet PT+) when Güney joined Deep Purple in 2001.

The "Fall Plan": Text Versus Context

A project such as Royal Fleet PT can generate two kinds of organizational tension that are interwoven, and these became the focus of Güney's research. There is, first, the planning dynamic itself: how a large company such as Deep Purple works through to a corporate strategy that reconciles the pressures exerted by what the market calls for, on the one hand,

---

7   In server technology, firmware is an interface function between the hardware and the operating system. This function helps minimize the impact of hardware design changes on the use of a particular operating system.

and what the firm can deliver, given its strengths (and its weaknesses) in technology development, on the other. Planning generates friction as different functional perspectives rub up against each other: the marketing people and the long-range planners, notably, versus the "down-to-earth" (as they see it) development people.

The official responsibility for planning future marketing strategy and which new products will be given priority is the domain of a division called the "brand function." Brand managers in Deep Purple are made up of representatives of different corporate divisions (Research, Development, Marketing, Sales, etc.) involved in the production cycle. The major brand function for a given product line is to keep on top of market trends as they impact on it. The brand division's role involves studying trends, soliciting feedback from customers, reading the other signs, and then producing, at the end of August, what is called the "Fall Plan." The 2001 Fall Plan, for example, arrived on Anthony's desk as an attachment to an e-mail, in the form of 100 plus pages of graphics and text. "'You missed it ... I will have a copy made for you' was an e-mail note from Anthony to me on August 29," Güney reports.

The Plan describes the "icons" (icon stands for a product) for the coming year—products and product features that were "on the roadmap" (jargon is abundant in contexts like Deep Purple). People in the production centers call this the "wish list" of the brand people: what they thought would sell, or could be, as the developers said dismissively, "marketized." If a topic is in any way related to customer use, developers call it a "brand issue." If something is a brand issue, it does not, almost by definition, concern the developers. Marketers, in the developers' view, were a nuisance they had to live with: "something we [developers] have to deal with," "a threat to getting our job done." Their context—their frames of understanding—was different from those in Head Office.

The Plan as the Opening Move in a Complex Game

Güney explains the organizational significance of the Fall Plan in this way:

> Fall Planning is a corporate-wide annual process within Deep Purple. As some members of the hardware development organization described this process:
>
> - It is a proof process to ourselves through which we come to believe that we have made the right decisions.
> - This process is designed to help cope with the question of implementation. It is about making provisions for resources on which everybody agrees.

- It is the process through which the business, with its variety of disciplines, attempts to establish a connection between the budget and commitments for the deliverables of the coming year, predominantly, and of years beyond, to a certain extent.

We can therefore think of the Plan as a text that sets out the rules of a development game: a map that must be authenticated if it is to be "naturalized" (see Chapter 2). It establishes the goals, delimits the area of play, defines how the refereeing will be done. It includes lists of names of team leads, chief engineers, project managers, program managers, and development executives responsible for the delivery of the coming year's products, as well as the specifications of the latter. The document also indicates (a crucial component!) the brand division's decision on what percentage of the total allocated budget will be spent in which area of development: x amount of dollars to hardware development and y amount of dollars to software and firmware development, for example.

Not surprisingly, given the stakes, every division within the corporation—research, development, marketing, etc.—plunges into its own version of the Fall Planning process. It is here, after all, that they all have their opportunity to influence the company's dominant account of where it is going. Güney observed it from one perspective, but a vital one, since technology development is the company's primary business, and hardware is essential to it. She writes:

> My descriptions . . . reflect the significance and experience of this process among the members of the hardware development organization. Members from other organizations in other divisions, or even members from other organizations within the larger server development division, will have different views.

In the Game? Or on It?

That is our point: "different views." Since it is the document that sets out the rules of the game, the negotiations that are triggered by the Fall Plan, to the extent that they conform to its rules, are what we meant when we earlier used the phrase "playing *in* the game." But there is a second agenda: reinterpreting what the Plan says so that it in effect says something else. That is playing *on* the game. The stakes are high. In Güney's words, "the publication of this document indicated the beginning of negotiations over product definitions and was a phase-shifting event for the Hotville development organization." Richard, for example, called it "chaos," an "endless back-and-forth." According to some members who had participated in these negotiations, the organization did not get out of "utter

chaos" until the end of the year or early January, when "the plan closed."
"Some argued," Güney adds, "that the plan in fact never closed."

Thus, the Fall Plan, far from being set in stone, itself became the object
of continuing negotiation, since the priorities the brand division had laid
out in the abstract (the "icons") were only as viable as the capabilities
the development centers had of realizing the targets that had been
identified. As Richard put it:

> This is a cultural difference between brand and development. Com-
> puters are not baked overnight like cookies ... You can't run this
> operation like a utility, where you turn the power on and off to save
> money. When the brand tells me to stop spending on that and instead
> to spend on this, well, I have *already* made 2/3 of the investment I
> need to make on that other thing.

Naturally, therefore, centers try to maximize their leverage over the
overall development process by talking up their own priorities, while
downgrading the ones that contradict their sense of what should have
priority and what should not.

The negotiating process works like this. After receiving the icon map,
groups on the development side initiate a process of "content optimiza-
tion" to arrive at an "executable" roadmap, i.e., one that takes account
of operational constraints of personnel, current technology development,
and realistic timing. It involves cost calculations for the proposed projects
and may result in a changed definition of products, scheduling, and so
on, even to the extent of taking icons "off the roadmap."

The Fall Plan obviously impacts dramatically on the centers where
development takes place. One center may, for example, find itself assigned
a higher development priority, and thus its prestige and budget are on
the up. Another discovers that its budget has been reduced, and its role
in development risks being rendered peripheral because the product it
specializes in is now out of favor. Its status slips in the network. Within
the boundaries laid out by the Plan, the various research and development
centers must therefore compete to protect their own interests (and,
incidentally, that of their members).

This competition, "playing both *in* and *on* the game," is the focus of
Güney's account. Except that playing *in* and playing *on* the game are
realized as a single complex interplay of inter-connected conversational
sequences, all centered on the objectives defined by the Fall Plan. There
are, simultaneously, interpersonal tensions, inter-center tensions, and
inter-divisional tensions at work (development versus brand/marketing,
in particular, or research versus development). Each is a dimension of
the same field of play; each implicates actors who embody in their persons
both individual and collective identities.

As Güney observes,

> Fall Planning involves different sets of negotiations among partici-
> pants at different levels in the development organization. One set
> of negotiations takes place between development executives and the
> corporate finance group over financial parameters. Another set of
> negotiations goes on between development and brand organiza-
> tions over product definitions. Yet another set of negotiations takes
> place between development executives and representatives of groups
> within development organizations over budgets for programs and
> functional teams.

And in the background, of course, lies the competitive contest the
corporation is itself engaged in, where the "game" is the marketplace,
and "winning" is determined by volume of sales.

It is the interplay of these levels and the way they reflexively and
recursively shape each other that make organizational communication
such a complex phenomenon. As Güney herself remarks, "observing everyday interactions among organizational members as they went through this
process . . . was quite astonishing."

Some sides of organizational life only become visible in periods of
crisis. For this reason, Güney found the Hotville–Snowfield exchange
especially revealing, since it pointed up, not only the differences between
development and head office functions such as the brand department,
but divisions within the development universe itself.

Two Communities, Two Cultures

The achievement of Royal Fleet PT+, as we have seen, was predicated
on the collaboration of two development sites, Hotville and Snowfield.
The cultures of the two communities could hardly have been more
different. During the course of one of Güney's interviews with a member
of the Snowfield development organization, for example, her informant
asked her to take a good look around, to try to understand some of the
organizational implications of converging two previously distinct Deep
Purple brands. He explained his own perspective this way:

> People who work here were probably born in this area and have
> been here all their lives. They like working here. Life is quiet and
> simple here. Everybody comes to work by 7:00 in the morning, and
> the whole plant will be empty by 5:30 in the afternoon. That's the
> way we live here.

That was quite a contrast to the work life of the Hotville center, where
workdays could start as late as 9:00 in the morning, but people would

often stay until 9:00 in the evening, or later, if there was work to be done. And working hours were only the most obvious difference between the organizational patterns of the two. The deeper divergence was rooted in what they had each come to represent, both within and outside Deep Purple. The differences between their product lines, and their preferred market niches, had encouraged what they themselves called "radically different brand values." Each had a different image of what development means and how to do it—images that had become consolidated, over time, as the two centers had grown and thrived. Their "stories" were very distinct from each other, in content and in frame.

Perhaps because most of the organizational members in the Hotville location were, as some called themselves, "migrant workers of technology," coming from every corner of the world, they had acquired a nickname in the company at large: the "Hotville cowboys." The label "cowboy" identified the Hotville members' attitudes to their work. It differentiated them from other Deep Purple development locations, especially from conservative "Old North" in the northeast, where the company's history had begun.

The nickname, "Fort Snowfield," also conveyed, in its own way, an attitude of independence from the "Old North Mafia." The image of the Snowfield organization as a secluded stronghold was strongly held among the members of the Hotville organization. When, Güney reports, she told members in Hotville that she was about to travel to Snowfield to attend a workshop, she would get remarks such as "Be careful where you go there. They will shoot you if you walk down the wrong aisle." Internal discipline and a self-conscious sense of community were defining characteristics of the Snowfield culture. "Hotville cowboys," on the other hand, were portrayed as lacking in discipline. They were seen by others to be endlessly discussing, arguing, and then revising the same decisions they had already agreed on as being settled. Individualism, even orneriness, was tolerated, even celebrated.

Leo, the director in Snowfield responsible for establishing the software strategy for the collaborative development of the Hot-Box and Cool-Box products, was one of the members Güney interviewed during her trip to Snowfield. An edited excerpt from Güney's field notes illustrates how he perceived differences between the Snowfield and Hotville "styles" of making decisions. Even the ways people asked questions, he observed, might "rub wrong" when they interacted. The Snowfield style was to work through a problem and look for details and facts to come up with a solution. It was a style that involved asking for the next fact and probing for particulars. But then, when decisions were reached, they were closed, like, he said, decision-making in a socialist–collectivist environment. On the other hand, he observed, Hotville seemed to take a "free form," open-ended approach to decision-making. It was difficult to be sure in Hotville when decisions were actually final. The discipline was missing.

There were thus fundamental differences in the way precedence and order emerged and hierarchy was enacted, in the two centers. This contrast of styles seemed to have become part of the collective knowledge shared by all Deep Purple members—an element of their collective culture. The juxtaposition of images of "cowboys" versus dwellers within a "fort" thus indexed more than personality differences or heterogeneity of background. It pointed to a significant difference between the ways in which participants from Hotville and Snowfield communicatively constructed and presented themselves as part of a larger community: their "story." The difference seemed guaranteed to make joint decisions problematical when their fates were linked in the invention of a new technology. Not a promising basis for success, it occurred to Güney.

The Management Perspective

Management, at least at the operational level, was not unaware of the dynamic that might be triggered by such an imposed cooperation. Her sponsor, Richard, for example, told her during their first encounter that he was interested in an outsider's perspective on the way they were dealing with complexity in his organization, under the pressure of constant change, which he described as often "change for the sake of change." He invited her to advise him on what he called the "organizational complexity" that might result from the convergence of distinct product lines. "I would like to know whether we are making our life more complicated than it needs to be and what we can do to reduce complexity in our organization," he said to her.

He was prescient. "Reducing complexity," as things turned out, was a tall order.

The "NuevoHyp Episode": Partners? Or Competitors?

The tension implicit in any collaboration between two cultures as different as Hotville and Snowfield boiled up to the surface in the immediate aftermath of the circulation of the 2001 Plan. At issue was a Snowfield proposal to include an innovative hypervisor feature they had developed, NuevoHyp, into the 2003 roadmap for the Royal Fleet PT+ machine.[8]

8   A "hypervisor" is part of the firmware capabilities in server technology that organizational members also refer to as engineering software. While these capabilities may not be visible to the user, they enhance hardware functions, especially those related to system maintenance and reliability.

The Plan document listed a Hot-Box version of Royal Fleet PT+, the high-end server system, showing converged versions only for mid-range and low-end/entry boxes. The Snowfield counter-proposal initiated by the head of their design team, Greg, was to integrate NuevoHyp into the high-end as well as low-end boxes. This would mean removing the current service processor, designed in Hotville and used in previous generation products, from the Hot-Box version of Royal Fleet PT+ and replacing it with NuevoHyp. This change, the Snowfield designers argued, would result in significant progress toward building a "fully converged system-architecture" for Royal Fleet PT+. The Snowfield team had tried their new design on Cool-Box products, and, they reported, the results had been entirely successful.

Including NuevoHyp would guarantee that it would be an integral feature of the system definition for the first shipment of Royal Fleet PT+. That would be a coup for Greg and his team. Anthony's objections to including NuevoHyp in Hot-Box products were based, he said, on the grounds that to do so would put an impossible strain on already scarce resources and would jeopardize new product release for the entire year of 2002. Incorporating NuevoHyp in the 2003 Royal Fleet roadmap, Anthony argued, could not be reconciled within the timeline the 2001 Fall Plan projected.

The "NuevoHyp episode" began, Güney reports, on August 31, when Anthony learned about an e-mail note from Greg, the senior architect of NuevoHyp in Snowfield. She writes:

> I met Anthony in his office (in Hotville) before a Royal Fleet PT+ project meeting, as I had been doing for more than a month by then. That day Anthony's face was different from how he usually looked in the mornings—it was unshaven and expressionless. He said to me, "A key guy in my team is cutting the life blood to my computer." According to Anthony's account of the e-mail exchange, the participants from Snowfield were trying to isolate Anthony from the discussion on NuevoHyp, because they were "seeing him as a threat" and "they wanted his badge."

It was this e-mail message from Greg that, as Güney describes it, "pushed the negotiations between Snowfield and Hotville 'out of control.'" Greg, it transpired, had in the meantime addressed his campaign to guarantee the inclusion of NuevoHyp (without informing Anthony), in the next iteration of Royal Fleet PT+, to higher-ups in the company: directors and vice-presidents. They, in turn, seemed sympathetic to the idea of accelerated convergence. This aggressive act on Greg's part, as Anthony read its meaning, provoked a similar response from him. Anthony, not surprisingly, interpreted Greg's e-mail as a polemically charged "end of discussion" dismissal of Anthony's position, and an attempt to finesse him out of the project. He therefore responded vigorously. Now the conflict was out in the open. As interpreted by some members in Hotville, this was the beginning of a major "execution interruptis" in the harmonious development of Royal Fleet PT+. Everybody was getting in on the act.

Notice how what had started as a project involving collaboration had been transformed, for Anthony, into a story of conflict, involving high stakes, with himself as protagonist and Greg as antagonist. This is what we meant earlier by schismogenesis.

Conflicts Generate Processes

A follow-up conference was now convoked by the overall director of converged server hardware design (including Royal Fleet PT+), John, on Tuesday, September 4, to see how the issue could be resolved. Since Anthony had not been included he invited himself to the meeting.

Why all the heat, one is tempted to ask? There were seemingly both personal and institutional factors at work. The personal issue, the conflict involving Greg and Anthony, we have already mentioned. The underlying issue, however, beyond the interpersonal antagonism, was who would claim ownership of the new product. "Ownership," Güney observes, is a term that Deep Purple members themselves use. It signifies the credit for the accomplishment of a project. In the development of Royal Fleet PT+, the "owner" would have, not simply the accountability—and therefore the jobs—for this particular project, but for the entire new version of the converged system, with all that this implied in terms of its significance for the company's future direction and viability. As things stood, it was the design team in Hotville that was responsible for extending the usefulness of existing technology for one more generation and for laying the groundwork to facilitate the transition between technologies for the next generation products. The design team in Snowfield, on the other hand, was developing another advanced technology, one that promised to be a significant step toward creating a common system-architecture interface between the two Deep Purple brands. This leading-edge innovation, however, needed a "delivery vehicle" to get it to market. The first shipment of Royal Fleet PT+ would allow this innovation to be integrated in the very near future as part of a product with high visibility, within and outside of the company. The question about the ownership of product definition resolved to this question: "Whose interests best represent the interests of the company in the context of the common initiative?"

Resolving Conflict in Organization Occurs in Phases

The onus was now on the two development centers to buttress their arguments with data citing the cost and/or feasibility of including NuevoHyp into the immediately executable roadmap for Royal Fleet PT+. Güney found herself included in the first of a series of intense teleconference sessions where the respective participants were called on to defend their positions. The following people were involved:

From Hotville: *Richard*, located in Hotville, was the director of the hardware program management. He oversaw the development process of "converged line" products for both centers (Anthony's immediate superior). Then there was *Anthony*, the program manager of Royal Fleet PT+; *Cindy*, director of engineering software; and *Dave*, located in the Old North complex, who was the director of converged server hardware design and who had overall responsibility for the hardware development of the converged product line that included Royal Fleet.

From Snowfield: *Leo*, director of converged server software design; *Greg*, chief design architect of "NuevoHyp"; and *John*, "distinguished engineer, converged server software design."

In addition, *Frank*, company vice president responsible for converged server design (splitting his time between both Old North and Hotville), was also present as an observer ("Old North," we recall, is Güney's term for the principal company facility in the East, close to Head Office).

Richard, Anthony, Cindy, Dave, and Frank were physically present in the conference room at Hotville, where Güney was observing the interaction; Leo, Greg, and John joined them on the phone, from Snowfield.

The sequence of interactions is the following, as Güney describes them.

Richard, as the overall director responsible for the management of the programs of the two centers, put the question this way: Could the people in Old North who were pushing the agenda on immediate convergence justify the investment in the development of a technology for one product, if it meant risking the shipment of a whole family of products for the year of 2002? Anthony chimed in by emphasizing what he took to be a significant mismatch between the official timeline of the Fall Plan and the resources available to meet the deadlines it foresaw. Integrating NuevoHyp at this stage would seriously disrupt the approved line of development, Anthony argued, since significant work remained to be done on NuevoHyp to make it compatible with other components of the system. As the Hotville program management team saw it, he said, this mismatch posed an unjustifiable risk.

As the meeting went on, Richard repeatedly quizzed the Snowfield participants on how, given Anthony's objections, the risk in investing in NuevoHyp could be justified. Leo, Greg, and John all cited the advantages of NuevoHyp, notably the opportunity to create a common (field) service between the two product lines that would address maintaining the server at customer sites. None of them responded in so many words to Anthony's argument about the immediacy of deadlines and the shortage of resources. At the end of the meeting, Dave showed, both by his comments and through the tone of his voice, his irritation with Anthony's insistence on the risks incumbent on including NuevoHyp in Royal Fleet PT+. As that person who represented convergence on the hardware side, and answerable to his masters in Old North, his mandate was to ship out converged products as soon as possible. He insistently underlined the necessity "to put numbers on the table and executize [*sic*] to show why it does not work" (by "it" he meant immediate convergence). Anthony needed, he emphasized, to formulate the cost assumptions more precisely for the different options. Cindy requested a list of options so that her team could do a sizing[9] based on the checkpoints defined by the timeline. She repeatedly expressed the need to create clear and crisp guidelines concerning scheduling, content, and cost for two different options: the first being what was originally described in the Fall Plan, the second the variation assuming accelerated inclusion of NuevoHyp. In the end, no decision was taken. Instead, a follow-up meeting was scheduled, this time to delve into the specifics of the two options, based on data to be assembled by Anthony and his team.

More Meetings

The next day, Wednesday, at the "Plans and Status" meeting for Royal Fleet PT+, Anthony tasked the development team he headed up with "going and getting data to show what it costs." What he meant was a precise count of how many people and machines would be needed if they were to proceed with the technology option that included NuevoHyp. The Hotville development team did not react very well to this executive order. They strongly believed, they made clear to Anthony, that the NuevoHyp variation was unjustifiable, and its immediate integration undoable. Wasn't that obvious already? Anthony spent an hour explaining to his frustrated team members why, nevertheless, they had to do a sizing. He started out with an account of Tuesday's meeting. When his account seemed to increase the team's confusion about the rationale behind the demand for a sizing, he got up to draw a diagram on the whiteboard about the current debate over the Fall Plan. That did not go over very well, either. Then he shifted metaphors to compare what they were being asked to do with "working on a mathematical proof"

---

9   This term refers to an estimation of resources—people and money—required to do a project.

in order to understand what has to happen to get to a particular point. When objections continued, he raised his voice noticeably to tell them that he needed the sizing to be completed before his presentation to the executives on Friday. No further room for discussion.

On Friday, September 7, again in the course of an inter-site conversation, Anthony's executive overview summed up the risks involved in adding a new technology such as NuevoHyp to the established definition of Royal Fleet PT+. Again, Dave and Cindy were present in the conference room, and Leo and John joined them on the phone. John (Snowfield) opened up the meeting discussion by presenting the current roadmap for different versions of the 2003 Royal Fleet products. He began his intervention by saying, "I don't know what to call this any more. It has changed so many times that I don't want to call it a roadmap any more." After John's presentation, Anthony took the floor and began to describe the already existing challenges for the team because of late machines and the unavailability of key resources. Under these circumstances, he argued, investing in a new technology for 2003 might mean losing all the revenue for the intervening year, 2002. As Anthony went down the list of items in his overview, he gave completion dates and bring-up durations (the time it takes to have a hardware function up and running after it is adopted in design) to illustrate the risk of incorporating a new technology at this juncture. Dave listened to Anthony's list of reasons for "why it would not work," with a frozen expression of frustration on his face. His voice sounded more impatient each time he challenged Anthony's assumptions. Leo also objected to Anthony's projections about feasibility by observing that the "information originally asked for" had not been forthcoming. What *exactly* would it take to include NuevoHyp into Royal Fleet PT+, he wanted to know. Leo then added a comment about how problematic it was to rely on the Hotville service processor team to complete even what was *already* in the plan. Cindy, who was the director of this team in Hotville, did not take kindly to this comment. Her loud response to Leo only added to the already heightened tension in the room.

Anthony actually had the information Leo was asking for in the slides that were meant to follow up and support his executive overview. However, before he could go into detail, Dave broke his frozen expression to say, in a loud, agitated voice, that Anthony's overview was not even close to what they could take up to the "Big Boss" (the development general manager in Old North). Anthony's documentation of the shortage of people and machines, and the effect of this shortage on the program schedule, was, in Dave's opinion, unacceptable. He made it clear that there was "nothing to be swizzled" about the 2003 Product as it was described in the Fall Plan. (By "swizzle" he meant shuffling icons/products around by dropping some and changing others, based on the capabilities of the development organization). In order to generate revenue, they needed everything specified in the Plan and more. Dave told Anthony to "go fix it!" Cindy summed up her understanding of what needed to be done to make Anthony's pitch presentable to the Boss as two main action items: (1) stabilize what is in the Fall Plan, and (2) work on the feasibility of the second option that would include the new technology, NuevoHyp.

This intervention seemed to crystallize the discussion. The participants agreed to work on the Fall Plan definition the following week, and on the second option (inclusion of NuevoHyp) the week after that. They also concluded that technical leads (working to debug and improve existing software to go into Royal Fleet PT+, according to the Fall Plan) needed to be included in these discussions. Dave turned to Anthony one last time and said that Anthony's pitch should be put together in a way that would show the Boss, "We lifted up every rock." He told Anthony to base his pitch on answering two questions: what would it take to build what is asked? And how soon can I make it happen? He also advised Anthony to go over his pitch with Frank before it went anywhere else. He then went on, in a more teasing tone, to wrap things up and ease the tense atmosphere of the meeting, "This *is* the Fall Plan. We re-invent it every year."

It had been almost an hour since Anthony began taking attacks on his presentation. He kept his upright posture the whole time; however, the strain he was under showed on his face. He blinked twice and said, in a faint but deep voice, "Okay . . . I'll tee it up for you . . ."

Toward Resolution

In the meetings that followed, Anthony again cited the risks in making NuevoHyp part of Royal Fleet PT+. Greg again countered by emphasizing the technical capability that would be gained with a fully converged system-architecture.

"Intense" was the word that the conference participants used during that week (and long after that week) to describe the general atmosphere of these face-to-face verbal contests. Hotville members regularly made reference to the "turf fight" between the two design teams. When no resolution was immediately forthcoming, development executives instructed the representatives from Hotville and Snowfield to have it out, once and for all, in face-to-face meetings in Snowfield to take place in the week of October 15, 2001.

> At that meeting, and after hearing a synopsis of the technical discussions among the representatives of different views, the development executives decided to keep the service processor (designed in Hotville)

as part of Royal Fleet PT+. They decided to include NuevoHyp in the definition of the low-end system of the converged server family and not in Royal Fleet PT+. This decision came after members of the Hotville and Snowfield organizations—who were almost literally locked up in a conference room in Snowfield—had argued eight hours a day for three days over the risks versus the advantages of including NuevoHyp in Royal Fleet PT+. The participants from Hotville went out to dinner in the evening of the fourth day, which was the last day of their trip to Snowfield. One member from Snowfield, who was managing the Hotville-based design of the "support function" for NuevoHyp, hosted the members from Hotville. No one else from Snowfield attended.

Conclusion

There are, of course, alternative perspectives that we could adopt in analyzing the sequence of events we have just been describing. Güney chose to emphasize the question of identity: of the individuals who were involved, the centers and the functional interests they represented, and the company itself. In privileging this dimension of the accounting process, out of which a company's identity is forged, as well as that of its members, she opens up for our attention a central issue of organizational communication theory: the nature of identity and its role and genesis in the arena of interaction.

How Communication Theory Sees the Genesis of Identity

There is a long history of preoccupation with the concept of identity in Western thought, dating back at least as far as Descartes, and his famous dictum *Cogito ergo sum* ("I think therefore I am"). The only thing we can be sure of, in this classic view, is that we exist as individuals. Everything else is an add-on, an expansion of that core precept. The psychological conceptualization of identity remains to this day centered on the individual: his or her emotions, needs, and sense of self.

Communication theory, as we saw in Chapter 2, proceeds differently, in that it portrays identity as a *consequence* of relationship, not as its origin. Identity is established in and through communication; it does not pre-date it. To cite Mead (1967 [1934]: 135), "The self . . . arises in the process of social experience and activity, that is, develops in the given individual as a result of his relations to that process as a whole and to other individuals within that process." Goffman (1959) portrayed the individual's self-affirmation in quasi-theatrical terms, as the acting out of a role. When we enter society, we are obliged to adopt, in his terminology, a *line*, and it is the coherence of the line that enables us to claim an identity. It is that coherence which enables others to understand the meaning of our acts by indexing them with respect to our claimed identity. This is why the maintenance of *face* is so crucial: to "lose face" is to have one's very identity called into question, like Anthony, when his interventions went unheard.

Harvey Sacks (1992), from the perspective of ethnomethodology and CA, saw identities packaged as sets, not as isolated individual definitions: mother implies child, and vice versa; student implies teacher; manager, managed. Labov and Fanshel also explored the consequences of having, or being accorded, an identity as part of a set: it comes with rights and privileges, but also duties and responsibilities to others. Identities are forged *within* a relationship. Bateson's Palo Alto school showed the devastating consequences for the individual psyche when the individual is accorded no identity at all: neither loved nor hated, but treated as not even present. To have one's identity questioned is, of course, painful, but it may also be, alternatively, a stimulus to self-affirmation. To be totally ignored, on the other hand, to be treated as being *without* identity, is intolerable.

The NuevoHyp episode that is the core event of Senem Güney's chronicle of how accounting occurs in an organization such as Deep Purple could be seen, it is true, as a clash of individual identities. But the real foundation, Güney concluded, was organizational. Anthony and Greg were pushed by the Fall Plan to confront each other competitively as leaders of their respective communities in the larger game of the corporate process of developing a strategy. It was a strategy that implicitly pitted center against center, individual against individual. The identities now made salient were collective, and not merely personal. To affirm their own identity, confronted with those of other communities, the contestants had to come up with the right "story": a convincing chronicle of where development was headed, in which they would emerge as legitimated agents of the company, justified by the authority the story conferred on them.

Each side in the controversy thus chose to frame the evolution foreseen in the Plan or roadmap in a way that made their own role preeminent, and that of the other secondary. The issue was precedence: hardware versus software. One interpretation, the Snowfield version, had software as the primary agency that would best realize the objective of the Plan for a new product, with hardware, in effect, as an accessory. Hotville, where the hardware was developed, argued back that you could write any software you liked but, if the hardware was not there to embody it, then it was no better than vaporware. If there was no "box," there was no product. A whole year's line could be shot, according to Anthony, if the company plunged prematurely into NuevoHype. Both sides portrayed themselves as the legitimate agents of the company, with the authority this role conferred on them.

It was an instance of the frame game. They framed the sequence differently, and, as they did, the game itself evolved, from meeting to meeting. In the process, the Plan ceased to be merely the framework of the development game. It became its object. As John from Snowfield remarked, the roadmap had changed so often he no longer recognized it. And as David added, every year the Fall Plan gets "re-invented."

They played in the game, but the game itself changed because they played on it as well.

Through the Researcher's Eyes

Güney first witnessed the impact of this institutionally grounded challenge to identities from a special angle, that of a summer intern watching the reaction of her mentor and principal informant, Anthony, to, as he saw it, a threat to his identity—literally *excluded* from the conversation. Written out of the story. As we reported earlier, the day he received Greg's message, Anthony looked different from how he usually did: "the first of a number of mornings where Anthony appeared disheveled during the NuevoHyp episode." Only afterwards did Güney grasp the full significance of this physical manifestation:

> Later in my fieldwork, there were other days when Anthony came to work, looking like he had not held a razor or a comb for a week. I learned on one occasion that for Anthony not grooming was an act of "putting on war colors." He would tell me that years ago during a project, he and one of his "buds" working on the same project did not shave or get a hair cut until their project "GAed."[10]

Anthony's reaction was, thus, not merely a personal idiosyncracy. "Putting on war colors" when your program is threatened is part of what it meant for these individuals to have, and to play out, the identity they did. "Program managers," she noted, "sometimes talk about their role as one of creating a clear vision and as one of 'dragging one's knuckles' until those who do not share their perspective give up."[11]

---

10 This is the acronym for the General Announcement of a product.

11 " 'A knuckle-dragger' in the development organization, I found out, was someone who focused on a task and used his weight and relentless pretense to stupidity to get that task done. A knuckle-dragger would 'sit on the plan and drool' until all others who did not relate to the immediacy of delivering the committed products went away" (Güney, personal communication).

Güney observes,

> Competitiveness is part of the fundamental norms and values of the participants' larger interactional contexts—the company and its market environment ... Deep Purple was full of instances where distinct development groups competed with each other and the loser of the competition paid with the price of lay-offs, plant shutdowns, and "killed projects" at their site. These instances are part of the collective knowledge of the organizational members as they interact to develop a common family of servers.

Implications

A modern hi-tech firm is certainly a special kind of organization. Its future depends on the skills and originality of professionals and technicians, so specialized in fact that they cannot easily be told what to do or how to do it by a manager, because, as Barley (1996) points out, *they* usually know more about their subject than their ostensible superiors. They are, moreover, well aware of their status as an élite in contemporary society. Since the technology they develop is so complex that the design of a "box" must be thought of as a collaborative accomplishment, as Güney discovered, the sense of a collective team identity, grounded in a local practice, is also powerful. They form into communities with their own internal mechanisms of precedence and authority.

Arriving at a corporate strategy of development is thus a complex process of frequently tense negotiation out of which the identities of individuals and groupings of special skills emerge, some enhanced, some diminished. To phrase this insight in ethnomethodological terms, the process is highly reflexive: self-reaffirming. Losing the game is hard enough; losing your right to play *in* it is intolerable. The account of what the *company* is doing is forged in the fire of heated exchanges such as the one we have been describing, but it then subsequently forms the context for these same exchanges, and structures *them*. As Güney observes, "the negotiations over these plans create platforms of interaction among participants from different corporate organizations, specifically from the brand and development organizations." The totality of those "platforms" is the organization. It is also a world of texts. The battles come down to how the text is written.

And the Identity of the Organization Itself?

One consequence, as Güney writes, is that

> It is difficult to define organizational identity as a stable structure. Members continuously construct the meaning of who they are and

what they do as an organization in their routine as well as non-routine encounters. During these encounters, members flesh out their interrelationships as part of an organization and communicatively construct the boundaries of their organization's roles, interests, and frameworks of action, which make up their organizational identity. These constructions evolve over time, as members continue to interact. An organization's identity, in this sense, takes form and meaning in the interactions of its members against the backdrop of the formal structural definitions of what the organization is and what it does. When we observe how members engage in communicative acts to orient each other to the core elements of their organization's interests, we begin to understand organizational identity as a dynamic construct that is the product of co-evolution between members' communicative constructions and the organization's formal structure.

Concretely, in Deep Purple, the enveloping organizational story is concretized annually in the plan for the following year—a "roadmap." It is the Plan that establishes, in the immediate future, through its material manifestation as a map, the thirdness of the organization. This is Peirce's "law," seen differently, as by common accord endowed with the right to govern the operations of the centers, now inscribed in a text that is accessible to all. It is in the text that the authority of thirdness is found: where and how identities are legitimated or invalidated. It is therefore, for the development centers, a crucial context, one that affirms the value of their own operations (or fails to).

But, as Güney documents, the two centers she focused on had their *own* plans, and thus their own interpretations of the organizational thirdness. It is therefore hardly surprising if emotions ran high. Laws, after all, are open to interpretation, and ultimately to alteration. They need to be applied, and, as they are, they may be rewritten. What the researcher witnessed was an intense struggle to interpret the Plan—the "law" of corporate strategy—in a way that would make *its* thirdness consistent with their *own*.

"Organizational identity," as Güney writes, is "dynamic." As we will see in Chapter 7, issues of identity, authority, and the turbulence that are stirred up when a "Plan" meets the reality of daily life are by no means unique to Deep Purple. In the next chapter, we continue to probe the same phenomenon, but now in another environment: not one where technology is developed but where it is implemented. The "plan" is no longer something to be actualized *in* hardware/software by designers as a product. It is instead the image of organization the system designers have already inscribed in the "boxes." It is the plan—the "map."

Suggested Supplementary Readings

Denis Wood's *The Power of Maps* (1992) is a penetrating analysis of the role of maps in human communication (we drew on it freely in our 2000 book). It is readable and opinionated, but stimulating. On the role of conflict, coalitions, and the role of a third actor, try to get your hands on Caplow's now somewhat dated but intriguing *Two Against One* (1968), especially the first two chapters. He provides a summary of the seminal work of Simmel at the beginning of the twentieth century. On boundary objects (a "roadmap" is a boundary object), the original analysis is that of Star and Griesemer (1989).

Chapter 7

The Organization as Text

Lawrence and Lorsch (1969), as we saw in Chapter 2, identified the tension that exists in any large organization where there are pressures toward greater *integration* at the same time as its specialized divisions tend to become increasingly *differentiated*. It is a challenge that confronts all organizing in the large. We have seen instances of it in all the chapters that preceded this one. On the one hand, there was a local practice: the construction of a large new building, developing the hardware for an innovative integrated system, mounting a campaign requiring the collaboration of numerous volunteers covering a region of Chile. The people involved were caught up in a practice that kept confronting them daily with problems that needed to be solved *now*. They had each developed a specialized set of skills, as well as a body of experience that allowed them to generalize over time about what was going on and how to deal with it. Inside their communities, they worked together collaboratively, sharing a common body of knowledge. They became experts in their area: Anthony and his servers, for example, because he knew how they are constructed and what they do. These are the accounts of people who possess the requisite skills and knowledge for dealing with a hybrid material–social world: the ultimate object of the organization.

That capacity of skilled people to understand what they are doing, to see a pattern in their work that others cannot, is what confers on them a special authority, an authority that is grounded in knowledge, painstakingly acquired over time, as a result of learning through accumulated experience. As recognized experts, they belong to a community whose principles of performance they abide by—a shared script, in effect. Responses to situations take on the authority that acting with legitimacy (literally, according to law) confers, because it is confirmed by competence and experience. They are doing, as acknowledged experts, the *right* thing.

Authority as Established in Uplinking

Those domains of practice, however, are imbricated within a larger, non-local network. They must all contribute to the attainment of their host organization's over-arching goals, because if *it* fails, so do *they*. The local spokespersons know they must therefore offer an account of their activities to their hierarchical superiors. But those same superiors have an agenda of their own, one that focuses on the integration of the parts of the organization. Their authority is thus also legitimated, in *their* "larger" view, by a different set of understandings from those who report to them. They too work in a context of thirdness: as executives they are expected to exemplify managerial skills, by wisely and skillfully leading the organization and enunciating its policies and intentions.

There are, accordingly, imbricated domains of thirdness at work: layered and intersecting, a composition of many (in principle) complementary practices, crosslinked and uplinked. It is hardly astonishing to discover that they do not always quite match up with each other. Up until now, in our chronicle of research projects, this has meant that the imbricated accounts of those who were downlinked had to fit the criteria of those to whom they were offered: tailored to meet their superiors' expectations—submitting a budget update, a report, a grievance, a response to the corporate plan. In this chapter, we consider a different case, where it is sometimes unclear who is "up" and who is "down." The "game" is played differently. At stake again is who will write the text of the organization.

The Organizational Text

The *organizational* text, as opposed to any version of it offered by a member, however entitled, is ultimately forged collectively in the heat of what are often intensely involving conversations, as Güney's study of Deep Purple illustrates. Members had their own idea of what company strategy should be—their own "text" of what it was about. In this chapter, we continue to probe the tension that is created when a text that has not yet been tested in the crucible of performance is introduced. We consider how people's special knowledge of the *existing* organizational text—"how things work around here"—becomes for them a tool to be now put in play in the frame game of organizing. People who work *in* an organization already possess a view of what the text is, and what it should be. The designers in Hotville and Snowfield had worked for Deep Purple for years and were proud members of it. They had no hesitation about criticizing the corporate strategists at Old North if they felt the latter were getting the company text wrong.

People who work in an organization know that their text has been validated in their practice, and they are empowered by that awareness. This becomes evident when "outsiders" attempt to translate the organizational text in the language of their *different* thirdness, grounded in another practice: software design, in the instance we look at in this chapter. In the case study we now consider, outside consultants are directing employees of the company through the steps of implementation of a new software system. Those in the organization, it turns out, are in a better position to play "on" the game while playing "in" it than the consultants, because it is *their* game and *their* organization.

This is the topic that Sandrine Virgili addressed in her doctoral research (2005) at the University of Nice Sophia Antipolis in France, influenced, she writes, by our earlier analysis of the interaction of text and conversation (Taylor, Cooren, Giroux, & Robichaud 1996; Taylor & Van Every 2000); she now teaches at the Université de Metz, in France. She took seriously from the outset of her research the injunction that an organization is, or at least can be thought of, as a text. Taking ethnographic research as her basic model, she set out to study the implementation of a new computer-supported, mixed information/communication system into a large pharmaceutical firm. The system, known in the trade as Enterprise Resource Planning, was supposed to join up all the disparate activities of the organization so that they could be supported from a single computer-based server.

Some Background

Introducing such a system supposes that the consulting firm that has been engaged understands the operations of the client firm: it can offer a system that corresponds to the latter's needs. They would have, as Sandrine interpreted their task, to map the text of the organization onto their own textual representation of it, and vice versa—and furthermore in a way that would permit the integration of the parts of the company's operations into a mixed hardware and software equivalent.

In practice, such object-oriented texts, inscribed in computer code, become standardized across whole sectors of activity, according to how the company that develops and implements the system understands the sector's "best practices." Such pre-packaged systems, however, never quite match up with how people envisage the map of their own organization. The latter have, as we have emphasized, their *own* organizational text, even if it may never have been verbalized as such. They perceive the mismatches between the familiar text and that of the newcomer. They can hardly be expected to passively adapt to the new text, since the one they already have is quite legitimate, in their eyes: sanctified by practice and sanctioned by the evident success of their company. It is *their* context, *their* company, legitimated by a proven track record. They are going to resist. This is no longer merely an interpersonal stand-off, like that of Anthony and Greg. Reconciling the two texts now becomes the object of an intense dialogue between the software company and its contracted experts and the employees. It can easily lead to a symmetric escalation of competitive skirmishes to establish the correctness of one text (the invader's) over the other (that of the "natives"). Each party to the interaction aims to see *its* option dominate, because it is the "right" one, the one that "makes most sense': not *a* thirdness but *the* thirdness.

"La Construction Mutuelle de la Technologie et de l'Organisation en Phase de Développement: Une Perspective Communicationnelle Appliquée à l'Étude d'un ERP"[12]

There are interesting coincidences between the projects of Virgili and Güney. In both cases, for instance, their involvement in their respective projects began in the spring of 2001. For both, the period of intensive implication in the ongoing life of the company was initiated in September of that same year. Virgili's fieldwork for her dissertation stretched over a period of 18 months, three or four days a week. Like Güney, she had a sponsor who saw in her presence and her regular reports during the implementation of a new technology a way of keeping himself informed about the progress of the project. Virgili also, like Güney, conceived of her role in the organization as that of a participant-observer: unintentionally a participant only because she was quite aware that her role made it likely that her interpretations might subtly influence those most intimately involved. She too, like Güney, encountered initial suspicion of her motives: a "management fly on the wall." Virgili was equally confronted with the task of progressively establishing confidence in her discretion and creating a climate of what she calls "empathy" that would allow her to talk freely with those most closely involved. As she wryly notes, it was not surprising that people in the company might find it a bit disconcerting to meet up with a young doctoral student wandering the halls carrying a notebook, ready to whip out her pen at the drop of a hat and start writing. She dealt with this natural reserve by declining the offer of an office, since this might connote a status other than that of observer. Instead, she elected to hang out in meeting rooms, where she would temporarily take up residence, especially if there was a meeting going on and she could sit in. Mostly, she found herself in rooms along with the consultants hired to implement the new technology.

If, at first, her principal preoccupation was to become integrated, after a time she realized that she now faced the opposite danger, of having become, as she puts it, "naturalized": so identified with the preoccupations

---

12 "The mutual construction of technology and organization during a phase of development: Applying a communicational perspective to the study of an ERP." See also Taylor & Virgili (2008).

of the people she was interacting with that she risked surrendering her objectivity—too much participant, not enough observer. They had become used to her and increasingly included her in their ongoing conversations—in its own way a seductive trap.

Virgili began with a clear idea of what she was looking for, even if, initially, she was much less sure how to go about finding it. As she explains it, her approach rested on two assumptions: (1) that communication is in essence a continuing construction of sense; and (2) that collective formations such as companies are by their very nature "moving, dynamic, changing." The organization is a construction of human interaction and reflects the multiple interpretations that are at work in it. Methods that privilege set interviews based on the researcher's pre-established questionnaire will inevitably sap the juice out of the process, and produce an artificially tidied-up version of the real thing. Given her theoretical commitments, it followed, there was no alternative to plunging into the maelstrom of the conversation, talking to people, listening, asking questions, trying out interpretations—making, like everyone else, sense of what she was learning.

She calls the resulting approach to research, as we do, "abductive." This does not imply, she explains, starting with a blank slate. Rather, you begin by formulating some preliminary ideas and lines of questioning. Little by little, as your impressions take shape, influenced by what you have learned (both confirmatory and not), you are led down new alleys of investigation. It is a methodology, she clarifies, that is not merely abductive, but iterative. There is no exact starting point, but neither is there really a conclusion. Any single research project is part of a larger geography of continuing investigation. What it aims at, above all, is authenticity: grounded in an encounter with the experiences of the people who, through their communicating, *are* the organization.

Reconciling Contrasting Visions and, Therefore, Texts of the Organization

Her initial hypothesis was this. Any advanced technology having the complexity of an ERP incorporates, as we saw in Chapter 6, a mix of hardware, firmware, and software. If it is to be used to support the mix of operations typical of a large modern organization, it must make assumptions as to their nature and complexity. Once the components of what Anthony called the "box" (Chapter 6) have been configured, however, they are not easily adaptable to environments that exhibit incompatible configurations. The advantage, but also the bane, of the incredibly sophisticated composite systems now available in the market-place is precisely this complexity: it makes them powerful tools, but it also makes them dauntingly hard to reconfigure when they are implemented.

The main problem with introducing such systems, therefore, is that they are not merely assemblages of hardware/firmware/software. They are also texts, or what Hoppenbrouwers (2003) evocatively calls, from a design perspective, instances of "frozen language." Their components are encoded descriptions of the organizational processes they are meant to support. This means, Virgili observes, that they tacitly project structures of signification, of domination, and of legitimization (Giddens 1984). The configurations built into the system convey an image of what the object X is, who is responsible for dealing with it (A), and who benefits from the process (B). ERPs treat these encoded computer configurations as meaningful and legitimate, indeed as the norm: both descriptively and prescriptively. The issue this poses for the implementation of a new technology is that people in an organization already have their *own* idea about the kinds of configuration of task sequences that work best and how authority over functions is distributed. Like the Fall Plan, the technology that is aggressively marketed as the "ideal solution" to your problems of integration needs to confront the reality of what *can* be accomplished, given previous investments: the "sunk costs" of the organization in its own plant and people.

As Virgili conceptualized this situation, it meant that there were, at the beginning of the ERP implementation in September of 2001, two texts that would have to be reconciled with each other. It is her concentration on the process of reconciliation, and the often painful compromises it necessitated, that gave her project a direction, and her investigations a structure. It did not take her long to discover that the initial attitudes toward the new technology of members of the firm were negative. People perceived it as a threat to both their personal and their collective autonomy. Those most affected would be middle management. They feared they would see their sphere of discretion radically curtailed and their status downgraded. In the future, it would be the system that would make the decisions, regulate activities, centralize control. The ERP looked to them like Big Brother. No wonder they were apprehensive.

The question was how this would play out in the crossfire of conversation involving implementers and implementees. This is Virgili's topic.

The Research Site: "Labopharma"

Labopharma Laboratories (again all names are fictional) is the European leader in the field of phytotherapy (basically, naturalistic medicine and medical practice using plant products). It dates its start-up from 1986, with an initial staff of 166, and has grown rapidly in size ever since, as interest in naturalistic medicine has ballooned, especially in Europe.

By 2000, the firm was listed as among the 100 most profitable in France and had attained the position of fourth largest pharmaceutical enterprise in the country. Its products are marketed in more than 50 countries, and, at the time of her study, it had subsidiary operations in the US, Spain, Italy, the UK, Ireland, the Netherlands, Belgium, and Germany. Its current sales are more than 160 million euros (about U.S.$300 million when this chapter was written). It looked back on an unbroken record of success.

In 1996, the company went public by listing its stock on the Paris exchange. One implication that flows from trading publicly is that investors expect up-to-date and factually detailed reports on the company's operations. Over the years, Labopharma had accumulated no less than 14 different computer-based information systems, each tailor-made to fit the operations of a particular sector, such as finance, purchasing, operations, warehousing, and sales. The company lacked a central integrated server, and, since the diverse systems regularly encountered problems of compatibility, it was difficult to project a coherent picture of the state of affairs as a whole, in conformity with the norms that apply to publicly traded firms. Furthermore, as we have already observed in the previous chapter, technology was undergoing a sea change in the 1990s. The new ideal was a fully integrated accounting system, supported and driven by a central server, exactly Labopharma's weakness. Investors expected better. It was time, management decided, to do something.

In 1998, the company hired a consultant firm to analyze its present systems and to advise it on how to proceed. The consultants strongly reiterated the problems of inter-system incompatibility. They pointed out their negative effects on the quality and accuracy of the company's integrated accounts. Not only did they find a proliferation of accounting systems, but also administrative practices that themselves varied from domain to domain. The company lacked, as a result, a coherent, up-to-date picture of the state of its own operations. The consultants recommended that Labopharma implement an ERP, the current standard for centralized computer-based information systems.

Prodded by the consultants' analysis, in January of 1999 the company tasked its internal computer service to come up with a strategy. Top management attached two conditions: stay within a limited budget, and make sure that the special needs of the firm, as a pharmaceutical enterprise, were met. The search for a vendor was on. One effect of the conditions imposed by management was to eliminate as candidates the giants in the field, such as SAP, Oracle, and IBM, all of whom were at the time marketing systems tailored to the multinationals. The computer service thus invited offers from a range of mid-sized firms. By February, the head of computer services had established a short list of potential suppliers: JD Edwards ("Oneworld") and RS. To evaluate their proposals, Labopharma set up two committees: one a steering committee chaired by the CEO, with directors from the principal affected divisions; the other a working group, staffed by user representatives and their associated computer advisors. The latter committee was asked to define the requirements of each section, using a checklist provided by a national advisory service and designed for that purpose. In March, the results of the survey were forwarded to the suppliers, with an invitation to indicate their capability to meet the requirements. In April, two companies arrived to do their "show-and-tell." In the aftermath, on the advice of the head of computer services, the steering committee was invited to confirm the choice of RS. The telling factor seems to have been price: RS had made the most attractive offer. Sandrine discovered in her talks with operational people, however, that the choice elicited no great enthusiasm on their part:

> We were not exactly swept away, you know. We were even pretty skeptical ... We just had those two to choose from. Anyway, we wouldn't have chosen either; it was the head of computer services who was running the show.

How well adapted were the suppliers to meet the special needs of Labopharma, Sandrine asked? "It was impossible for us to find out ... We knew it was mostly marketing, meant to seduce us."

The project was launched with some fanfare in September of 1999. It foresaw the implementation of the system as a "big bang": the whole operation to be launched at a single time. In the meantime, storm clouds were gathering in the international hi-tech sector. Smaller developers were being squeezed out. As a result, long before the project could be completed, RS found itself in trouble financially and decided to close down its operations in France. It reneged on its contract with Labopharma (who sued).

It was not the kind of experience to inspire confidence among people in the company who had been involved in the choice process. Their estimation of their own in-house computer "experts," as well as the competence and reliability of vendor firms, had been shaken.

The Next Step

Labopharma shut off its planning process for the moment, in order to take stock. However, at the beginning of 2001, the project was revived. The previous head of computer services had been thanked, and replaced. This time, Labopharma turned to the market leader in the ERP field, SAP, inviting it to submit a proposal, again with some financial limits imposed. By this time, however, SAP and its closest competitors had begun to see the sector of mid-sized firms as a priority, and Labopharma had become an attractive target. In the space of two months, SAP, in collaboration with a small firm of implementation consultants it was accustomed to work with in France (SAP is a German firm), was ready with a working plan. Because the project was already behind schedule, senior management at Labopharma set a requirement that implementation be expeditious. SAP agreed it could respect the exigency and accordingly established a target date of August 2002 for a full implementation of the system. But, it cautioned, there were conditions attached. First, Labopharma would have to live with a standardized system, based on SAP's previous experience with, and understanding of, pharmaceutical operations. Second, a rigid schedule would have to be adhered to (employing what they called Rapid Implementation Tools and Services (RITS)). The process that they envisioned was comprised of five phases: project start-up (July–August 2001); analysis of any discrepancies between the system configuration and present practice (September–October); fixing new parameters where necessary (November–March); integration of data from previous systems (January–June 2002); training and start-up (July–August). Any adaptations to the system configuration to accommodate the special needs of Labopharma, they stipulated, could not exceed 10 percent.

First Steps Toward Implementation

Phase 1 (July–August 2001) was preoccupied with preliminary activities, taken up with detailed planning, based on the requirements data gleaned from the earlier exercise, and putting a team together. September (when Sandrine began her fieldwork) was the first time that people working in the various sectors of the company got an actual look at the new system. The structure of the committees empowered to oversee the implementation was like the one adopted by the company in 1998. There would again be a representative central steering committee, with the CEO as chair. And then there would be workshops (*ateliers*) depending on the sector (purchasing versus financial, for example). Workshops would be comprised of operational managers from a sector, their associated computer specialists, and representatives of the consulting firm employed to supervise the implementation of the ERP module corresponding to that particular activity. Thus each workgroup would take on a dimension of the system, depending on the sector. Production people, for example, would look at planning, handling stock, database operations, labeling. Commercial reps would study client files, sales flow (sales, delivery, billing), prospecting future commercial operations, etc. SAP, through its consultants, would act as the integrating central server.

What this phase thus obliged people to do was to stand back and to take a close look at the usual operations they were engaged in without, under normal circumstances, paying them much overt or critical attention. Even more novel, they soon found out, was to be confronted with how other people (the consultants representing SAP) envisioned these same operations. Perhaps for the first time ever, the managers now were required to make a public account of how they organized their work. It was one that would have to stand up to scrutiny, if they were to respond effectively to the outside agents who were there to restructure their work patterns. Virgili used this necessity they now faced, and their response to it, to buttress her argument that the organization could be read as already having a virtual text. It was only when confronted with a different and unfamiliar text that the managers began to understand that their own practices had one all along.

What they were confronted with was complexity: or what Virgili calls the "somewhat ambivalent nature" of SAP. Some features were a clear improvement, people conceded, on the systems they already had. Planners, for example, discovered they could more freely explore a range of strategic alternatives than before. There were problems as well, on the other hand. For example, the shipping department normally packaged its deliveries in shipments of several products at a time, depending on what the customer needed. When a pharmacy orders 30 different products, it expects they will be delivered in the same shipment. SAP, however, worked on a different logic, line by line. This would complicate delivery schedules considerably and leave customers unhappy. As the people in shipping pointed out, there would also be supplementary costs: "It's going to cost us plenty, and the pharmacy too. This is not the way we work at Labopharma, and it's clear that the commercial department and Madame X (president-CEO of the company) won't buy it."

As one sector representative put it, "For sure, some things are going to change, and others are going to be improved. And there are others that are not going to budge. It makes for a complicated mix, all that."

Clearly, they were concluding, an SAP ERP is indeed a complex tool. What was now becoming evident was that the envisioned transformations of practice would affect more than local operations. There were implications for the global strategy of the whole firm, the kind of question that preoccupies top management.

The Negotiation Process Intensifies

The disparities between SAP and current practice were accumulating: how to handle transactions between Labopharma and one of its subsidiaries; commercial rules for complimentary products; shipping (as described above); problems with reporting procedures in the financial control division. The people in the workshops now requested a meeting with the steering committee, to be given guidance. There was still not enough clarification of the issues, however, for the latter to pass judgment, they reckoned. The workshops were instructed to go back to the drawing board, in close collaboration with the consultants, and to come up with more precise analyses. We are, by now, up to December. Phase 2 should have been completed a month before, and we are already embarked on phase 3, with many, many issues not yet resolved. The one that looms largest, and drives all the others, however, is whether (a) to modify the program to fit Labopharma's special needs, or (b) to revise the strategies, processes, and the documents of the enterprise itself. In effect, people were asking, which text will take precedence?

The consultants were reluctant to budge: don't forget, they reiterated, we're limited to changes of at most 10 percent. Anyway, some of the configuration parameters were inscribed in the hardware and firmware of the SAP ERP. It would not be practical, even possible, to change them, notably where accounting was concerned.

Nevertheless, in spite of these and other reservations, the process, Virgili reports, was beginning to follow its own trajectory: one that was different from what had been envisaged at the beginning. The participants in the process were starting not only to understand better the characteristics of the ERP but to learn more about their own patterns of work. They were not going to be stampeded, they decided. They had learned enough about the system to understand how much they didn't know.

For example, there was the issue of how to handle incoming invoices. This was initially treated as being connected only to accounting. Now people were obliged to recognize that it had wider implications that affected the organization as a whole. For example, where special orders were concerned (office supplies, for example, that are not part of the usual warehouse complement), budgetary control had always been local, service by service. With SAP, it would be handled differently: item by item. It now became clear to those involved that there would be no way to trace the path of the order across divisions, and so the question was posed: how will the authorization be handled? Previously, decisions had been taken locally, to respect sector budgets. This would no longer be feasible. Here, even the consultants finally had to admit there was a problem. The consultants were also having difficulties explaining the SAP logic: sometimes an explanation given in one meeting seemed to be contradicted in the next, people were complaining (which the consultants themselves sometimes grudgingly conceded).

Crosslinked Tensions

The most vexing issues, it now seemed evident to those participating, were the ones that crossed divisional lines. They had also discovered that the consultants were, to cite Virgili, "hyper-specialized" in their own module of the system (for example, accounting). Their repeated mantra of "zero specific, 100 percent standard SAP" was not helpful, people felt. In fact, insistence on the precedence of SAP was starting to grate, especially since the more deeply the people in the company probed into the new system, the more intractable the inter-divisional issues appeared to be. Given these perplexities, the operations reps and their computer advisors now turned to the project head, requesting, first, that special inter-section meetings be formally set up and, second, that they be given permission to access modules other than their own, by being issued the relevant password. This request generated a controversy. The project head replied in the negative:

> I insist on the principle that your profiles and your authorizations must be restricted initially, to be enlarged later, because there are so many transactions in SAP that you are going to get lost, and furthermore you risk going into someone else's module and destroying data by an incorrect manipulation of the data that he has created, or something like that. There are too many risks, you won't be able to handle it.

To which the rep from the commercial division replied,

> Look, I think I'm speaking in the name of everyone here. If we don't have those authorizations, how do you expect us to do our work and how are we going to learn the tool, and do the analyses and treat the particular files if we can't see how the whole flow works? It is out of the question, we can't work like that, we won't make any progress.

The project head backed off a bit: "OK, end of the discussion. We'll see, I'm going to have to think it over. But, for the moment, that's the way it's going to be."

Pandora's Box Opened

He was wrong. They didn't wait. Instead, they organized themselves— formed a coalition. They began to invite each other to their meetings, where they interactively explored alternative scenarios. They traded passwords and authorizations, so that they could each access other modules and transactions, whenever the latter were, they knew, directly relevant to their own preoccupations. But even that was not enough: they were still unable to link up using a single password. Enter the consultants, who agreed to let them use their own passwords. This opened up the entire package of modules to those involved. The question of "official" authorization was thus shelved for the moment. But the interaction between divisions had become an established principle, and would continue to be so throughout the rest of the project.

Not that all was sweetness and light. On the contrary. There were, Virgili reports, "clashes, sometimes heated, between the representatives of the different modules." The source of some conflicts was the hypothetical transfer of task responsibilities between sectors and, more generally, which current rules of practice would be scrapped, modified, or implemented. Nothing appeared to be tied down: a standard that seemed to have been agreed on earlier might now have to be once again reopened for questioning. Choices of how to proceed were left unresolved for the moment. New discrepancies between SAP and current practice were unearthed. On the other hand, some things that seemed to have been problematical before now turned out not to be so intractable: the perceived problem came down to no more than a hitch in translation. SAP is composed in German, and there were difficulties that arose with translation into French: it was hard to match up terms such as purchasing agent, buyer, procurement clerk, for example. Whole discussions could hang on the connotations of a certain word.

Sometimes, the problems they encountered could be traced back to technical features of the system. Manufacturing products such as pills, syrups, creams, and the like requires very precise measurements of the weight of ingredients, such as plants and powders. The current computer system for manufacturing at Labopharma allowed for a precision of up to nine decimals. The best SAP was capable of was five decimals. As people in manufacturing told Virgili,

> That, you may not realize, is absolutely catastrophic for us. That will make an enormous difference, and it is going to have to be managed. What's more, we're going to have to find a solution, and that takes time. Here we are, only three months away from start-up, and we're just learning about this problem now? That is not acceptable.

What transpired was that plans for the switch-over and training of employees, then underway, were suspended for a month while they worked frantically to resolve the problem.

Phase 4?

The hypothetical transition to phase 4 (January–June 2002), as laid out by the original plan of work, slipped by without anybody even noticing. As one person remarked to Sandrine, in June,

> You know we didn't even realize we were already in phase 4. Did you? Be honest ... It's not important. What matters is to move ahead ... That's just consulting and keeping up appearances for people outside, to satisfy management, and give them something to hang onto. But in reality it's all the phases going on at the same time. What do you think, isn't it a complete shambles [the word he actually used was *bordel*, which translates literally as "bordello," but is commonly used by French-speakers to mean any really confused and messy situation].

People were not unaware of the need to keep management informed, however. One sector representative put it this way to the researcher:

> You understand, Sandrine, when we send an e-mail we always copy it to Madame X (the president-CEO). That way, she keeps up to date, because she'll know that things are not going so well. So at least, if the project is behind schedule because of the directors, because the key decisions have not been made, we won't be made to carry the can, we warned them. Because they don't seem to be tracking (*s'en faire*) ... The other day, when we had the meeting about codes, for example, we talked about shipping using LM (a module). And you had H. G. and C. C. (director of marketing and of commercial, respectively) who said, "Oh yeah, OK, but anyway that is classic SAP, don't worry." All that because they'd heard it talked about three times, and now they think they know everything. They're soon going to find out what SAP is all about!"

More than one respondent told Virgili the same thing: they had sent a copy of their correspondence to the chief executive.

Still More Delay

In June of 2002, training was suspended, and the start-up date was pushed back from August 2 to November 4. By August, three months from the *new* D-Day, there were still 543 points unresolved, not merely organizational but several of them technical. RITS has been scrapped. Cross-divisional meetings were still the norm. Virgili calls this the period of the "hesitation waltz." Three weeks from the new start-up in November, no test had yet been run for the system as a whole. There were still technical problems, such as frequent server breakdowns. Data transfer from previous systems had still not occurred. Training was still incomplete. There were still perceived inadequacies in the SAP architecture. "It's purely technical and there is nothing we can do about it," one informant told Virgili. Actually, it proved to be hard, in retrospect, to sort out what was technical and what was practical; it was too complex. In October, with so many issues still unresolved, the steering committee met and accorded a further delay, this time to put off the starting date to January 5, 2003.

Finally, although without total unanimity, a strategy was being patched together. For some functions, SAP was found acceptable, although with the provision that it might eventually need to be modified. A number of issues went on a new list labeled "after the implementation." In the meantime, people had come up with ways to "fool the standard system," as they put it, so that it would approximate the current strategy and practice. In other sectors, an interface would have to be constructed to integrate the SAP central server to link up with a limited number of systems currently in use—five, in all. Overall, the initial expectations of what the ERP could deliver had proven unrealistic. What had emerged was a hard-fought compromise, an improvement over the old system, but also far removed from the original vendor dogma. The tension the process had generated, at the interpersonal level, is perhaps summed up in an exchange that Virgili was privy to:

Project chief (an ERP consultant):   I sincerely think that the commercial success of Labopharma is being used as a pretext to preserve the present habits that sometimes contradict the rules of management that SAP defines.

Commercial rep (the company):   It's not up to us to adapt to the tool. If our commercial policy is working so well it's precisely because we are more original than our competitors. It's up to the tool to adapt itself to our situation. Furthermore, if we bought it, it's not because we want to do things less well, it's to make the work go better ...

And then the human dimension of such inter-group interactions to achieve some kind of reciprocity emerges:

Commercial rep: ... And anyway, you're a computer scientist and its understandable you'd reason like that. But we're on the operational side and we can't ...

Project chief (interrupting):   Oh no, I'm sorry, but I am in no way a computer scientist. I am a consultant in information systems, and it's not the same thing. And furthermore I worked for 10 years as the head of commercial operations at [name of company] in Belgium, so I know as much as you do about operations and the profession!

There was one consolation for all the investment in time they had made. Their principal competitor, located nearby, had just completed its own implementation, and its ERP, after a month, had crashed, shutting down production and leaving the personnel *de facto* unemployed. They would be out of operation, totally, for three months.

Meanwhile, at Labopharma, the new system was finally launched in March. A week later, Sandrine finished her fieldwork and addressed the writing of her dissertation.

The Conversation in the Text, and the Text in the Conversation

Virgili describes her approach as *émergentiste*. This neologism is her umbrella term for a variety of perspectives on technology and organization that include, she notes, studies in the social construction of technology, actor–network theory (Callon, Latour and Law, among others), activity theory (Engeström), and structuration theory (Giddens, Poole and DeSanctis, McPhee, Orlikowski, and others). The unifying link between these otherwise diverse sets of ideas is the common conviction they share that organization (or society) is constructed from the interaction of people, through the medium of the language tokens that they use to do so. Her immediate inspiration, however, for the work we have been reporting was, she explains, a claim by members of the so-called Montreal School (Cooren, Taylor, & Van Every 2006; Taylor, Cooren, Giroux, & Robichaud 1996; Taylor & Van Every 2000) that organization is generated in the cross-over translation process from the more durable constructions of language, or texts, into the fleeting processes of human interaction, or conversations, and vice versa. It is in this alternation between the *crystal* of text and the *smoke* of talk (Atlan 1979) that the permanent features of organization are both constructed and perpetuated (the role of text), and the re-interpretation and transformation of organization in response to current realities is renegotiated (the role of conversation).

What this process entails in practice is better illustrated than explicated. To this end, we look closely at two conversations Virgili recorded. They illustrate two crucial features of emergence. First, they display the structuring power of text as people put it to use in interaction to establish what they claim to be real, what they think is legitimate, and where they see authority as being vested (these are what Giddens calls the dimensions of "structuration"). Verbal compositions based on a text are a potent means to justify a mapping of a particular tissue of complementary relationships, with everyone slotted neatly into a position, either one-up or one-down, depending on the context. Like a machine in its logical hierarchy of functions, there is precedence. Text, furthermore, always has an author, and it thus conveys and aims to legitimate the singular perspective of this author, whether individual or collective. It thus enshrines authority.

Conversation instantiates, however, by its very configuration, a mixed symmetrical and complementary relationship, positioning one individual or community horizontally with respect to the other. They literally *confront* another, each endowed with their own notion of what the authentic text really is. How this sometimes discrepant interaction of perspectives, complementary versus symmetric, works out in practice, and how organization emerges out of the dynamic of the ensuing game that it inspires, is one phenomenon that Virgili set out to explore. It is what we have been describing as playing on the game and playing in the game, all at the same time: not merely acting *in* frame, but also recognizing and sometimes reconfiguring *the frame one is in*: re-framing it and, by doing so, evoking a whole different set of players and rules.

The other dimension of communication her work illustrates is an affirmation of an insight developed in some depth by Cooren (2006) and by Robichaud, Giroux, and Taylor (2004). They argue that one conversation is made present in another through the mediation of a verbal account (which is also, in its own way, a text, since it too must be "authored" for the occasion—spoken by someone). This is the principal mechanism by means of which organization is enabled to extend itself *beyond* the immediately local to transcend boundaries of space and time. The verbal accounts of those who are physically present *in* a conversation become channels for the dissemination of a text that was assembled in *another* place, at *another* time, by *other* actors. How such tele-acting, as Cooren calls it, works in practice, to impose the constraints of organization, is illustrated by Virgili's reports on interactions between the computer system consultants and the Labopharma managers.

Conversation 1: Different "Maps"

The first exchange we consider is taken from a session observed in February of 2002 (6 months after the initiation of the project). The ERP consultant, Frédéric, is explaining to Babas, manager of logistics management (LM) shipments, Karl, the sales division representative, and Pierre, computer adviser to sales (not their real names), how the relevant SAP module handles LM. This is a recognized problem area in Labopharma. For some 8 years, the company had a problem with breaks. The system they already had in place to deal with it is not efficient: unable to handle the volume expeditiously. The company hopes SAP will lead to reduced breakage, leaving LM to handle the simple task for which it was originally intended: to prepare the invoice. In this way, they anticipate, the company will be more responsive to customer relations and needs.

We pick up the conversation with the consultant, Frédéric, explaining how SAP works.

Frédéric: Today, we're going to see how SAP handles breaks [*ruptures*]. Here's how it works. It functions on a line-by-line basis. Everything in stock or ready to ship is entered directly into LM, which prepares the order. The delivery slip is generated in SAP, it's then sent to the commercial clerks who can then easily trace the customer order. For those orders in breakage, SAP initiates control availability, which allows products in stock to be set aside, to trigger an estimation of MRP requirements in the module MM/PP. Here's how the flow works (*he illustrates the process using a diagram*).

Everybody turns to look at Babas, the manager of LM shipments, at this juncture, to see his reaction.

Babas: Okay, we've got a problem. We don't work like that, and I mean not at all like that. For breakage, it won't work. I think we haven't understood each other on the question of handling breakage. Apparently, it doesn't mean the same thing for you as it does for us. What we do, we enter LM, and we input the number of orders and the number of breaks. And generally we don't ship the order if there are too many breaks. So it's like very much a decision that is made by people when it comes to shipping. We go directly into the command "verify." But there, at the beginning of the season we know we are already up to 80 percent of breaks. You understand, at the moment that's not the way we do it. We don't look at the availability. And more than that, don't forget our concept of special customer. There, what you are proposing, that'd work for ordinary customers maybe. But we have a lot of special customers [*clients privilégiés*]. Those orders, they have to be given priority over the others. With SAP, if I understand correctly, that's not going to be possible?

Frédéric: Right, but there again, you have a whole lot of empirical notions, like "special customers." SAP is standard, it can't manage case by case, I've already told you that.

Karl: Yeah, but look, I can't understand why for someone who is already configured for the pharmacy sector, you've never come across this with your other clients, like Boiron, Sanofi, and so on, the idea of special customers?

Babas: Look, it seems to me you are oversimplifying real life management to the ultimate degree. But anyway, it's one of the features that was laid out in the original list of requirements. Okay, it's true that you couldn't know in advance too well how it works . . . Could you at least add a rule so that SAP does not scan the line of commands by date?

Frédéric: Absolutely not. It's impossible in R/3 [a term referring to the basic architecture of SAP, comparable, for example, to a version of Windows]. It's you who perhaps have a problem of logic. You do too much case by case, you are too empirical [*vous faites trop de cas par cas, de l'empirique*].

Babas (*now visibly upset*):   Well look, I'm sorry, but with that system there we're headed straight into a wall. You're not following me. Sure, we talk about fluid logic. There's no computer rule that can explain commercial considerations, the guy is going to negotiate . . . it's a problem I meet up with every day.

Frédéric: Yeah, but you have to understand that working on the line by line principle, SAP launches the availability control, and that is necessary so that the assistants will have the information, and follow up. Somewhere it has to be, the clerical staff have to realize that by this time it's finished. SAP, it's an integrated system, everyone is involved.

Karl: In my opinion, we would have to change the people before implementing the ERP.

Pierre: It, it's the problem of the special customers.

Frédéric: Look, you can't make an exception into a general rule. The situations you describe, they're what you are focused on, but . . .

Pierre: Sure, the thing is that he is often in these situations. He's adapted to a system.

Babas: From what I can see, with LM, I won't be able to select the number of lines I want. I would be happy if SAP could download the re-shipment lines then.

Frédéric: No, sorry, that's not possible.

The conversation continues for a bit, much in the same vein. Finally, they have to admit they have reached an impasse.

Babas: The problem is that there, it's that SAP works on the line principle, and we do it by order. Can we make SAP work on the order principle?

Frédéric: Impossible. And you, can you work on the line principle?

Babas: So then there is no solution. Unless we change how we do things completely [*changer de direction générale*] . . .!!!

Pierre: Yikes . . . so we're going nowhere. We will have to go back to the system we have now.

Constative? Or performative?

Consider the exchange, as interpreted by Virgili. Frédéric, the consultant, is working from a text (and visibly so). In Virgili's reading of this kind of encounter, he is using the text to establish three things: (1) to transmit in the form of a disciplined account the *meaning* of logistics management, as SAP understands it; (2) to insist on the legitimacy of his account (and incidentally of his own role as its expositor); and (3) both to *portray* a distribution of authority in the carrying out of tasks, and to *assert* his own authority as instructor. Every function of logistics management, as SAP interprets it, is assigned a meaning and is described by a term. The entire span of task performance making up sales is given an interpretation that is grounded in SAP: its "signification, legitimation, and domination" to use Giddens' terms.

Frédéric's training role, to interpret what is happening differently, using Austin's terminology, thus has both a constative and a performative dimension. Like a magician, he dazzles his audience by his manipulation of the objects he encourages them to concentrate their attention on (the "constative" part), while simultaneously distracting their attention from what he is actually doing (the "performative" part). The "constative" side of his performance takes the form of a show-and-tell: a display of visuals firmly embedded in a web of talk. This, he says, is how we handle breaks. See? The listeners are supposed, he implies, to concentrate on the content of his presentation, a diagram, for example. The "performative" part is conveyed by the *illocutionary effect* or *modality* of his discourse: he is *telling* them how to do their work, with the SAP ERP as the agency to which they must all in the future defer. They are meant to respond to his presentation, it is clear, by "up-taking" what he says: learning from him how to do their job when the ERP is up and running.

When they prove recalcitrant, he displays considerable irritation. "You have a problem of logic," he says dismissively. But why should they take what he is saying at face value? There is a clear mismatch between the system that this consultant is describing to them and what they experience as their everyday reality. His explanation of the SAP logic doesn't, in fact, make sense to *them*, and because of that they question its legitimacy and resist its domination. The "significance" is wrong. Is it merely a matter of words, Babas wonders? But then no, it seems, the problem goes deeper. When Frédéric, for his part, encounters opposition from Babas and his colleague, he accuses them of being too "empirical." He again insists on the solid basis of "sound logic" that justifies the SAP procedure. It is based on the "standard." He points to its capacity to integrate activities (as opposed to the lack of integration that has previously reigned in sales, he intimates).

Hold on, retorts Babas. Legitimacy, in a manufacturing company, is not determined by any abstract system of logic. There is a different kind of logic people in sales have to bear in mind: commercial logic. Customers insist on negotiating. It happens every day. I've got practical problems to deal with. If the SAP ERP can't help me do my job, why should I use it?

What is rock-solid logic for one person, it seems, is excessive rigidity for the other. On the other hand, what is flexibility for the latter is mere empiricism for the former—a want of discipline. The two parties are now in a symmetrical position: neither prepared to concede to the other the right to decide. If Frédéric reposes *his* authority on the well-worked out text of SAP (the "standard"), the people in the firm can counter-pose their *own* text, grounded in the hard realities of the commercial practice they live with, and its inevitable constraints. It is, for the moment, a stand-off.

Virgili's point is that what is at issue, ultimately, is the text. In the absence of an integrative text, the everyday work world of Babas and his colleagues would be no more than a disconnected sequence of disparate encounters. It is the existence of such an integrating text that renders it possible for them to make sense of their work life: to indexically "connect up the dots," in effect. Frédéric vaunts the "integrative" feature of an ERP as one of its main selling points. But the people in sales, they begin to realize, have their own integrative text. It is merely that, as a well-established (and successful) community of practice, they seldom need to verbalize it to each other, in so many words. They are, however, perfectly conscious of the trajectory of success of their company, with its singular modes of practice, and it is this awareness that legitimates for them their own virtual text: *their* thirdness.

Who Is Acting, Individuals or Their Principals?

Two corporate entities, it seems, SAP and Labopharma, are vicariously present in the discussion going on in sales: each "tele-acting" through the agency of its respective spokespersons. The interaction between consultant and company personnel is thus *simultaneously* complementary and symmetrical. The interaction between those present in the conversation is itself, in fact, a confirmation of the agency, and identity, of the respective bases of authority that motivate their actions. SAP and Labopharma are virtually interacting. It is the text, as interpreted by their agents, that mediates their co-presence.

The meeting we have been looking at led to several weeks' discussions that were dedicated to a search for a compromise between the technical configuration and the commercial policy. All in vain. Virgili offers again a transcript of the exchange, now with two others present, the consultant project head and the company project head. The meeting she recorded had been called, as Sandrine notes, "without much conviction," in the hope of resolving the impasse. The participants in this last encounter still trotted out the same arguments as before, one emphasizing the logic of the machine, the other the logic of the product and of work (*logique du produit, logique de travail*). SAP is incapable of resolving the problem of breaks that led them to search for a new solution in the first place, because to solve this problem it would introduce another that no one had foreseen: problems with customer relations. This turned out to be, in the final analysis, one of four existing systems that were retained: SAP would do no more than download information onto the local system. Neither text was the clear winner; the combination was a kind of hybrid text no one had envisioned at the outset.

Conversation 2: "Telepresence"

The phantom presence of absent agents in conversation—those of organizational thirdnesses—is illustrated by another recorded exchange, this time in a different division, purchasing (for a more detailed analysis of this extract, see Taylor & Virgili 2008).

As before, the encounter takes place in a small meeting room. There is an SAP consultant at the head of the table (let's call him Paul). He is addressing one of the eight operational heads assigned by the purchasing sector to supervise the project. We'll call him Gilles. Seated beside him is his second in command, Méla (short for Mélanie). Across the table is the company computer specialist for the same sector, the purchasing department, Alfred (again a fictional name). Sandrine is at the rear of the room, taking down what is happening in shorthand. The consultant is facing a screen on which he is projecting a PowerPoint presentation that outlines the features of SAP the others will need to learn in order to implement the new system.

Paul: There, that's the MIGO transaction that the purchasing agent initiates when he has completed checking out the purchasing order.

Gilles: But wait, I don't understand. He "initiates" it . . . what does that mean? That's already several meetings we have had about this module, and the way you are talking about the purchasing agent, that's not the way it is done here, not at all. How can the purchasing agent who is supposed to look after the requested purchase, how can he initiate this transaction . . . That seems to suppose that it is he who takes the decision. Here, with us, I'm not sure that it works like that. What do you think, Méla?

Méla: Oh, let's see. I'm thinking about Noëlle, when she does that. No, no, it's not exactly like that. For us the problem is that it is not the purchasing agent who initiates the order, he merely enters the order into the system, he does the entry of the order. So there (*turning to Paul*), according to you, it's the purchasing agent who issues the order, is that right?

Gilles:	There, you see, that's what I thought. You, when you speak of the purchasing agent, but it's not like that here, it doesn't have the same meaning, here with us the buyer is not the same as the purchasing agent, it doesn't have the same meaning, it's not the same function. Here, in our operation, the purchasing agent doesn't do the negotiation; it's split up into two. It's the buyer who does the negotiating. And then the buyer enters the orders in Page [an existing software] and then into Skep [another software]. Do you understand? That's why we couldn't understand the logic, we couldn't grasp it.
Alfred:	I think it would have been a good idea to make a glossary of terms before we started working on this, because look it seems like there are a number of things that have the same term here, with us, and in SAP, but that don't mean the same thing. Look, we're really going to get lost this way.
Gilles:	Yeah, and then the more we go on, and get into detail, the more we are going to have this problem, I think. Because it's not the first time this has happened. We need to be really clear, otherwise we're going to be wasting our time, for nothing.
Paul:	Well I'm sorry, but you'd better get used to it, because that's the SAP terminology. But in the present case, let me know if you don't understand (*he turns back to his presentation, and pulls up a new slide on the screen*). So now we're going to look at the organization of the purchase.
Alfred:	The organization of the purchase, what's that, is it the purchasing department or the buyers, or both?
Paul:	What do you mean by that?
Gilles:	Well is it the purchaser or those who enter the orders, is it all one operation, or is it instead one or the other? Because here, with us, us using Page, it's not like that. Here, it involves several people. There's the administration of the orders, for example, the first thing to do is to consult the source file to check up on the contracts, it's the purchasing agent who does that, you see, he'll pick up the phone and call the supplier. He negotiates on the basis of the contract that is recorded in Page. It's like that, Page shows him the different contracts. And then he gets in touch with the buyer and transmits the order directly. It's always in a direct relationship, each time.
Méla:	Are you sure? But it seems to me that Noëlle [a user in the purchasing department] told me that she also had a role to play in the process.
Gilles:	Yeah, I think you're right. Wait though. But I think she comes in at the end, for the PMS 400 [name of a sequence of purchasing transactions].

Paul: Well if you two can't even agree among yourselves, then (*spoken in a joking tone*)!!!

Gilles: Hey wait, I'll phone Noëlle, she'll tell us right away. Better to check directly with the source.
            (*He gets up, goes to the back of the room, and calls the person on the telephone. The others wait.*)

Gilles: Yeah, that's it, you're right. So in the process we have to also add her and the PMS 400 of Page.

Paul: Okay, I understand.

The common feature between the two sectors, sales and purchasing, is their recourse to a rationale of practice, contrasted with the more abstract logic of the ERP system. Both Gilles and Babas buttress their position by citing "empirical" considerations, but Gilles, with the help of Méla, does more: he dramatizes the contrast by inserting into this conversation another with Noëlle ("the source"). "Yeah, that's it, you're right," he reports, thus embedding one interaction within another, making Noëlle's reality now vicariously present in this ongoing exchange of talk.

The conversation, after the interruption, continues.

Paul: Yeah okay, I understand. But first let me finish showing you the things I have. Afterwards, you can compare. OK, we're going on (*he shows a slide*). There, you can see in the file purchasing information, and the list of sources of purchasing. You see?

Gilles: Yeah, okay, that's a nice screen, not bad. It's user friendly. But you can enter just like that into the FPI [file purchasing information]?

Paul: Yeah, yeah, it's pretty flexible.

Gilles: Personally, I'd say it was even on the lax side. Wait a minute, does that, does that mean, if I understand you correctly, that anybody can modify the FPI? So, if I pursue that line of reasoning a bit further, that also means that even if the FPI is not up to date, you can enter an order into it, is that right?

Paul: Yeah. You see SAP is not so rigid as all that. Often, it's very flexible. Afterwards, it's true that there, it could be dangerous, so it's up to you to do the organizing.

Gilles: Myself, what really concerns me now, it's that all that, that's calling into question pretty much our whole organization of the purchasing/buying procedure. That's how we see things, if you like. Okay so, SAP is flexible for some things, but not where we would like it to be. The problem is that it's getting at, after all, the very heart of the process. Apparently, SAP doesn't distinguish between the two. And then also the interface with the planning department is doubtful. Because, with SAP, the risk is to screw up [*shunter pas mal*] the planners' work. We'll have to see if that makes sense or not. We're gonna have to ask ourselves if the way we organize things makes sense any more, or whether SAP, you see, can help us out in some way. But that's not a decision that we can make, among ourselves. We'll have to bring in the director of purchasing. Furthermore, for him, we've got to know if he favors more flexibility, but not so much that the FPI is so accessible to everyone, like that. In my opinion, we have to build in some more structure, some barriers. We'll really have to give that some serious thought. And then, after that, there is that whole business of the orders. For us, that's a real roadblock if we don't have them. Maybe make some more specific, but we're not going to budge on that.

Paul: Look, we're just at the beginning here, you shouldn't get too worked up. So we will have to consult the purchasing director, and then we'll see. So now you can make a note of the problem areas, just to keep track, and tomorrow we'll have to call in CA [the director of purchasing] or somebody he delegates, and we'll talk it through.

Now Gilles has pulled off a second displacement of the conversation, this time by embedding it in a *future* encounter that he has verbally evoked, involving the director of purchasing (who was, incidentally, one of the founders of the company). Nice move, one is tempted to say! He has managed to call up, in the course of a short exchange, the entire organizational structure of Labopharma, where his section is concerned, from the boss down to the clerical staff, and, in so framing, to assert the authority of practice. He has effectively evoked the unspoken text of the organizational structure of the company.

Conclusion

Jacques Derrida (1988) once analyzed the signing of the American Declaration of Independence, the founding document of a new state, in this way. The people who met in Philadelphia, he observed, did not represent their country, because, when they assembled, there was no such country. It was merely an insurrection. It was their signature that created the country: "We, the people of these United States of America …" It was also that signature that instantiated them as authentic spokespersons for the new country, and thereby legitimated their role as signers. The signer writes the signature is how we usually think of such an event. Derrida's point was that, in this instance, it was literally the signature that authorized, and created, the signers as having the identity of those who are entitled to sign. It was the text that they devised, and signed, that endowed them with the authority to sign such a text.

This is pretty much what Garfinkel meant by reflexivity: it is the interactive talk of people who create the conversation, but it is the conversation, now materialized as text, that authorizes the same conversation. Virgili's analysis suggests this is the usual basis of organization, not an exception. The advantage of studying a disturbing situation in the life of the organization, such as an implementation of new technology, is that the disruption of everyday life makes the emergence of organization in conversation visible. Only when challenged by the outsiders did it become incumbent on the people who worked in the organization to, in effect, "write the constitution" of their particular enterprise, by making it explicit in text to order to re-establish its authority.

In Chapter 8, we extend this analysis in a very different context, one where there *was not* a common text to start with. We consider the inception of organization, engendered in conversation, but progressively constituting itself through the generation of an authoritative text. Up until now, we have been considering examples of organization that announce themselves as such: companies, agencies of government. But this risks once again reifying organization: seeing it as a *thing*—a regression to machine logic. That is not what we mean by thirdness. It may be the case that any socially recognized entity, such as an enterprise, must establish its thirdness; otherwise it cannot long survive. But thirdness has many manifestations or embodiments. Organization, we claim, is conceptually defined by thirdness, not the other way around. It is an achievement, not an entitlement. Chapter 8 tracks both the emergence of thirdness and the role of established thirdness in its inception.

Suggested Supplementary Readings

The principal reference here is Chapters 2 and 3 of our earlier book, *The Emergent Organization* (Taylor & Van Every 2000). For a somewhat different interpretation, influenced by the actor–network theory of Michel Callon and Bruno Latour, see Chapter 6 of Cooren's *The Organizing Property of Communication* (2000).

Chapter 8

The "Western," Twenty-First-Century Version

Mapping the Boundaries Through Texts

The idea of reflexivity is at the heart of the approach to research we have been considering. If we assume that people are continually in the business of constructing and reconstructing the self-same world of meaning that supplies the context and essential point of reference for their own activities, it makes no sense to assume an a priori existence of that context, as if it were written in stone. It is still *under* construction. To imagine otherwise would be to return to the discredited way of thinking that Smith (1993) called the metaphor of communication-*in*-organization. That route leads to a reification of organization, treats it as merely a fixed parameter of interaction, a house built by someone else and temporarily occupied by the current members. At best, they can decorate their own offices and hallways to make them livable. At worst they feel alienated, dismayed, depressed.

The thesis of reflexivity illustrates an alternative thesis, that those who make up the organization are also its architects, both for better and for worse. People such as Vasquez' Mariana and Fernanda, Güney's Anthony and Greg, Virgili's Babas and Gilles, or Fauré's Georges, Alain, and Jacques are far from being no more than passive boarding-house roomers. They take on with a will the responsibility for their own actions and those of their organization. They know that the construction of the organizational context (and its text) is a collective achievement. It transcends the authority of any single person. Everyone is part of the construction process, not excluding the CEO and management generally. Authority may not be homogeneously distributed, its pattern can even be (and often is) gravely distorted and unfair, but neither does it radiate from a solar source identifiable with any single person. Not even in a dictatorship.

Given a commitment to the thesis of reflexivity, the task of the researcher is to go look, listen, and ask how, in the course of conversations, an ongoing reconstruction of a text and its context is accomplished an organization that continually emerges as both a process (an "organizing") and an entity (an "organized," with an identity: a corporate personality). In this chapter, we broaden the horizon even further, this time by examining a context where there *was* no shared text, initially, and, as a consequence, no common organizational commitment or identity to start from. The phenomenon we look at is the construction of a text, and the emergence of the kind of organization that it enabled, in and through the flow of the conversations of the people who produced it. We look at the progressive consolidation of text-fixed understandings leading to the birth of an organization, again through the eyes and ears of a recent doctoral graduate, this time Andy Blundell at the University of Calgary, whose dissertation inspired this chapter (Blundell 2007).

We use this research to explore in greater depth a phenomenon that we have repeatedly evoked in preceding chapters: the capacity of text, spoken or written, to both inform and reconstruct its own context. Explora, BTP, Deep Purple, Labopharma—all *began* with an inherited text and an already established organizational track record. What Blundell's research explored, in contrast, was a context where there was, initially, *no* shared text, certainly not one of the participants' own making. They entered the arena, each with their own well-practiced "stories-so-far," their own constructions of a context they had separately constructed: landowners versus petroleum resource development companies. The people with whom each side became engaged in conversation, as Blundell observed their interaction, were more likely to be construed as adversaries than allies or members of a larger community of interest. And yet they eventually did arrive at a tolerable compromise, a *modus vivendi* that they got to by building a text they could both live with: a framework of mutually acceptable principles and interpretations—including, literally, a *map*. They, in effect, redefined their context in a way that shoehorned their respective agendas into a livable accommodation. The key, we will argue, was in their eventually arriving at a common understanding, translated into a law that would be both constatively and performatively binding on both parties. Not merely finding a shared thirdness, in other words, but—and this is fundamental—materializing it in a text, to define a shared boundary (Star & Griesemer 1989).

"Communicating in the Field: The Role of Boundary Objects in a Collaborative Stakeholder Initiative"

Rewriting the Genre of the Western?

Alberta is a province of Canada. It is a big slice carved out of the North American continent, 20 percent larger than France, situated just to the east of the Rockies and to the north of Montana. It is part mountain, part foothills, part bald-headed prairies, and part northlands. In the beginning, it was settled by cattle ranchers, in the southwest foothill country, and by wheat farmers on the plains further east, leaving the far north no more than sparsely populated. The native population was (and is) still very much a presence, however drastically sidelined and decimated by European conquest and settlement. Like in most of the West, settlers started moving in one by one in the nineteenth century, part of the westward migration of that century in North America. Faced with the prospect of the loss of this rich territory to the United States, the Canadian government embarked on a proactive policy to stimulate the building of not one but two transcontinental railway systems. With the railways came a more systematic settlement and a diversification of the origins of settlers, again partly as a result of government policy, and partly just an effect of international movements of people in search of land and a better chance at life. Alberta and its neighbors to the east, Saskatchewan and Manitoba, developed a way of life and a culture in striking contrast to the ways of being of the eastern provinces, Ontario, Quebec, and the Maritimes. People in Quebec who live and work in French like to think of themselves as forming a "distinct society." The truth is that Canada is a nation composed entirely of distinct societies. Nowhere more so than in Alberta, which soon developed its own literature and distinctive modes of political and cultural life, even though it was still very much a rural society (the first author of this book, notably, wrote his master's thesis on its first important novelist, Frederick Philip Grove).

This all began to change in 1914, when oil—"black gold"—was discovered in Turner Valley, to the south of Calgary. The oil rush did not, however, turn into a stampede until 1947, when there was a significant oil strike a few miles south of Edmonton: the Leduc oil field. Once that happened, the dam was breached. By the end of that same year, 1947, 147 more wells had been drilled in the Leduc–Woodbend oilfield (if you travel there, you can still see the remaining pumps and pipelines dotting the fields of an otherwise bucolic countryside, even though they have all long since been capped).

That was just the start. Then the boom really took over. From what had once been mainly a rural and agricultural society, conservative in its modes of living, if radical in its politics, Alberta morphed bit by bit into a different kind of place, with fast-growing urban centers (Edmonton and Calgary) and provincial coffers stuffed with the royalties from oil exploration. What had once been a poorish area, economically, became gradually the richest province of all in Canada, per capita. In the 20 years from 1941 to 1961, the population grew from about 800,000 people to about 1.3 million. Compare that with the latest census figures (2006) of about 3.3 million people. The province has continued to expand ever since: probably, by the time these lines are being penned, more than 3.5 million inhabitants. Oil reigns supreme.

Except that . . . does it really? Not in everybody's mind, as we shall see.

Once upon a time, the classic Hollywood western built stories around the conflict between the vast ranching empires of Texas and the encroaching farmers who were moving in to settle on the fringes of the cowboys' extended domains. Many such movies showed an image of a farmhouse, burned to tinder by the ruthless barons of the cattle country. That never happened in Alberta, principally because the rolling hill country of the southwest where the cattle thrived was not tempting for wheat farmers, and the flat expanses of the prairies were not suitable for ranching. We had to wait for the petroleum boom to get the kind of friction that generates a conflict of interest similar to the olden times of the West, even though resolving issues with six-guns has long since gone out of style. It is one of those phenomena that only become evident over time. From those few wells in Leduc in 1947, the number kept expanding, to 48,000 in 1974; to 140,000 in 1989; to 250,000 in 2005. In 2005, the projects to drill for oil submitted to the agency of government set up to authorize them amounted to 55,000 for that one year alone. Most were given the green light to go ahead, without dissent. Alberta is a big province, but that is a lot of oil wells!

It all had a good deal to do with the way mineral rights work. The constitution of Canada began as the British North America Act. Its provisions set out how federal and provincial rights over a wide range of jurisdictions would be carved up. Among those provisions were those covering mineral rights. They were assigned to the provinces, with a certain number of exceptions, such as aboriginal treaty lands that remained under federal jurisdiction. At the beginning, both surface and mineral rights belonged to the purchaser of a certain property: all part of what went into the deed. But towards the end of the nineteenth century, a different policy began to come into effect, affecting Alberta a bit later, in the twentieth century. From that point on, the Crown (the government, that is) would grant a title of ownership only to the surface of the property, which was defined as "the depth of a plow."

The government thus reserved for itself inalienable rights to everything below the surface, including petroleum. Any subsequent exploitation was conditional on the obtaining of a lease. Mineral rights, including oil, could no longer be bought. They can only be leased by application to, and on conditions established by, an administrative body established for that purpose. In Alberta, the 1948 Right to Entry Act set up the Surface Rights Board, which was authorized to determine what compensation was owed to the ostensible land "owner" for the inconvenience of having a development team moving in on "his" or "her" land. But notice the consequence. As an individual landowner, you might end up one day with a drilling rig in your backyard, because some exploration company had purchased the rights to dig for oil on what you thought was "your" property. You can haggle over the right of access, but you can't block the project completely, because those rights belong to the government.

It is a recipe for confusion and conflict. As an owner, you may get compensation for the inconvenience but you cannot easily head off the incursion.

If that is not material for a rebirth of the western, it is hard to think of what might be. The days of the classic western, however, are over: a century and a half behind us. Instead, a rather more complicated dynamic ensues these days, just as intense in its way, but attenuated by the multiple folds of a society that has long since ceased to depend on the gun-slinging marshal to bring law and order. Nowadays, politics reigns. Law and government take over. The church-going gentry and the cautious merchants in Dodge City and Tombstone won out. The outlaws have gone elsewhere: mutated into the Hell's Angels, perhaps.

So, let's see how this new kind of rubbing up against one another in disputes over property works out in practice, as observed by a researcher.

Here is how the project came about. Andy Blundell was, by profession, active in the oil industry before he entered the doctoral program at the University of Calgary, having worked in companies involved in the petroleum business. The idea for the doctoral research he conducted goes back to 2003 when, on the suggestion of a vice president of the Canadian Association of Petroleum Producers, with responsibility for environmental and stakeholder issues, he attended a meeting centered on what was called "synergy." It sounds like a buzzword (and it often is, including in the oil industry), except that, in Alberta, it has a special connotation, as we shall shortly see. Before we develop that part of the story, however, we need to introduce the indispensable third party in any respectable western: the sheriff.

The Alberta Energy and Utilities Board (Recently Re-named the Energy Resources Conservation Board)

Back in 1914, when the Turner Valley strike began, there was no regulatory agency. Oil wells sprang up overnight, with little or no control. The waste in resources was appalling: precious gas was simply burned off, so that the developers could get at the oil below. It was chaos. Not for nothing did residents call Turner Valley "Hell's Half Acre." The night sky was often an inferno, fueled by burning gas. By 1938, more than 80 percent of the field's gas production had simply been wasted, burned off, the equivalent of 25,000 tons of coal per day! To cite one historian (Breen 1993: 4): "The essential requirement was that one had to obtain consent of the mineral rights holder, then one might dig, burrow, blast and drill at will."

The first stabs at regulation were simply shrugged off: on appeal, the courts refused to recognize them as legitimate. In 1938, however, using precedents established in Oklahoma, and this time with considerable industry support, the Alberta government moved to set up an agency with real regulatory powers, the Petroleum and Natural Gas Conservation Board (PNGCB), the progenitor of today's Board. Its role? "To ensure that the discovery, development and delivery of Alberta's energy resources and utility services take place in a manner that is fair, responsible and in the public interest." The Board was invested with sweeping authority. Its decisions could not be challenged in court, and any appeal was restricted to narrow grounds, such as a failure to notify a directly affected party. The Board thus had exceptional autonomy. While industry might sometimes chafe at its hegemony, it also depended on it for market access and needed financing. Order was re-established. The interests were roughly balanced.

This changed in the decade of the 1990s when, as Blundell observes, "low prices and ideology combined to reduce the size and influence of the Board." The effect was to dilute the confidence of the general public in the independence of the Board. In one observer's view, it was "no longer viewed as an ombudsman with a foot in both camps" but "very much seen in rural Alberta as being on the side of the producers." As oil development accelerated in the province, so did the tensions, culminating in occasional sabotage and the murder of an oil company executive on one farm in central Alberta. The industry itself was divided. Large, established companies prefer orderly development and are prepared to work to promote good relations with the public. They see it as in their own long-term interest to do so. So pressure was building at the century's turn for the powers of the Board to be extended, and for it to become more proactive in promoting better citizen–industry relations.

To respond, the Alberta government appointed a new chairman with a mandate to restore public confidence in the regulatory process, especially among rural residents. One of his early initiatives was to issue guidelines requiring companies who proposed energy developments to conduct "significant and meaningful public consultation with involved members of the public." The chairman's vision was that of a "fundamental cultural shift" in the organization and development of mutual accommodation between the public, energy companies, and the Board itself. One new step he took in this direction was to encourage the formation of local consultative organizations known as "synergy groups," which would stimulate the search for a livable compromise at the local level, through the participation of both companies and citizens of the area.

This was the context of Blundell's fieldwork, which concentrates on the years of 2005 and 2006. It centers on one case, located in what he calls the Heron Lake Watershed (the name is fictitious, as are the names of all the individuals and companies he refers to).

Heron Lake Watershed

Heron Lake is a little treasure of nature, once, not so long ago, an unspoiled paradise. It is a medium-size lake in a narrow valley, surrounded by wooded hills and situated in an extended watershed, no longer prairies but not yet quite the foothills of the Rockies. Lake fishing is good: whitefish, pike, perch, walleye. The trees come right down to the lake: aspen, poplar, spruce, birch, willow, and alder, all part of the great Boreal Forest covering that part of North America. There are wetlands, including what are called "water recharge areas" (namely lake sources). It is one of the few lakes in the province not fed by glacier run-off.

For a while, in the early part of the twentieth century, the main activity in the area was logging. Lumbering, however, ended in the 1940s, leaving a modest settlement behind, a few miles from the lake, subsisting on a marginal economy. Then, in the 1970s, a main road was constructed into the area, with the result that more farmers began to settle, although not in the immediate area of the lake. In the 1980s, activity in energy development was also intensifying, although, again, not yet in the immediate vicinity of the lake: more to the north. In addition, there was still a significant aboriginal presence in the area, mainly Cree, some of whom owned land that had been acquired following the same procedures as other non-native owners (not treaty land, in other words). But there was also another new community moving in: well-to-do, educated, middle-class professionals, many with continuing ties to (and good connections in) the big cities, Edmonton and Calgary. Some of them had once worked for oil companies. They were looking for a pleasant environment to build a home. Many of them came intending to establish permanent residences for their retirement.

These new elements marked the start of a considerable culture shift. As one person remarked,

> When I came here plying an occupation as an architect, designer and artist, it wasn't something that real men did. You had a 1964 Chevy pick-up, with a gun rack in the back, rolls of barbed wire rolling around in the box, drinking Black Label beer and your occupation was a broken-down back-hoe and a gravel truck. It was that kind of area. So I was really something of an anomaly at that point.

A New Sensitivity to the Environment

One consequence of the opening up of the area and the changing composition of the population around Heron Lake was an enhanced concern for the environment and its protection. In 1974, for example, the county council passed a bylaw designed to retain tree cover and inhibit development on the lake itself. Residents formed the Heron Lake Natural Area Preservation Society (HLNAPS) and mounted a successful protest—a petition signed by 200 landholders (out of 300 total)—in opposition to a county initiative to build a campsite in the immediate vicinity of the lake (in contravention of its own rule!). The preservation society then began to elaborate a petroleum development policy, to temper the trend to helter-skelter drilling involving an increasing number of companies with an eye on the potential riches lying under the ground around Heron Lake. It was a first step, but no more.

During the 1990s, Blundell was told, residents' relationships with the oil companies and the governmental agency, the Energy and Utilities Board (EUB), were mostly amicable enough, on the whole. The latter, for example, required companies intending to open operations in the area to contact the preservation society. As one of his informants told him,

> Most of them we didn't object to. Two or three of them, we asked them to modify the location so that they were away from the escarpment or a creek. And some of the companies found it worked quite well because rather than making a decision and then having to defend it and fight with the residents, they took these things into consideration ahead of time; they knew they wouldn't meet unreasonable demands.

Some companies could also understand the reason local residents were concerned. One large international, for example, had bought an old plant from the previous owners who had "rolled a truckload of amine into the lake and killed all the fish." That was not very good PR for the oil companies. The biggest problem, however, for some residents, was the rate of company turnover: "You're not dealing with the same company for very long. You establish some kind of a relationship but then there's a whole new bunch of people who don't know anything about it and in some cases couldn't care less." As this informant then went on to add: "It's a tiring and thankless job to try to deal with them as a resident."

The pace of development was also, if anything, accelerating. And people in the area felt the Board's philosophy had also changed:

> At one time we had a much better working relationship with the EUB's field office. We felt they were really acting in the public interest, in our interest, and it was a much more balanced approach. It's the pace of development and internal changes that have taken place within the EUB. Now it just seems it's pro-industry all the time.

It sometimes boils down to interpersonal relationships. Residents got to know the former EUB people because they had been serving there for a long time. They were familiar with the area, and its people, and respon-sive to them. After they left the field office to take positions elsewhere, in the second half of the 1990s, "it has never been the same since. That has been one of the components of the frustration felt by people in this area since."

There were some public regulatory hearings in the same time frame (most applications are dealt with administratively; only exceptions result in hearings, and even then citizen participation is limited). At one such hearing in 1994, however, the local preservation society expressed to the Board its desire to participate, with industry and other interested parties, in the development of a land management plan for the area, following the hearing. Nothing further ensued, but perhaps a seed had been planted, in the Board's as well as in the residents' minds. It took a while. The idea finally found a receptive climate to flourish only in 2005, a decade later.

A Chain of Events, 2003–2005

By 2005, there were 13 companies operating a total of 74 wells and 4 compressor stations in the watershed. And that is not counting another 21 companies who held licenses to 51 abandoned and 25 suspended wells in the area. What brought the growing tensions between residents and resource exploitation companies to a head, however, was a 2005 Board hearing.

Somewhat before, in 2003, one company, Cougar, drew up plans, in concert with another company, Bison Gas, to drill a well in what is known as a "Banff formation." By preference, Cougar set out to negotiate access rights with the owners, rather than resort to a lengthy application to the Alberta Surface Rights Board. The owners balked. The family "felt they were being overwhelmed by developments on their land" (there were already two operating wells on their property, with five more planned by Elk, as well as a sour gas well proposed by Antelope). Cougar then tried a different approach, what is called "directional drilling": that is, coming in on the target from a slant, rather then straight down. After further fruitless discussions with the landowners, Cougar finally filed what is called a "non-routine application" (i.e., one that requires a hearing since a landowner is "directly and adversely affected").

The hearing was held in December 2003. Those present included the family and its lawyer, other potentially affected residents, representatives of Cougar, and two Board staff. The company made 22 broad commit-ments to area residents, including specific ones to the family. Among other things, they promised to meet with the other companies, Antelope and Elk, to develop a coordinated plan for surface facilities in the section and its surrounding area. A month later, they informed the family they were making progress in their talks with Elk and Antelope.

Then, in February 2004, Cougar opened negotiations for a surface lease in the adjoining section of land, 1–27, to the northwest. In April, they wrote area residents to inform them they were withdrawing their application for the initial location. In August, Cougar received authorization from the Board for the new location, again in the face of residents' objections. Residents filed a copy of the survey sketch for the new site that indicated it was a wetland (covered by poplar and swamp spruce) and thus, in principle, exempt from drilling. Nevertheless, the application was approved by the Board. The well was drilled and completed by November of 2004.

Residents, in the meantime, filed a request to the Board to review their decision, in accordance with provisions of the Energy Resources Conservation Act. The Board, in its later report, noted local environmental concerns, voiced, among other resident submissions, by an expert who emphasized the interrelationship between land-use planning and water management, with a stress on "maintaining native tree cover and the impacts that tree removal would have on the watershed." Cougar, the residents argued, had "failed to demonstrate plans for protective measures in regard to the watershed, especially in light of their view of the impact that the oil and gas industry has had on the community" (from an official EUB document dated December 2005).

The review panel, in the face of these arguments, made a commitment to take up the matter with the full Board, and to recommend:

> that a meeting be set up with representatives from the oil and gas industry, the Heron Lake Natural Area Preservation Society, the County, the Regional Planning Agency, the newly established synergy group in the area, and interested members of the general public to discuss the possibility of setting up a pilot project to develop an area development plan for the Heron Lake Water Management Area.

Even though it had confirmed its earlier decision, the Board recognized,

> that the concerns of the area residents are legitimate and is very aware that future energy projects could impact the Heron Lake Water Management Area, particularly if development is not planned and managed properly as the density of development continues to increase.

The residents had found their story. As against the petroleum companies' account of the immense prosperity that oil exploration would bring to all Albertans, the residents had become the champions of the land itself, by insisting on its integrity as the ultimate resource for a sane Alberta future. A decision to make a distinction between surface and underground rights to property, taken a century and a half earlier, had now become the basis of two narratives: the thirdness of the environment providing the rationale for the residents, that which gave meaning to their position, versus the thirdness of resources and the wealth they bring, for the developers. Both accounts had apparent validity, and yet they contradicted each other, in practice.

Organizations as the Crosslinking of (Contradictory) Narratives

The irony is that it is precisely in that juxtaposition of contradictory accounts that the seeds of an eventual organization were planted. In fact, looking back over our previous chapters (Vasquez, Fauré, Güney, Virgili), it is hard to escape the conclusion that *all* the organizations we have looked at so far were sites of contradictory accounts. The function of organization was not to resolve them, but to reconcile them: to find a *modus vivendi*, or reciprocity, to use Bateson's term. Blundell's chronology of the events he witnessed, for example, is grouped in columns: the first records the activities of the companies, the second those of the residents' synergy group, the third the eventual reconciliation of the two in the form of an area development plan. Here, we have an initial firstness: oil exploration. Secondness (and the bone of contention): the practices of the exploration companies and their impact on landowners (who perceived the drillers as invaders). The initial thirdness justifying resource development thus highlighted a split between two contradictory narratives, each serving to explain what was going on, who was who, and, depending on the narrative, who was protagonist and who antagonist. *If* an accommodation could be found, it would have to lead to a common narrative.

Narratives are invested with perceptions of moral rectitude. This is what gives them their tone of legitimacy. But could the two competing narratives eventually be threaded into a single strand? If so, how? If not logically, pragmatically perhaps? Could someone find an integrative narrative? Could it be negotiated?

Heron Lake Watershed Synergy Group

There is more than one account of how the Heron Lake Watershed Synergy Group (HLWSG) got off the ground. One resident explained it to Blundell this way:

> Things got progressively worse because we felt, to get anybody to even pay attention to what the problems are out here, we had to object to everything. This is the approach we took. We decided as

a group of people here that we are going to oppose every single application. That's when our relationship started to build with the Board ... As the relationship with the oil companies went down, the Board started to get more involved. And that's when they decided they'd had enough. Everybody decided they'd had enough. So that's when the Synergy Group was started.

A different informant, Graham (a businessman who is active in ecologically oriented groups and one of those who would be the most active negotiators in the ensuing negotiations), saw it somewhat differently:

Well, it came about because I coordinated a meeting with some high level people at the Board, people from their law branch, Councillors, the MLA [Member of the Legislative Assembly or provincial parliament], to look at the oil and gas development in the area and try to bring some coordination to develop more thoughtful and careful planning ... This was October last year [2004] and for two days I had them out here. And on the second day the Board said I suggest you have Synergy, this is what Synergy is for. And I said I don't know, I don't see it happening. What I see here goes beyond Synergy, this is talking about reevaluating how we look at development, how we make room for people and communities.

It is easy to understand his reservation. "Synergy" sounds goody-goody: a talkfest that never quite gets around to doing anything concrete, no more than a way of "letting off steam." Graham wanted something more solid than that.

The First Meeting in 2005

The first meeting of the synergy group was held in February 2005, at a local inn. Ted, the local EUB representative, took the initiative for calling and organizing the actual event. He explained to the meeting what a synergy group meant, and how it should unfold: the rules of the game. He had engaged Phil, a practiced facilitator, for the occasion, who would remain for the meeting, three from the EUB, twenty-one from industry, representing eight companies in all (all on Ted's invitation), but only seven residents. Blundell was not there for that first meeting, but the moderator, Phil, later told him:

My recollection of those very first meetings was, the way I characterized it at the time, was the atmosphere was kind of bleak. People weren't very positive and there were far more questions than people could really answer. I went back to Calgary with my staff and said, "We've got to try and do something here."

Even that initial meeting, however, generated a text: a "mission and vision statement and goal." The purpose of the group would be,

> to provide an effective and proactive forum to allow Community, Industry and Government to communicate and share information respectfully and cooperatively, and to aid in an integrated approach to developing and planning oil and gas activity within the Heron Lake Watershed.

It would further "develop a forum to standardize acceptable practice which takes into account the needs of the Heron Lake watershed."

In addition, the facilitator, Phil, took it upon himself to compile a list of issues that had cropped up during the discussion, which he then handed out at the meeting in May. The list included topics such as how to address issues of sensitive or critical areas, how to deal with oil leaks, absentee ownership, impact assessment, environmental safety.

The process had kicked off. A sequence of meetings ensued that first spring, from February to June. After the first two, the attendance fell off, both among residents (only three turned up in June, for example) and oil companies (from more than 20 in February and March to fewer than 10 afterwards). In February, four Cree owners attended but, when they learned that the area would be restricted to Heron Lake Watershed and thus excluded them (their properties were in the vicinity of nearby Eagle Lake), they did not return.

What seemed to drive the process, initially, was local concern over ongoing negotiations with companies such as Cougar, but the burden of continuity of the exercise fell on the shoulders of a few dedicated individuals from the community, a handful of oil company representatives, and of course the EUB employees themselves. The companies (those most active, in any case), they insisted, were "looking for greater understanding and a new way of doing things." Len, a part-time Edmonton professional but active in local community affairs (a consistent spokesperson for the residents throughout the process), "wanted to establish a maximum threshold for activity that won't impact lifestyles and property values." The moderator, Phil, discouraged any move to enter the domain of what the legal rights and responsibilities were (that is the privileged terrain of the Board, he pointed out).

The group was still establishing its parameters: would media be allowed to attend, for example? (No, that would inhibit free and frank discussion, but they would issue a press release.) What about other government departments (energy, environment, local chamber of commerce, for example)? Shouldn't they be involved? Later, perhaps. Where should the geographical boundaries be set: only Heron Lake Watershed or more inclusive? Only Heron Lake. Industry participants chimed in to say they wanted a better fix on resident concerns so they could adapt their modes of operating to head off endless conflict with local property owners. They said they actually welcomed a development understanding. It would make planning their operations easier.

Once again, the group restated its initial "vision statement." Much the same for the meetings that followed. In April, for example, participants set about clarifying their goals even further: among other objectives, develop a collective understanding of the area ecology; standardize acceptable practice; provide for public participation and learning. It was noted that there were 13 companies active in the Watershed, operating 36 oil wells and 24 gas wells. Including other companies holding licenses but currently inactive, altogether there were 34 companies that had been or were active in the area, totaling 74 active wells and 4 compressor stations.

A Third "Party" Is Heard from: The Environment

At the meeting in May, the Regional Planning Agency made a presentation, reporting on results from a survey of local landowners, leading to a discussion of priorities such as lake water quality, maintenance of the habitat, restrictions on property development and density of habitation. Len, for example, made this comment:

> If you look at the maps, and we've actually undertaken this exercise, in the last 10 years the single biggest impact in terms of tree cover disappearing has been the oil and gas industry. There's been virtually no other clearing and that's why residents are here, because the oil and gas industry is not regulated. That's one of the reasons this group has been formed.

George, another local resident who would be among the most active participants throughout, remarked that residents felt they had been trampled on. Both the Board and the Alberta ministry of the environment simply ignored residents' concerns: they didn't even bother to reply to letters.

Once again, Phil used his role as facilitator to summarize discussions and identify issues and objectives. The meeting concluded by outlining future group activity, including, for example, moving toward development of a pilot project for how residents and companies could work together. A possible objective to aim for: shouldn't there be areas protected from drilling, such as the wetland sources of the lake (called "recharge areas")?

That of course would involve government intervention. As George remarked, "industry's only going to do what it's allowed to do."

People from industry responded by again expressing their continuing desire for a clarification of acceptable practice, but they equally made clear they *were* going to continue to drill wells, within the parameters set by the government. With respect to the idea of designated no-go areas, one of the community organizers working with a company replied that the companies,

> are not going to be happy but they'd live with it. It all comes down to you, as a group, you are going to have to lobby your government representatives. I don't think you're ever going to convince all industry.

The Environment Again, but this Time with a Different Voice

At the June meeting (only three residents in attendance), Alberta Environment made a presentation. They claimed that water quality in the lake, scientifically assessed, had not significantly deteriorated in the 20 years from 1983 to 2003. Peter, a scientist representing the department, conceded they could not predict at what point resource development centered on petroleum might start to impact water quality. A resident of 50 years standing in the area countered by observing that, while there used to be sitting water on his property (ponds and other wetlands), that was no longer the case in the aftermath of oil and gas development. The conclusion was that environmental restrictions on development at the level of government were unclear and not always respected, and the impact of further oil and gas operations on the ecology of the area was not well understood. With so few residents in attendance, however, the meeting ended inconclusively.

Summarizing the Activities of Spring 2005

What happened in those first encounters? Looked at collectively, it seems that three things occurred. First, the group spent some considerable time presenting itself to others not physically present in the meetings. For example, there were the media: the group would issue a press release directed to them. Then there were the agencies of government: the ministry of the environment, for example, as well as the EUB, their sponsor. They should be kept abreast of progress. The group was also obliged to present itself more effectively to a skeptical community (judging by the attendance in June). They had already advertised their meetings, but now they were also counting on the conversations of the faithful attendees, such as George, to talk it up with neighbors. For his part, he remarked,

There's only a few of us here tonight but we have our finger on the pulse and we know what the issues are ... We're going to make a concerted effort when this thing kicks back in the fall to make sure there's a lot more people here.

And, of course, the oil company representatives presumably reported back to their principals.

If, as Goffman remarked, it is in the presentation of oneself to others that one establishes an identity, then HLWSG had taken the initial step to claiming a distinct corporate personality.

Second, the group began to play the role of a mini-parliament: a place to debate issues within the orderly framework of a meeting chaired by an impartial facilitator, backed by the EUB, and with implicit rules of procedure: what Halliday calls a context, an accumulation of common interaction, talk, and minutes of meetings. Issues of current salience could be aired, and the contrasting perspectives of local landowners and developers voiced. We have seen one instance: Cougar's plan to do directional drilling from a site judged by local residents to be environmentally sensitive, and Antelope's projected tapping into the same site with its own operations. Both projects were vehemently opposed by local residents. But other, more mundane irritations could be brought front stage. At the May meeting, for example, this exchange occurred:

Company (David):   [We need] to let the residents know—and we'll do that by telephone as well—that we'll be taking our battery down on the 24th of May for turnaround for 4 days. We'll put signs up for additional activities on the road and when we take it down there'll be some flaring.

      ...

Resident (Brent):   You're going to be flaring?
David: Just depressuring the facility. It's a common practice.
Brent: How much?
David: Oh, probably about 25 e^3m^3 of gas.
Brent: That's sour gas?
David: Yeah, I guess it is. Taking it down will be about half an hour's process. So it's not like it's going to be continuous flaring. If you're not on the highway watching you probably wouldn't realize it's happening. What I'll do, being that Len and I have worked in the past together, I'll probably discuss with you.
Len: Yes, sure. David, just as an aside, we can hear the noise all the time now. I'll discuss it with you later.

Unless you are in the know about how petroleum mining works, you might not catch the significance of that clarification: "That's sour gas?"

"Yeah, I guess it is." Sour gas is not some innocent by-product of exploration: it contains a highly poisonous chemical, hydrogen sulphide, H_2S. It has a bad reputation in the West, where at one time it was burned off indiscriminately, in huge quantities, literally creating pollution. There had also been accidents. In 1982, for example, one well blew out, spewing out as much as 100 million cubic feet of gas per day containing 25 percent of H_2S. It was brought under control only two months or so later, and, in addition to a loss of life (two technicians killed), the sour gas was so bad that it could be smelled in Winnipeg, about 1,000 kilometers to the east. Companies are more careful now, as the sequence just cited illustrates, but it remains a sensitive topic. HLWSG meetings provided a venue where concerns such as this could be voiced and explanations offered.

Third, as we have already emphasized, HLWSG was becoming a reality to those who participated in it as a configuration of space–time: meeting at a local inn, once a month, three to four hours long, established room architecture (EUB at the head of the table, and mostly residents on one side, oil people on the other), and rules of interaction. It was developing its own distinct meaning for those who were caught up in it—at least for those who faithfully attended (Arthur and Paul from industry, for example, and Graham, Len, and George from the local community).

The Constructive Role of Sustained Interaction

Translated into Halliday's theoretical framework, this evolution takes on special significance. There is first the experiential dimension. Although all those who attended were reacting to the same events, they experienced them in profoundly different ways. From the owners' perspective, the drilling of a new well could be very disturbing, as for the owner cited earlier, whose family faced the prospect of *nine* active projects on their property alone. The quality of people's emotional response is conveyed by the way they translated it into their talk (what Halliday called the "logical" dimension of ideation, i.e., expressing what one sees and feels in language): George, for example, when he expostulated, "We lose every time. Industry wins; we lose. The community loses. The watershed loses." The very different experiential basis of other categories of participant is equally suggested by their choice of language. David, for example, who explains "We're just depressuring the facility . . . Probably about 25 e^3m^3 of gas." His experience is that of a professional, an engineer. The oil and gas companies' community specialists used a neutral language, but it was still that of a detached professional, phrased diplomatically; for instance, Sarah (in the May meeting): "One of the things you could do is lobby some of those interested parties in this area for some cash to develop some sort of study that you're prepared to live with."

But then she coolly went on, warning them that if they did, "It's a catch-22. If it comes out to being not what you want to hear you're still going to have to say, well we agreed." She speaks as someone who has seen several Heron Lake equivalents in her time with her firm. The representative from Environment, for his part, talked about "impact," "water quality," "vegetation disturbance," "risk of surface runoff": again very professional, with no personal stake in the process and no sign of emotion.

On the other hand, the mere fact of participating in a synergy group (more or less obligatory for the oil companies, at least the larger ones) meant that, to recall Halliday's second dimension of language, people were actually sitting down to talk to each other, for hours at a time. At the June meeting, for example, Antelope reiterated its openness to discussing their projected 1–27 well with residents. George replied that the residents wanted to wait for the outcome of the EUB review of Cougar's well, which the local owners had insisted on, before discussing further development at the site. The excerpt that ensued illustrates the contrasting voices residents sometimes heard when they talked to developers: Arthur is Antelope's community relations specialist, James its site foreman and engineer.

Arthur: We met with George but we still haven't had time to meet with others.

Phil: So you guys will have a lot to talk about when you meet in September.

George: No, hopefully not (*laughter*). As I indicated to Arthur, we would rather wait 'til the other issues with 1–27 are dealt with. We don't know when that's going to happen. The Board have contacted us for a pre-hearing meeting but we haven't heard back when that's going to be.

The Board gave their update, and then Antelope's foreman, James, spoke:

James: We're still planning to drill from the 1–27 location, October/November is the kind of timeframe.

George: You're planning to go ahead and drill that well before the issue is even resolved with Cougar?

James: Well, when's that going to be resolved?

George: I've no idea.

James: The Board hasn't given you any information?

George: No.

James: We'll I guess we're hoping things will be resolved by then.

Arthur intervenes:

Arthur: But that doesn't mean we don't want to sit down and work
            things out with you.
George: Well, as far as we're concerned it's all up in the air, we're
            waiting to hear back from the Board.

But the subtlest of Halliday's dimensions is that which evokes the power of text to constitute its own context. The accumulation of interactive exchanges, using both talk and documents, that had occurred over the February to June sequence had begun to constitute a singular kind of environment, with its own local rules and procedures, its own special habits of sensemaking, and a history, recorded in minutes and written reports. From now on, when they came back to meet in the fall, they would do so in a context they had interactively constructed for themselves. It would have its own integrity.

Or, at least, a first step had been taken in that direction.

The Fall Meetings, 2005

HLWSG reassembled in late September (eight residents present), after a summer break of 16 weeks. The principal point of order was another presentation from a specialist in the environment department, who explained the latter's concern over the progressive disappearance of wetlands in Alberta (64 percent lost or impaired in their estimate). The department was hoping to have a policy adopted in the next parliament establishing the maintenance of wetlands as a priority.

His presentation opened the door for some pointed discussion of the oil industry. Graham (the businessman with contacts in Edmonton) noted that the EUB application process currently relied only on the *developers'* estimates of risks to the environment. In its application, for example, Graham alleged that, "Cougar's choice of language about their drill site [this is the one already referred to above] did not trigger the Board's attention" (from Andy Blundell's notes). Len argued for the need for a cumulative impact assessment, since currently each developer addresses only the immediate impact of its *own* project.

Industry representatives, Blundell reports, made "no significant contribution to this discussion." Again on Phil's initiative, the meeting turned to reflect once more on its own mission and vision, this time in the context of, among other things, the rights of First Nations (there was a Cree owner in attendance).

Again as well, there seems not yet to have been any real clarification as to where the group was headed, other than providing a forum for discussion (Graham's initial skepticism might seem at this point to have been prescient). Especially since, while celebrating the benefits of dialogue in synergy groups, as a way to sensitize their own principals, the representative from Bison went on to announce an ambitious new venture, spread over "nine townships involving compressor stations, pipeline tie-ins, 38 multiwell pads with 14 deeper locations off the multiwell pad sites" (from Blundell's notes). Bison assured those present there would be a series of open houses in November "to discuss resident issues and concerns." About one-third of this development project would affect the Heron Lake Watershed district. Blundell reports that, "at the end of his ten minute speech, the Bison spokesperson asked 'Is this what this group wants to hear?', to which one resident replied, 'What *I'm* hearing is a declaration of war. That's what it sounds like.'"

November 2005

There was no meeting in October. The group reassembled in November. Over the first six sessions resident attendance had averaged seven, while industry participation was fourteen, double that of the locals. From November 2005 to May 2006, however, resident attendance shot up to an average of 15 per meeting, while industry participation dropped to an average of nine per occasion. At the November meeting, also, representatives from the county where Heron Lake is located attended. Arthur, one of the oil company representatives, from Antelope (he faithfully turned up for every meeting of HLWSG, except one in September of 2006), contributed topographical maps of the district. This was a tool used by the developers in designing their operations, offering a perspective residents were less familiar with: an instrumentality whose value would later become evident in how it enabled planning.

Once again, the facilitator, Phil, returned to the discussion of what it was that people expected to come out of the synergy group's meetings. The oil company representatives reiterated their desire for a more orderly development program. The residents complained that their worst headache was small, fly-by-night companies and the endless turnover of leases on their land to a new developer. Ted, from the EUB, confirmed that, whereas the Board had to deal with only 75 companies active in Alberta in the 1980s, the figure now stood at 1,600.

One company representative remarked that his principals had concluded that, "nothing short of the complete removal of the oil and gas industry from the watershed would be acceptable to area residents." But even this skeptic agreed his firm would live with guidelines the group arrived at. Phil, the moderator, kept pushing for more concrete discussion of best management practices. They needed to be clearer about what they envisaged as an acceptable process. Why not, for example, take Bison at their word? Set out the rules of the game. The project Bison had presented at the previous meeting could be a vehicle for clarifying things such as the development process, what the regulatory issues are, how to respond to the energy department's concern for water quality. How could they be more involved "up front"? George responded positively, but he was still preoccupied with the Antelope project, as well as Bison's. Bison's representative, Bob, also a regular attendant, assured the group his company was prepared to respond to concerns to identify sensitive areas in the watershed.

The group, quite evidently, was still looking for its "synergy."

December 2005: Turning the Corner

Everything was the same in the next meeting in December and in the meetings that followed in 2006, and yet everything changed from then on. For one thing, the increased participation of local residents altered the atmosphere from involving only a few, exceptionally committed individuals from the community meeting the professional community relations people from the principal oil companies, to the more complex dynamics of an open forum with many people participating. On the other hand, the many discussions that had preceded, involving people such as Arthur, Bob, and Paul from industry, and Graham, Len, and George from the community, meant that they, at least, had established the kind of working rapport that is characteristic of an ongoing conversation. They could shift gears from confrontation to teasing, and back, because each had become familiar with the others' moves. Blundell paid attention throughout his observations to a variable he calls "laughter." In September, for example, he noted no instances of laughter. His notes on the December meeting, however, report this:

> The introductions to the meeting caused lots of laughter. One resident introduced himself as so-and-so's neighbour and successive residents introduced themselves as neighbours, to much laughter. For the first time that I noticed, an industry representative deliberately introduced humour when talking about the possibility of hiring a minute taker and joking about the current minute-taker's salary. Later on, Harry produced laughter when he said, "I'm going to be positive." In the second part of the meeting the facilitator asked, "is that a hand waving?" and was told, "No, I'm just scratching."

That meeting in December, with 40 people in attendance (25 area residents), still provided a forum for the airing of industry–resident tensions: a pipeline break on Elk's land, and the lake pollution it risked. George felt he had been, perhaps deliberately, given less than fully truthful information from company representatives, who, he complained seemed unable to speak in a single voice, since the engineer had one story, the company representative another.

But the December meeting also included a more positive discussion of how to resolve issues in a more comprehensive framework of mutual understanding about limits. This was a step toward an eventual reconciliation of competing interests—a contribution that Blundell saw as a crucial turning point in the reconciliation process.

Len's Report

One of the most active spokespersons for the community, Len, with support from the industry, had attended what was known as a "One Circle Conference": a grouping of people who are active in promoting concern for the environment. His report to the meeting was inspirational in tone.

> Where this all starts from is finding common ground, and where we find common ground, whether you are an oil and gas operator, or whether you are a logger or whether you are a farmer or . . . whether you're a professional person and you live in an area, I think we can all agree on what we want our lake to look like in 25 years from now, one generation away. And I think that is the place we all start. I think we can all agree that we want clean air, clean water, a safe and quiet community and that's where we start to build our common vision. And that was the fascinating part about the conference, every one of these models for sustainable community-based planning, all have a vision of what they wanted their community to look like 25 years down the road.
>
> The industrial operators can agree on that, the residents can agree on that, and that's what the conference was about, what we called the One Circle. That we are all connected to a bigger circle of life that sustains us, that's the Earth. When we are planning, if it's going to be sustainable, it has this one circle, just like we are tonight, where we're all part of the community. And community means everybody. I think sometimes we as residents see ourselves as the community. But because we have various interests here overlapping and sometimes competing, to be a community we have to realize that oil and gas operators are also part of our community. And if we're going to have sustainable long-term planning, they have to be part of that circle.
> [. . .]
> What we have at Heron Lake, if we are going to maintain the ecological integrity, if it is going to be a safe community, if the water's going to be safe and abundant, if our forest is going to be intact and if we're going to extract oil and gas, which we are here. It's not a case of whether we are, it's a case of how. That's really

the only question that's out there. We're going to need to accommodate residential, agricultural, recreational, and industrial interests, and they all have to be brought into the circle.

[. . .]

What has been happening here in the past, we have faced each other across the table but we've never talked about being inclusive, about being part of that bigger circle. The base of that is trust and we heard a lot about that and that's the first bridge that needs to be built. The fact of the matter is that at a lot of levels the residents don't trust the oil and gas industry and the oil and gas industry doesn't trust the residents. And that is what we need to change. How we change that I certainly don't have the answer. I'm just the messenger here. There are a lot of people out there that are capable of assisting us in this process. Who do we need at the table? We need the residents, we need our county, we need representatives from the provincial government, we need our Regional Planning people, we need the oil and gas operators and we need the regulator at the table. And we also need a liaison with scientists, researchers, and consultants. But we can't do sustainable planning if we don't have the science and we don't have the knowledge. And that's where it has to start. We have a common goal and the information has to be open and transparent and available to all of us.

Len received a receptive hearing from both parties, residents and company spokespersons. It is difficult to judge the impact of his testimony, but he had earned the respect of all parties through his consistent participation in the process. For the first time, those present were confronted with an evocation of thirdness—sustainability—reflecting neither the special interests of the oil companies, nor those of the property owners, but of the larger community to which both belonged: sustainability as the *sine qua non* of a healthy and prosperous society.

In any case, something else of crucial significance had just happened.

The EUB is Heard From

A second transformation occurred in the December meeting, perhaps even more significant. It involved an actor who was not even physically present that night at the Heron Lake meeting, the EUB. The Board was not there at the meeting but in Edmonton, and yet it had nevertheless been, throughout the entire synergy process, an "absent presence" at all of the local meetings, frequently evoked by the parties there: a phenomenon we have seen illustrated in previous chapters—a different kind of thirdness, a common point of reference, an authority.

Residents, we recall, had convinced the EUB to review their earlier approval of Cougar's plan to drill in 1–27, a borderline case because the area could be described as wetlands. The Board's decision, subsequent to the review, came down at about 4 o'clock in the afternoon on the same day HRWSG met in December. It reconfirmed its earlier approval of Cougar's application, but recognized the validity of the community objections. It therefore recommended setting up a pilot project to develop an area development plan for the next year, "and to see how the joint use of facility sites, existing rights-of-way, and access roads could be incorporated into such a plan."

After the coffee break, the meeting approved setting up a small committee of two residents, two industry representatives, and Board staff. We have already met the members of the committee: Arthur from Antelope, Bob from Bison, and Len and Graham from the community. Simon, the Board agent, would manage the process.

It took time for this project to get off the ground (waiting for the Board to draft terms of reference, for example, and inviting input from companies and the people in the community), but eventually it did. Beginning in March, it was involved in discussion of the planning process. By April, the terms of reference had been finalized and agreed to by the Board. By May, Graham was able to report on the formation of project teams, as well as an agreement with Ducks Unlimited to do a wetlands inventory. Maps were coming to the fore: a base area map, a land use map, including development locations, hydrology, soils, and vegetation. Mailings to citizens were being prepared. They were already envisaging a delivery date for a final report: the November meeting. Industry representatives were contributing without apparent reservation: Bison, for example, had made available its unique source of data describing the area. A consultation process involving residents was being planned.

The Mood Had Changed

At the June meeting, the project team reported it had met in late May and taken a two-day tour of the area, including the swamps, to get a real feel for the character of the lake and its surroundings. They were trying to see the lake ecology through the eyes of those most intimately close to it because this was where they lived. Bob (from Bison) remarked:

> We felt like the African Queen going up the inlet at the north end of the lake, dodging tree stumps and that kind of thing. It was very worthwhile and I think there's a lesson in there about understanding and getting a sense of the watershed.

Bob was manager of community affairs for his company, and had actually grown up on a farm south of Heron Lake. That led him to assume that, like the farmers he knew, owners would be swayed by economic considerations (payment for right of way to sites). He perhaps underestimated the depth of feeling people in Heron Lake had developed for their natural environment. It is this theme that Graham picked up:

> Well, a lot of the people who don't live here don't understand the emotional attachment we have here. Taking them out there and showing them the fern glens, bald eagles' nests, the pelicans and all that. I mean, who doesn't like to be on a lake? You're looking at mergansers and grebes and loons and that stuff. And you're telling them stories about the moose, and the cougars and the bears, and the wolves and all that kind of stuff we see out there. That surprised them, I think. Everybody has a bit of outdoorsman in them you know. If they didn't make the emotional connection, they maybe understand ours a little more.

Simon from the Board perhaps best summarized the sense of camaraderie the project has generated by making a joke:

> I felt at one point that Graham was too gleeful as he looked back from the bow and said "I wonder what many landowners would give the EUB and an industry guy in a boat in the middle of Heron lake" and I wondered if the life jacket I'd been given was made of something that floated or if was filled with lead shot.

Everyone in the room laughed.

Fruition

The project team presented its final recommendations to the October 2006 meeting, attended by 53 or more people, a record turnout (with so many people straggling in late, Andy had difficulty keeping count). The report established three tiers: tier 1 would be a no-go area: a "sensitive area where new disturbance should be avoided," including wetlands, lake edges, public lands, and natural areas. Non-routine EUB applications for operations in a tier 1 area would be mandatory. Developers of new sites would be expected to assess and implement means to minimize disturbance to tier 2 sites, "such as low impact seismic, reduced facility site and right of way clearing and early restoration of natural cover following disturbances." For tier 3 sites, the usual rules currently in application would still be valid. The formation of a Heron Lake Operators Group was recommended to share information, as well as to work together to minimize proliferation of facilities and surface disturbances in the area, and to better manage heavy traffic. A protocol based on mapped information pulled together by the project team, including map designation of the three tier areas, should be made available to companies planning Heron Lake developments. Companies would be expected to make site visits to verify suitability of potential oil and gas well locations before finalization of any plans. It was further advised that the HLWSG finalize the recommendations respecting acceptable practices as part of a continuing normal planning cycle, as well as develop a communications strategy, and continue the dialogue now established with industry representatives. The project should be re-evaluated in two to three years.

There were criticisms from both residents and company people, and lots of discussion. The members of the group were themselves conscious of the constraints imposed by the laws and practices of the province imposed on them. But the plan had been written, and, with the authority of the Board behind it, it became a reality.

Blundell's informal contacts with the Heron Lake people continued, but the data collection phase as such ended with the October meeting.

Conclusion

Earlier, we evoked two images of organization that have frequently figured in the literature, organization as *machine* and organization as *game*. The research we have been considering in this chapter might seem to confirm, with reservations, the validity of both metaphors. A crew engaged in drilling for oil *uses* highly sophisticated machines. But it is not much of a stretch to think of them as themselves *exemplifying* the property of machine-ness. Given the constantly present danger involved in pumping high-energy and potentially explosive gas and oil, there is no room for carelessness. Their performance must be flawless. They thus exemplify what Weick and Sutcliffe (2001) called a *high reliability organization*, which is to say one where not merely the machines but also the human components are specialized, the coupling is tight, and the operation must be conducted flawlessly. They become, in their reliability, like a machine: by definition, an apparatus "having several parts each with definite function" (Concise Oxford English Dictionary).

The limitation of the machine metaphor is scale: it applies most persuasively in contexts of what Weick (1985) called "tight coupling," like an oil well drill crew. Most of what Blundell witnessed during the meetings he attended, involving players as diverse as landowners, for-profit companies, and government bureaucracy, looked anything *but* machine-like. The Heron Lake synergy group's interaction, for example, was clearly game-like. There were two teams of players, more or less organized: the residents and the oil people, each side competing for rights to the same property. There was also a third party, the EUB, whose role seemed to alternate between that of referee (no discussion of regulatory issues was permitted, it made clear: that is the prerogative of the Board) and coach (here is how you organize a synergy group).

The organization that evolved out of this "game," however, eventually transcended its initial game-like dynamic by finding a synthesis that was concretized in a plan. HLWSG, as an organization, started out as a game whose members competed by authoring accounts while countering those of the opposition, wherever they could, by offering a more convincing version. But the organization that emerged to produce the actual plan went beyond the accounting game. By affirming its identity through the authoring of a text that embodied a by-now recognized authority, the authors started out as players, but then rose above the game to collectively generate an organization, however limited its reach.

The plan *literally* "authorized" a new organization, HLWSG: made *it* an actor.

The committee, with its mixed membership, had manifested teamwork. Andy was not privy to its internal discussions, but it is safe to speculate that there would have been differences of view, and arguments, but the group still succeeded in working as a unit. They carved up the work and directed themselves to a common goal.

In the background, both enabling and stimulating this collaboration, was the authority of a government whose "inalienable" property rights were the prize that was at stake. The EUB furnished the crucial instance that sanctioned the plan they eventually produced, and thus infused it with its own authority. The cloak of legitimacy conferred by the EUB made the difference for HLWSG. It supplied the indispensable *thirdness* of the exercise, a thirdness that allowed the local organization known as HLWSG to itself emerge as a social entity: constituted now as an organization, a continuing reality, and not merely an incidental by-product of a sporadic set of meetings.

Thirdness Reconsidered

"Thirdness?" It strikes one on first acquaintance as an odd idea (which may be why Peirce's insight has received over the years at best a lukewarm reception). But when we examine the idea with greater care, the strangeness begins to dissipate. Blundell's research illustrates why.

Thirdness, as Peirce explained it, is that which gives meaning to an individual practice or project: its script or program. Its essence is not material, but formal: that which allows human actors to perceive the pattern in what they are doing, and thus be able not merely to understand it, but to innovate as well. The examples we gave in earlier chapters, gardening or scientific experimentation, for instance, display an ordered sequence of actions, a recognizable configuration of activities that, in their patterning, constitute it *as* a practice. An oil crew, in the field, exhibits the kinds of synchronized and disciplined performance characteristic of disciplined team activities, where we understand that a thirdness (Peirce's "law" meant essentially this) is shared by all.

Where problems arise is when the actors' attention is directed to the same object *without* shared thirdness: a crossing of practices that are incompatible with each other. Then there is a potential for schismogenesis: either dominance on the part of one at the expense of the other (complementary schismogenesis), or sequences of conflict (symmetric schismogenesis). In the high-reliability environment of disciplined team work (Weick & Sutcliffe 2001) the object is shared, even though the roles deviate from symmetry because there is a complementary distribution of powers and responsibilities. Thirdness, in other words, does not merely cover the sequential performance of a task: it defines equally a social configuration of roles and a complementary distribution of authority.

At Heron Lake there was, initially, little if any shared thirdness. Both parties laid claim to the same object, access to and use of property. The situation thus created has interesting parallels with the inter-tribal rivalries that led Bateson to formulate his theory of schismogenesis in the first place: competing tribal claims to the same territory on a South Pacific island. Resolution of this kind of stand-off can only be accomplished by the construction of a common thirdness, a recognition of a larger domain of practice where all the parties find their place and where their respective goals are seen to be compatible with an over-arching common framework.

In the tightly coupled practice of a small workgroup, especially where the challenge is technically complex, thirdness, once established, hardly needs to be explicitly stated, since the script is already understood by everyone, as are their respective roles in it (Hutchins 1995). The back-and-forth of grounded conversation is enough, as both Chapters 6 and 7 illustrated. When non-coincident practices overlap, however, talk is necessary, as Blundell's case study illustrates, but also not enough. Now thirdness must be inscribed materially, either in a person (individual or corporate) or in a text, or both. The practices are not going to merge. Each is going to continue. What becomes crucial is therefore an accord or contract that will regulate the boundary between them, in a manner that preserves the autonomy of each but guarantees an orderly resolution of boundary disputes. For that to happen, the thirdness must be materialized, first in an understanding of the rules, and, second, in the establishment of a human agency that will act as arbiter: literally a third "person" (or agency) possessing the authority delegated to him, her, or it by an accord; the EUB, in Blundell's case.

What makes it work, however, is the existence of a text that has been jointly authorized. Metaphorically, a "map." In the case of Heron Lake, it was literally a map, complete with all the usual features, such as zones and "no-go" areas.

It didn't start that way. It began in an often agitated and even aggressive arena of talk, but that is how it ended—managed to arrive at closure. As one of the oil people, Bob, put it:

> at least you'll have some type of road map with the constraints map that you can put on the wall when you're doing your development planning and say "that's a no-no, this looks like it's doable"; it helps with the overall planning.

The EUB materialized an initial thirdness by establishing rules for its territory, Alberta. Heron Lake chafed, because that thirdness was too abstract, too distant, not easily applicable in the special conditions that reigned in its singular ecology. The Heron Lake Watershed Synergy Group was legitimated by the EUB, but it also translated the latter's provisions into something more concrete and local, to become, Blundell thinks, a model for other similar situations in the oil industry of the province.

Suggested Supplementary Readings

It is not an easy read, but try applying ideas Taylor and Giroux developed on "The Role of Language in Self-Organizing," Chapter 6 of Barnett and Houston's (2005) book on *Advances in Self-Organizing Systems*. The genesis of organization remains very much a question open to new research. The classic treatment is Chandler's *Strategy and Structure* (1962, re-issued in 1990), but it is slanted to corporate organization in the private sector and largely leaves unexamined the organizing dynamic as such. Weick's 2003 article on "Enacting an Environment" (reprinted in 2009 in *Making Sense of the Organization*, vol. 2) offers a self-critical look at common interpretations of enactment by emphasizing the role of materiality, "reading what one has written," as well as "knowing what one has thought by seeing what was said."

Part Three

Synthesis

Chapter 9

The Organization as Thirdness, or How to Do Organizational Communication Research

Introduction

This book has been written with a single objective in mind: to show the power of taking communication as the starting point for an understanding of organization, whether we conceive of it as process ("organizing") or alternatively as entity ("an organization"). There is, to be sure, a long and honorable process-oriented tradition, spanning many decades, that takes the individual as the starting place of research and analysis, culminating in a prolific social psychology dealing with interactive process where the context is organizational. There is an equally well-established, entity-inspired tradition, grounded in sociological and managerial theory dating back at least to Durkheim and Weber, on the one hand, and Taylor and Fayol, on the other, that builds a platform of theory which predicates a social unit that already exists. Process theories study communication *in* organization; entity theories of organization assume its existence a priori, and thus demote the role of communication to a means, among others, to realize the organization's goals. One is micro in its emphasis, the other macro. Neither addresses the issue of the genesis of organization: where and how it came to *be* in the first place, what it *is* now, and how it *goes on* being so.

To study an organization from a pragmatic perspective obliges us to regard both micro and macro worlds of experience as products of communicating: both process and entity. This in turn requires a fundamental inversion of our research perspective, from communication as merely a medium to its role as generator of not merely social but material reality as well, or at least insofar as we have shaped the latter to suit our purposes and to act for us.

Pragmatism does not mean that we avoid theory. On the contrary, Peirce, Simmel, James, Dewey, Cooley, Mead, Hughes, and others (including Goffman) bequeathed us a treasure trove of complex thinking about knowledge, personality, communication, and society. Pragmatism does, however, mean tying one's theories tightly to experience. It enjoins us to accept the principle that stubborn reality is the touchstone of all knowledge and of all scientific research. It is the constant tension arising from the perception that we have not yet explained the phenomenon of organization—that the theory does not yet quite match up with our observations—which motivated the plan of the book: three chapters devoted to theory, five to an examination of the results of in-the-field, "getting-ones-hands-dirty" empirical research.

The goal of this concluding chapter is two-fold. It aims to take a reflective look at how to conduct inquiry—how to do research—when we elect to take communication as our point of departure. But before we do so, there is some unfinished business we need to take care of: conclude the review of our communication theory by summarizing how the various empirical investigations we have reported on have both clarified and extended the ideas that we reviewed in Chapters 1–3. It is the play between theory and research analysis that has obliged us to rethink, even as the book has been in the writing, how we have traditionally approached communication research that is focused on organization.

Organizational communication research, we hoped to show, is alive and well!

Theorizing Communication

The point of departure for the theoretical exploration offered in Chapters 1–3 was the perception that the rationale for any kind of collaborative activity, and indeed the reason why people need to organize in the first place, is that all meaning is grounded in *doing* something: acting. It is the "doing" that links an actor to an acted-on: what Peirce identified as secondness (the doing) and firstness (the done-to). The action takes on meaning, however, only because it is an exemplar of an a priori understanding of how things "like that" usually are: what Schank and Abelson (1977) and, more recently, Latour (forthcoming) have called *scripts*—how to garden; how to do research; how, for contributors to Wikipedia, to construct an encyclopedia (Bencherki 2008). Other terms would do as well, probably: *project, program, plan*, for example.

We could have used Weick's term "enactment" (and his notion of "cause maps") to explain our conceptualization of communication, rather than thirdness, but if we had done that, we reasoned, the reader would have felt less obliged to go back to understand the logic that lies behind Weick's theory, since the latter is by now so well known and widely accepted that it tends to be taken for granted, left unexamined. We wanted to open up inquiry, not foreclose it.

Inspired by Austin, the theory that we have proposed further innovates by extending the idea of human activity to see communication as *itself* a doing. When the acted-on is construed as an agent (i.e., one subject acting *for* another, and thus the "object" of a communicative exchange), we must understand communication differently: no longer as merely a conveyance of information, but as the performative basis of a social unit, emerging in and through a jointly configured, coordinated two-person performance. Communication, mediated by language, is thus conceived to be "illocutionary" as well as "locutionary," "deontic" as well as "epistemic," "performative" as well as "constative" (the terminology, as we have seen, varies). *You* and *I* are in consequence constituted by the act of communication as a *We* that is now "organized"—capable of dealing with an *It*.

This is known, technically, as a *ditransitive* relationship (see Chapter 3).

It follows logically that one person may not only act *on* someone else, but *through* someone else, thus turning the latter into an agent who acts *for* the former (who is thereby identified as both *source* and *beneficiary*, depending on whether we focus on before the action or after). If there is to be anything approaching permanence and stability, this implies a contractual relationship: the actor who is regularly delegated to act for another may reasonably expect recognition and recompense for doing so. Acting on, to the extent that what is acted on has value (thus explaining why both parties have an interest in it, although not ever identical), thus assumes a reciprocity that can only be arrived at by metacommunicating, since the "object" of communication is now the relationship itself and how it will frame subsequent acts of communication directed to the common object. It is this reciprocity of benefits, although often far from equal, that led us in Chapter 1 to see the relationship as synergetic: one where both parties are motivated to sustain the relationship since both have something to gain from its continuity.

Every other step we have taken has been predicated on these elementary insights.

Frames

Peirce's theory makes it clear that all knowledge, all meaning, is always from a perspective. A sign, he wrote, "is something which stands *to somebody* for something, *in some respect or capacity*" (Peirce 1955 [1940]: 99, emphasis added): a sign that implies both a signified object (X) and an interpreter (B or A, for example). We have until now been looking at imbrication by taking a bird's-eye view: standing back, as an external observer and analyst, to think of it as a system. Those who are themselves involved in the imbricated chain of agents, however, because of its relational commitments, will see it otherwise, as a *situation* in which they are themselves actively involved as actors (and interpreters). The bird has landed. Their perception now has, consequently, a horizon that, borrowing a term from Goffman, we have called a "frame." Because, in an imbricated chain of agencies, the positions are always going to be *complementary*, then the framing cannot, by definition, ever be identical: no longer A–X, but rather B (A–X). A and B occupy *reciprocal* positions in the relationship.

Every chapter addressed to research has illustrated the consequence: the incompatible framing of a situation that emerges whenever one community, having worked its way through a prolonged and highly situated conversation, to a compatible sharing of perspective, rubs up against another community that frames the interaction differently, thus infusing it with different meaning. The consequence is, both logically and empirically, friction. The research question becomes to account for how the organization manages to remain integrated, even though it is differentiated, characterized by seemingly incompatible interpretations that regularly confront each other in the forging of a chain of imbrication.

As a guide to understanding the resulting dynamic and how to focus research, we then introduced the concept of a frame game. A frame game is initiated whenever two communities confront a task that necessitates collaboration, but where the frames of understanding of what the task is, what roles each must play, and how authority is to be distributed, are incompatible, or at least different enough to require resolution. The result, we argued, will usually be playing simultaneously *in* and *on* the game: "in" to the extent that each must play complementary roles if the action script is to be respected, and "on" because now their attention is focused on the writing of the script itself. No longer *in* the relationship, but taking the relationship *itself* as their object.

Thirdness, but in a Different Guise: Now Embodied

The problem, to reiterate, is this: there are now two modes of under-standing of how a common project is to be conducted—two *incompatible* thirdnesses. If the interaction is not to result in schismogenetic symmetry (an all-out turf war) or destructive complementarity (relational dictator-ship), then a third party of some sort must be enlisted as mediator, referee, or arbitrator, thereby incarnating authority in a person since he, she, or they is/are thereby entitled to author the collective thirdness. The flaw in this "solution," however, is that the impartiality and/or competence of the arbiter is always open to question (the "stupid" people in Santiago, Chapter 4; the accountants in Chapter 5; the brand function in Chapter 6; the computer consultants in Chapter 7; the EUB in Chapter 8). This is what Simmel (1950 [1908]: 154) called the issue of "Tertius Gaudens," namely the *supposedly* "non-partisan" or neutral third party who may be tempted to "use his relatively superior position for purely egotistical interests," thereby profiting from the stand-off.

The solution to this problem, discussed in Chapter 2, is to embody the authority of thirdness differently, by constituting it in a text that claims to have the property of both objectivity and durability. The image of how such an authoritative arbiter might be conceptualized was that of a map. The well-designed map claims the authority of capturing in its inscriptions, both written and graphic, "what everyone knows." True, the map must be authored, and, therefore, respecting the reasoning of Peirce, it will be from a perspective: a point of view that has, by definition, built into it the implicit interest of the maker(s). But, once authored, the map begins to assume its own authority: the author disappears from view. The magic, indeed, is that once the map has been "naturalized"—recognized as incorporating an authority tested in the conversations of the communities who take it as their point of reference—then its authority now transcends that of its author, since the latter is *also* made subject to its provisions. As Derrida observed, once the constitution of the United States had been signed, its signers were themselves made subject to its authority, like everybody else.

A key issue, then, for the researcher, is *how* a map's authority gets established—or not! This too was a theme that was taken up in every one of the case studies: in Chapter 4 a poster (!); in Chapter 5 a budgetary account; in Chapter 6 a strategic plan or roadmap; in Chapter 7 a software-based system; in Chapter 8 a resource exploitation plan, built around a survey map. It is here, in the naturalizing of the map, their findings show, that the frame game gets played out: the authority of the map is something to be established in the crucible of practice. That is the whole point of pragmatism, and the source of the dispute involving Dewey and Russell: knowledge is more than a cognitively based image of reality, captured in a text. It is, as both Dewey and, later, Wittgenstein kept reminding us, grounded in practice. If it can't stand the heat of the furnace of practice, then the "map" is not valid, however exquisite it may look in the abstract.

The Role of Language

At the heart of the science of organizational communication is a preoccupation with language: how people use it, and how it in turn shapes the context of their activities to determine what they take as their object, and how they understand it. As Karl Weick has many times written, "how can I know what I think until I see what I say." Chapter 3 was thus devoted to a review of what we know about language.

Language, we found, has three roles to play in communication.

It is first a way of representing experience in a symbolic product that confers on the speaker the ability to be both engaged in action and yet to simultaneously be able to reflect on the experience: to be *in* the activity, as a participant, and simultaneously *out* of it, as an observer: to (literally) *reflect* on it, like a mirror. To see language merely as a representation of something else, a cognitive abstraction, is to miss Wittgenstein's point that language is not merely a code; it is a *tool*. Any instance of languaging is deeply impregnated with subjectivity. We can *only* perceive what is happening by framing it, so that it takes on a focus, and a point of view, like Vasquez' camera.

Second, language furnishes the instrumentality of interaction involving people who each, individually, sees things from the perspective of a space and a time that he or she has constructed experientially: what Vasquez in Chapter 4 called a "story-so-far." The world of conversation is a rich field of research because it is so much more than simply how one individual communicates their experience to another. It is that, to be sure, but it is also, as Goffman thought, a game of expression/impression whose stake is the negotiation of identities. It is also, as Labov and Fanshel wrote, about relationships and obligations. There is, conversation analysts have shown, a complicated grammar of interactive precedence and order, as participants try to balance the contrasting imperatives of a preoccupation with the objects that constitute their domain of practice and the negotiation of the relational framework within which the practice is embedded, imbricationally. One still-to-be-explored area of research, for example, is how different individuals resolve this tension inherent in every organizational context: on the one hand, becoming highly skilled in the conversational game, but typically less concerned with the object, versus a passionate technical preoccupation with the object, at the expense of an indifference to its social embedding. One thinks of Fauré's observation that the threesome in the office, where he was observing the construction of a budget update, glossed over the actual state of the project in the interest of accounting for themselves. Or of Güney's Anthony, who was so proud of his machines, but a good deal less adroit in handling the interactive exchanges she observed.

Finally, the third property of language-in-use is its capacity to shape the set of contextual expectations within which every activity occurs: no longer viewed so much as a text (mode of communication), but rather as a context (endowing people with a continuing framework of understandings and expectations that liberates them to concentrate on their current preoccupation). This power of text to serve as context for itself, reflexively, explains the continuity of organization (and why people are tempted to take its entity status as a given). It is text-as-context that enabled the communities of practice described earlier to have a history and a continuing identity. But it is also the constructed "story-so-far" of the organization that explains *its* continuity.

So What is an Organization?

To begin with, an organization can be seen as an accommodation that empowers some grouping of human beings to deal with a mixed material and social world. That world is experienced as situations. Any situation, encountered repeatedly, leads in time to a practice: actors who deal with a particular object that exacts a skillful performance. As the object becomes familiar, and the actors develop their expertise, the consequence is what Peirce called "thirdness": namely an assumption that the world that the actor now confronts conforms to a certain class of situations that is already known and understood. Thirdness, achieved through the establishment of a collective belief, is, as Dewey wrote, the basis of community.

Situations, however, never repeat themselves in exactly the same way as before. When the divergence between the expected and the experienced becomes too great, Peirce argued, people are pushed out of their comfort zones and begin to experience doubt. For both Peirce and Dewey, it is the doubt that leads to learning—organizational learning and change as well as individual.

What makes organizational learning complicated is that, in order to coordinate many agents' activities, make them orderly, thirdness must be inscribed in one agent (whether embodied in a human being or inscribed in an artifact such as a map), an author of the third, while the encounter with the reality of practice occurs through the actions of a *different* agent, a second. If doubt arises as a result of the activities of the delegated agent, since he or she is the one who is actually embedded in practice, a mismatch between the established thirdness and the actuality of experience is created: one actor's belief is disconfirmed by the other's experience, and vice versa.

Such divisions of perspective can only be resolved by communicating, because, to be shared, thirdness must be authored. Each of the empirical studies we have looked at, to illustrate our point, can be interpreted as attempts to correct a discrepancy: Santiago's poster as interpreted in a regional office; what is happening on the building site versus what the budget predicts should have happened; the differential impact of a strategic plan on two centers of development, leading to its consequent modification; the discrepancy between software and established practice in a company; and the tension between landowners and the oil well drillers in Alberta.

This analysis suggests that, on an enlarged scale, organizational process is a *continuing* reconciliation of thirdness (established belief) and second-to-firstness (the genesis of doubt in practice), through communication. Concretely, this means that organizations can only "learn" (to the extent that this analogy holds) through the friction generated by the rubbing up against each other of intersecting communities of practice (including management)—encounters that exhibit the characteristics of a frame game.

We have, until now, conceptualized thirdness as established practice, activities such as gardening or laboratory experiments. Peirce, however, was a philosopher of science and he meant us to understand thirdness in a second way, not merely as that which is *already* enshrined in our belief systems, but also as those hidden regularities of practice that we have *yet to discover* and give a name to: patterns that are there but that we haven't recognized. For him, that is the task of science. We have been looking into the enigma of organization: what it is. Our inquiry, part theoretical, part empirical, has led us to conceive of it as a con-figuring of diverse agencies, human, artifactual, and technical, held together, in spite of (and perhaps even because of?) their differences, by communication. *How* that happens is an empirical question. *That* it happens is in the domain of theory.

We've Been Learning too!

The book you have been reading, like every instance of ongoing inquiry, offers its own illustration of the pragmatic concept of human knowledge as the quest for belief in the face of an insistent doubt. We have not merely been reporting on the scholars' work described in this book. We have been learning from them: from Vasquez, the importance of spacing and timing in the constitution of organization; from Fauré, the complexity of accounting as an interaction of constative and performative perspectives; from Güney, the importance of seeing maps as boundary objects; from Virgili, the idea of texts as normally unverbalized texts of organization; from Blundell, the complex dynamic leading finally to an embodiment of thirdness in a plan. The writing of the introductory, theoretical chapters did not precede, historically, the analyses of the empirical chapters (other than as a first, preliminary draft), but has been continually in evolution as we have tried to absorb the understandings these new additions to our field now make available.

So now, to conclude, a few words on the conduct of empirical research as we have come to understand it in the course of absorbing the implications of this important new body of research.

On Being an Organizational Communication Researcher

Each of the five projects described in Chapters 4–8 conformed to one model: the authors adopted what might be broadly described as an "ethnographic" perspective on the conduct of inquiry. This meant, in essence, immersing themselves in the organization they were studying and staying there for a prolonged visit (Taylor & Gurd 1996): observing and recording (in a variety of ways and contexts), talking to people informally, sitting in on their meetings, continually asking questions, developing privileged relations with informants. In one context, filming. But, above all, being open, listening.

The term "ethnographic research" runs the risk, however, of encouraging a misunderstanding. Ethnography, as it became the norm in anthropology, meant literally *writing* (from the Greek *graphos*) a comprehensive account of an entire *society* or *race* (from the Greek *ethnos*), typically foreign to the ethnographer's own, and often, historically, tribal in its organizational forms and practices. Contemporary ethnographers have become uncomfortable with this model, partly because of its racist overtones, but also because of its methodological limitations (Van Maanen 1988; Marcus 1999; Couldry 2003). For Couldry, the problem is that the account of the ethnographer is always partial in its perspective. It tends to be infused with a particular point of view, a here-and-now, especially that of one or a few privileged "informants."

Communication as the Object

This is not, however, the challenge that an organizational communication researcher faces: to write a comprehensive account of a certain society, or of its kinship relationships, or of its culture. We can leave that to the ethnographers. Nor do we aspire to generalize to the properties of a population of organizations, like the so-called "ecology school" of organizational theorizing (Taylor & Giroux 2005). Instead, our focus is on the communicative mechanisms that come into play to sustain and reconstruct the organization in and through its daily practices. Whether it be a government agency, a private firm, a developer of technology or one of its users, or even an "organization" that did not start out by being very organized at all, is not the point. What we aim for is a science of *organizing*, not because we do not care about or are ignoring the entity status of the organization (Nicotera forthcoming), but because our theory tells us that entity and process are mutually constitutive.

For just this reason, there are also many connections with the science of ethnomethodology. All of the empirical chapters have included analysis of interaction, and some of the researchers have drawn explicitly on techniques developed in CA, a branch of ethnomethodology. As was the case with ethnography, however, the end object is somewhat different: to discover the organization *in* the conversation, as opposed to the organization *of* the conversation.

As we have been at pains to emphasize, our stance involves a shift of emphasis away from the individual as the primary unit, or alternatively the organization as entity, to thinking first and foremost of the inter-mediate ground of communication. It means focusing on the "daily miracle" of the reconstitution of organization (Krippendorff 2008).

What communication science aims to describe is the linking process, recognizing, to be sure, that both downlinked and uplinked perspectives are valid in their way, and far from irrelevant. The problem is that these micro and macro perspectives leave unexplored the middle ground of communication, where the up-/downlinking occurs. It is here, at the intersection between the downlinked and the uplinked, that the individual is constituted as a *social* actor, and where the organization must become recognizable as itself an actor, socialized and materialized, if it is to have any existence at all. To cite one of the great figures in the American tradition of pragmatic thought, George Herbert Mead:

> We attempt, that is, to explain the conduct of the individual in terms of the organized conduct of the social group, rather than to account for the organized conduct of the social group in terms of the separate individuals belonging to it. (Mead, 1967 [1934]: 7)

As Joas (1985: 112) interprets Mead's insight:

> For Mead the primordial given is not a "Robinsonade", not solitary actors who must first enter into social relations with one another, and who must first constitute commonly binding values, but instead the "social act", the complex activity of a group.

What we add to this is the next step, how the "social group"—now thought of as the organization itself—must also be constituted as an actor in the "organized conduct" of the community composed of those who identify themselves with it.

How is this a different way of addressing research to be accomplished? It is to this issue that we now turn.

Toward a Research Strategy

The organizational communication researcher confronts both a theoretical and a practical challenge. Months of observation, note-taking, recording, both audio and visual, and accumulation of organizational documents, mean a huge store of material, out of which an account having theoretical significance must be contrived. What to focus on in the analysis is a first step. Having then zeroed in on some situation, the second question becomes how to go about making an analysis.

Developing Strategic Priorities

Qualitative research of the kind we have been encountering in this book requires judgment and discrimination, both in gathering information and in analyzing it. There is no shortcut. It gets worked over through trial and error, using whatever feedback from colleagues and other researchers with a preoccupation similar to yours that you have available. There is an irreducible artisanal character to research of this kind: "best practices" that accumulate and are passed along from one generation of researchers to another. But it also encourages originality of interpretation: problem-solving, pursuing intuitions. Sebeok and Umiker-Sebeok (1983), as we noted in Chapter 1, have argued that Peirce's concept of abductive inquiry has notable parallels with that of Sherlock Holmes, Arthur Conan Doyle's famous detective (and, incidentally, a contemporary of Peirce). Peirce, they point out, thought of the formation of a hypothesis, or a line of explanation for one's findings, as "an act of insight" (Sebeok and Umiker-Sebeok 1983: 18) that is not, strictly speaking, "subject to logical analysis." It highlights intuition and original thinking, not in the abstract, but in "the unconscious perception of connections between aspects of the world" (p. 19). Abductive analysis of data thus cannot, unlike inductive or deductive modes of dealing with data, be simply reduced to rote, standard procedure. What we ask of the researcher is a convincing account of whatever he or she has found.

It is possible, nevertheless, to suggest a few guidelines about how to proceed.

The Focus of Analysis

Consider, first, the issue of the focus of analysis. Here, the criterion for what to privilege in the mass of recorded observations your field research has accumulated is to show how the organization as thirdness gets constructed in the circumstantially grounded conversations of those who identify themselves as its members. Each of the empirical chapters illustrates what we mean. Fauré, for example, sat in on any number of budget reporting meetings. Most of them were routine. The one he picked out for special attention differed precisely in its being an exceptional situation: an occasion where tensions were elevated, and, as a consequence, where the usually latent reality of the larger context of accounting practices of the firm became salient in people's talk. Güney, too, spent months and months in the organization she was studying, soaking up its atmosphere, developing a rapport with people there. But she also, like Fauré, chose a moment of tension, the negotiation of the Fall Plan, for particular attention. As in Fauré's research, the conversations that ensued revealed fault lines in the geography of the organization. Similarly for Vasquez, Virgili, and Blundell: each selected a time of mixed motives, because the incidents they focused on were where organizational constraints were revealed as both operative but also malleable.

In privileging an opposition of perspectives as where organizing is most clearly occurring, we are mirroring a perception of Simmel, who saw conflict, not as the negation of organization, but, on the contrary, as essential to it: "Conflict is thus designed to resolve divergent dualisms; it is a way of achieving some kind of unity, even if it be through the annihilation of one of the conflicting parties" (Simmel 1955: 13). "Conflict," he went on, "resolves the tension between contrasts" (p. 14). And "a certain amount of discord, inner divergence and outer controversy, is organically tied up with the very elements that ultimately hold the group together (pp. 17–18).

Conflict is often treated in the standard literature as an aberration: an abnormal deviation to be countered. The pragmatic view differs: it assumes that conflict is endemic to any large organization, with its many communities, its inevitable fissures and contradictions. But this same diversity is what makes the organization adaptive. It is in the successful management of conflict, for example, that innovation is stimulated.

To reiterate the point, every large organization (and small ones too) incorporates many contrasting modes of practice and sensemaking: specializations (Barley 1996). It is not the absence of such differences that characterizes the unified organization, but its modes of resolving (or at least mitigating) them. Simmel's point is that hidden oppositions become visible in interactive exchanges, focused on some textually inscribed statement of supposedly "objective" policy or account. In rewriting the account, the organization learns.

It is in conflict that the organization as an entity reveals itself in its thirdness to the researcher. When interaction is harmonious, there is no need to evoke a third party's position in the conversation, as Fauré's regional director did in his conversation with the new site manager. Ordinary interpersonal rules of conversation suffice. When there is tension, however, the otherwise shadowy presence of the uplinked organization emerges in the conversations of those involved. Mariana briefing Fernanda on how to perform her task is one thing. Fernanda reporting to her that the professors are not stepping forward to volunteer and the schools are clamoring for clarification is another. Mariana's language changes. She cannot imagine herself reporting to her Explora superiors that she has failed to reach her quota, any more than Fauré's regional director can bring himself to turn in a sloppy report to his head office. At this moment, the lineaments of the customarily unspoken background of an enveloping organization become visible.

The researcher is always looking for an account that allows us to visualize the organizing dynamic. Narrative is the normal way to do this (Bruner 1991), because it is about action and interaction, the stuff of organizing. The researcher tells a story because this is the usual way to understand human interaction: as both association *and* dissociation, collaboration *and* conflict (Taylor & Van Every 2000).

Tactical Considerations

Having chosen a situation for analysis, the researcher now faces a second question: how to do the analysis. Halliday's notion of the three dimensions of language provides guidance on how to proceed.

Halliday called his first dimension ideational: how people translate experience into the maps or frames of understanding that the logical structures of language make available. The appropriate model is narrative: people make sense of their experience by narrating it, telling their "story-so-far." They see their own and others' relationships and experiences as an unfolding, centered on valued objects and the human dynamic that constructs and enfolds them, socially. Whether it be a computer hardware developer in a southwestern American city, or a landowner in the Alberta oil patch of Canada, they impute motives, and ascribe agency, to themselves and to others. People evoke authority by bringing actors that are not physically but conceptually present into the conversation: the Old North, a French head office, Santiago, the Alberta Energy and Utilities Board, SAP. There-and-then is being made present in a here-and-now, by procuration, in effect.

Now the analyst has something to work with: a way to understand how the circumstantially circumscribed communities have built an image of their context in such a way as to make their own and others' activities "organizational," since it is here also that the narrative of the organization itself is under construction.

The Interpersonal Dimension

Halliday's second dimension is the interpersonal role of language. Here, the analyst also has a rich research tradition to draw on: namely the body of empirical work done by conversation analysts in the tradition of Sacks, Schegloff, Jefferson, and their successors. What CA has demonstrated is that it is not only sentences that must conform to strictures of form. Conversation comes with its *own* built-in patterns and constraints: a discipline to be learned through practice, as the child matures. There are, moreover, distinct contextual models or "language games" to be mastered: interviews, joking, consultations, meetings, seminars, arguing, criticism.

For the organizational communication researcher, the essentials of CA are valuable tools of analysis and a rich source of inspiration. We recommend a grounding in CA to any aspiring researcher. CA, however, has one limitation. Our research goal is *not* to understand conversation per se, but rather to comprehend how organization, in the imbricated patterning of its agency relationships, is constructed by and for people in and through their talk. We seek clues in the analysis of conversational processes to the genesis and shaping of the organization as a whole.

Notice again that, in every empirical research report we have considered in this book, there was a difference of perspective, verging on open conflict. Links between the communities involved may have been mediated by interpersonal conversation, but those same conversations were translating underlying differences in thirdness into situated talk. The process is far from passive (Katambwe &Taylor 2006). On the contrary, a better description, we have argued, is that of a game, where coalitions form and re-form as people in the conversation strive to get the upper hand over their adversaries. Evocation of a text of the organization by one of the players is one technique, among others, to establish a bargaining advantage (think of the Snowfield–Hotville conflict). One way to achieve resolution of a dispute is to invoke thirdness through its material embodiment in a third-party adjudicator, such as the EUB, in the case of Heron Lake. For the researcher, this is not merely where the existing organizational arrangements are mirrored. It is where the organization is being reshaped, in and through those same conversations.

The Textual Dimension

Halliday's third dimension is textual: how texts create a context that informs and structures the play of agency. Texts, on the other hand, are also what people focus on in their meetings: budgetary statements, questionnaires, posters, plans, software protocols, regulations, and rules.

In interpersonal conversations, texts (other than speech) play a limited role. Those who are involved just talk, since that is the natural way to deal with others when they all meet in one place, at one time. People already know the contextual frame because they have internalized it: this is a friend, a relative, or someone you are meeting for the first time. Constraints are naturally built in, because the situations that usually arise are thoroughly practiced.

This changes when the "conversation" links whole communities, located in different contexts, each operating in dissimilar space–time configurations of their experience. Now tacit assumptions are not enough. Understandings need to be spelled out, if they are to compel the communities to come to an eventual accommodation of their differences. Texts of one kind or another take center stage.

People evoke what they understand the organization to be trying to accomplish in their evaluation of the text. Texts have authority, as we have argued: they "map" the territory of the organization. The organization comes to be because its authored account gives it an identity: it too figures in a narrative of interaction with, and sometimes, contesting of, other collective actors like itself. That is part of what the researcher is out to discover: how an organization comes to get a story, and how it is shaped and modified in the talk of those who subscribe to it and are legitimated by it.

Writing the "text" of the organization was the topic of each investigation we have described: the mission of Explora (seen through the different frames of Mariana and Fernando); the account of BTP (the engineers' view versus the accountants' view); Deep Purple's Fall Plan (a contested "roadmap"); the administrative system of Labopharma (the constitution of the firm as seen, alternatively, by ERP consultants and employees); and the development "map" produced by HLWSG (landowners versus oil companies).

What is Organizational Communication Research?

Organizational communication, as we said at the outset, is, relatively speaking, a new field. Its history stretches back no more than about four decades. It emerged initially as a loosely defined collection of research practices whose roots were in legacy disciplines, notably social psychology, sociology, and rhetoric. The need for greater coherence was highlighted in a defining moment, a summer conference held in Alta, Utah, in 1981, the so-called "interpretive turn" (Putnam & Pacanowsky 1983). But the reality of a field without a clear central mandate remained, and it is where it has largely stood until quite recently. We undertook this book in the conviction that such a lack of a central vision is now changing. It is an evolution that is being led by imaginative young researchers in widely scattered locations, but all of whom share a common commitment to modes of research that are both theory-driven and saturated by empiricism. It marks, among other features, a resurgence of pragmatism and a rejection of the straitjacket of positivism. In a real sense, it is giving new meaning to the old shibboleth of what used to be called "grounded theory." Go look, try to understand, listen to people as they talk, communicate what you have learned in an account.

The return to pragmatism is part of a larger movement. On the one hand, there has been a growing recognition over the past couple of decades of the importance of language in the constitution of organization. It has masqueraded under different headings, such as the "narrative turn" or the "discourse turn" or the "language turn." Jian, Schmisseur, and Fairhurst (2008), in their exhaustive examination of the literatures bearing on discourse, versus those in organizational communication, note an unfortunate disconnect between these lively fields and communication studies. One of the authors of this book went further to claim that "communication remains a black hole in the discourse literature" (Taylor forthcoming).

The approach we have described also resembles in important ways what is now called the "practice turn." This other trend in contemporary studies has roots in more than one tradition: Bourdieu (1980, 1982), Suchman (1987), Lave & Wenger (1993), Schatzki (1996), among others. The pragmatists we have cited, Dewey, Peirce, Mead, Wittgtenstein, are also sources this literature draws on.

Where we differ from these two streams (although we have much in common) is in emphasizing the centrality of agency in the making of an organization. An organization is more than a discursive construction. Nor is it merely a domain of practice. It is both of those, but also more. It is a system of authority. In the absence of authority, there is no organization, whether we use the term or identify it by another name, such as leadership (Fairhurst 2007). The problem is not authority, as is sometimes suggested. It is that we have never really explored what authority *is*. The research that we have been reporting on will hopefully have begun to stop that gap.

Earlier, we evoked physics and its comprehension of matter (atoms and molecules) as a congealing of energy. For us, an organization is also a "congealing" of people's actions to form what amounts to a kind of matter—a hybrid composition of the material and the social to produce powerful new constellations of action. That the bonding agents the physicists study are fundamentally different from those that preoccupy the organizational researcher is surely beyond doubt. The principle, however, is the same.

If we are to have a science of organizational communication, it will be in the investigation of how such a coagulation of agencies, human and material, As and Bs and Xs, works. What we have been investigating in this book are the principles of bonding that explain the emergence of human organization: how it ties agencies together.

The analogy with the atom is far from perfect. Yet it offers a point of departure, to discover through continued research what it is that binds the organization, in spite of its antipathetic tendencies. Somehow, organizations do stick together—mostly. The ultimate binding agent seems to be the organization itself: the thirdness that justified the formation of a ditransitive first–second link in the first place. The puzzle of organization is this: it is the communicative exchanges of people that constitute the indispensable instrument for the creation of thirdness. But it is the existence of that thirdness enshrined in a "moral person," the organization, that creates the force that binds them together. The logic is reflexive to the core.

Suggested Supplementary Readings

For a perceptive but critical analysis of the approach we have developed here, see Putnam (forthcoming). See also Nicotera (forthcoming).

Bibliography

Alvesson, M. & Kärreman, D. (2000). Varieties of discourse: On the study of organizations through discourse analysis. *Human Relations*, *53*, 1125–49.

Anderson, D. L. (2004). The textualizing functions of writing for organizational change. *Journal of Business and Technical Communication*, *18* (2), 141–64.

Armour, L. (1997). The logic of economic discourse: Beyond Adam Smith and Karl Marx. *International Journal of Social Economics*, *24* (10), 1056–79.

Atlan, H. (1979). *Entre le crystal et la fumée* [Between crystal and smoke]. Paris: Seuil.

Austin, J. L. (1962). *How to do things with words*. Oxford: Oxford University Press.

Barley, S. R. (1996). Technicians in the workplace: Ethnographic evidence for bringing work into organization studies. *Administrative Science Quarterly*, *41* (3), 404–40.

Barnard, C. I. (1938). *The functions of the executive*. Cambridge, MA: Harvard University Press.

Barnett, G. A. & Houston, R. (Eds.) (2005). *Advances in Self-Organizing Systems*. Cresskill, NJ: Hampton Press.

Barwise, J. (1989). *The situation in logic*. Stanford, CA: Center for the Study of Language and Information.

Bateson, G. (1935). Culture contact and schismogenesis. *Man*, Article 199, XXXV. Also in Bateson, G. (1972).

Bateson, G. (1972). *Steps to an ecology of mind*. New York: Ballantine.

Bencherki, N. (2008). Stabilization of facts on Wikipedia as the interplay of text and conversation. *Paper presented to the conference on materiality, agency and discourse, Université de Montréal, May 21–2*.

Bertilsson, T. M. (2004). The elementary forms of pragmatism: On different types of abduction. *European Journal of Social Theory*, *7* (3), 372–89.

Blau, P. M. (1956). *Bureaucracy in modern society*. New York: Random House.

Blundell, A. (2007). *Communicating in the field: The role of boundary objects in a collaborative stakeholder initiative*. Unpublished doctoral dissertation, University of Calgary.

Boden, D. (1994). *The business of talk: Organizations in action*. Oxford, UK: Guilford.

Bourdieu, P. (1980). *Le sens pratique* (Translated as *The logic of practice*, R. Nice Trans., published by Cambridge: Polity Press). Paris: Les Éditions du Minuit.

Bourdieu, P. (1982). *Ce que parler veut dire: L'économie des échanges lintuistiques* [What speaking means: The economy of language exchanges]. Paris: Fayard.

Breen, D. H. (1993). *Alberta's petroleum industry and the conservation board.* Edmonton, Alberta: University of Alberta Press.

Browning, L. D., Greene, R. W., Sitkin, S. B., Sutcliffe, K. M., & Obstfeld, D. (2009). Constitutive complexity: Military entrepreneurs and the synthetic character of communication flows. In L. L. Putnam & A. M. Nicotera (Eds.), *Building theories of organization: The constitutive role of communication* (pp. 89–116). London and New York: Routledge.

Brummans, B. (2006). The Montréal school and the question of agency. In F. Cooren, J. R. Taylor, & E. J. Van Every (Eds.), *Communication as organizing: Empirical and theoretical explorations in the dynamic of text and conversation* (pp. 196–211). Mahwah, NJ: Lawrence Erlbaum.

Bruner, J. S. (1991). The narrative construction of reality. *Critical Inquiry, 18* (1), 1–21.

Burke, K. (1966). *Language as symbolic action: Essays on life, literature, and method.* Berkeley & Los Angeles: University of California Press.

Burke, T. (1990). Dewey on defeasibility. In R. Cooper, K. Mukaio, & J. Perry (Eds.), *Situation theory and its applications:* Vol. 1 (pp. 233–96). Stanford, CA: Center for the Study of Language and Information.

Burke, T. (1994). *Dewey's new logic: A reply to russell.* Chicago: University of Chicago Press.

Bybee, J. & Fleischman, S. (1995). *Modality in grammar and discourse.* Amsterdam & Philadelphia: John Benjamins and Sons.

Caplow, T. (1968). *Two against one: Coalitions in triads.* Englewood Cliffs, NJ: Prentice-Hall.

Case, P. (1995). Representations of talk at work: Performatives and "performability." *Management Learning, 26,* 423–43.

Catasús, B. (2007). In search of accounting absence. *Critical Perspectives on Accounting, 19* (7), 1–16.

Chandler, A. D., Jr. (1977). *The visible hand: The managerial revolution in American business.* Cambridge, MA: Harvard University Press (Belknap).

Chandler, A. D., Jr. (1990). *Strategy and structure: Chapters in the history of the american industrial enterprise.* Cambridge, MA: MIT Press. (Original work published 1962.)

Cheney, G., Christensen, L. T., Zorn, T. E., Jr., & Ganesh, S. (2004). *Organizational communication in an age of globalization.* Prospect Heights IL: Waveland Press.

Chomsky, N. (1957). *Syntactic structures.* The Hague, Netherlands: Mouton.

Chomsky, N. (1965). *Aspects of a theory of syntax.* Cambridge, MA: MIT Press.

Coase, R. H. (1937). The nature of the firm. *Economica N. S. 1937, 4,* 386–405.

Concise Oxford dictionary of current English (6th ed.). (1976). Oxford: Clarendon Press.

Cooren, F. (2000). *The organizing property of communication.* Amsterdam & Philadelphia: John Benjamins and Sons.

Cooren, F. (2006). The organizational world as a plenum of agencies. In F. Cooren, J. R. Taylor, & E. J. Van Every (Eds.), *Communication as organizing: Empirical and theoretical explorations in the dynamics of text and conversation* (pp. 81–100). Mahwah, NJ: Lawrence Erlbaum Associates.

Cooren, F. (forthcoming). *Figures of communication and dialogue: Passion, ventriloquism and incarnation.* Amsterdam & Philadelphia: John Benjamins and Sons.

Cooren, F. & Taylor, J. R. (2000). Association and dissociation in an ecological controversy: The great whale case. In N. W. Coppola & B. Karis (Eds.), *Technical communication, deliberative rhetoric, and environmental discourse: Connections and directions* (pp. 171–90). Stamford, CO: Ablex.

Cooren, F., Taylor, J. R., & Van Every, E. J. (Eds.) (2006). *Communication as organizing: Empirical explorations into the dynamic of text and conversation.* Mahwah, NJ: Lawrence Erlbaum Associates.

Corman, S. R. & Poole, M. S. (2000). *Perspectives on organizational communication: Finding common ground.* New York: Guilford.

Couldry, N. (2003). Passing ethnographies: Rethinking the sites and reflexivity in a mediated world. In P. D. Murphy & M. M. Kraidy (Eds.), *Global media studies: Ethnographic perspectives* (pp. 40–56). New York and London: Routledge.

Czarniawska, B. (forthcoming). Organizations as obstacles to organizing. In D. Robichaud & F. Cooren (Eds.), *Organization and organizing: Materiality, agency and discourse.*

Daskalakis, C., Goldberg, P. W., & Papadimitriou, C. (2009). The complexity of computing a Nash equilibrium, *Communications of the ACM, 52* (2), 89–97.

Derrida, J. (1988). Declarations of Independence. *New Political Science, 15,* 7–15.

Dewey, J. (1938). *Logic: The theory of inquiry.* New York: Henry Holt & Co.

Dewey, J. (1944). *Democracy and education.* New York: The Free Press. (Original work published 1916.)

Dietz, J. L. G. (2003). Designing technical systems as social systems. In H. Weigand. G. Goldkuhl, & A. de Moor (Eds.), *Proceedings of the 8th international working conference on the language–action perspective on communication modelling* (pp. 187–207). Tilburg, The Netherlands.

Drew, P. & Heritage, J. (1992). *Talk at work.* Cambridge, UK: Cambridge University Press.

Eco, U. & Sebeok, T. A. (Eds.) (1983). *The sign of three: Dupin, Holmes, Peirce.* Bloomington and Indianapolis, IN: Indiana University Press.

Eisenberg, E. M. (2007). *Strategic ambiguities: Essays on communication, organization, and identity.* Thousand Oaks, CA: Sage.

Engeström, Y. (2000). Activity theory and the social construction of knowledge: A Story of Four Umpires. Comment on Blackler et al. *Organization, 7* (2), 301–10.

Engeström, Y. & Middleton, D. (1996). *Cognition and communication at work.* Cambridge, UK: Cambridge University Press.

Eyraud, C. (2003). Pour une Approche Sociologique de la Comptabilité: Réflexions à Partir de la Réforme Comptable Chinoise [Towards a Sociological Approach to Accountancy: Reflections Based on the Reform of Chinese Accounting]. *Sociologie du Travail, 45,* 491–508.

Fairhurst, G. T. (2007). *Discursive leadership: In conversation with leadership psychology*. Thousand Oaks, CA: Sage.

Fairhurst, G. T. & Putnam, L. L. (2004). Organizations as discursive constructions. *Communication Theory, 14* (1), 5–26.

Fauré, B. (2006). *Les activités de production de l'information budgétaire: Communications organisationnelles et regulations—le cas d'une entreprise de BTP* [The activities of production of budgetary information: organizational communications and control—the case of an enterprise in the construction business]. Unpublished doctoral dissertation, Université Toulouse III, Le Mirail.

Fauré, B., Brummans, B., Giroux, H., & Taylor, J. R. (2010). The calculation of business, or the business of calculation? Accounting as organizing through everyday communication. *Human Relations, 63* (8), 1–25.

Fayol, H. (1925). *Administration industrielle et générale* [Industrial and general administration]. Paris: Dunod.

Follett, M. P. (1941). *Dynamic administration: The collected papers of Mary Parker Follett* (H. C. Metcalf & L. Urwick, Eds.). New York: Harper.

Foster, M. K. (1985). *The history and culture of Iroquois diplomacy: An interdisciplinary guide to the treaties of the six nations and their league*. Syracuse, NY: Syracuse University Press.

Garfinkel, H. (1967). *Studies in ethnomethodology*. Englewood Clffs, NJ: Prentice-Hall.

Garfinkel, H. (2002). *Ethnomethodology's program: Working out Durkheim's aphorism*. Lanham, MD: Rowman & Littlefield.

Gherardi, S. (2006). *Organizational knowledge: The texture of workplace learning*. Oxford, UK: Blackwell.

Gherardi, S. (2010). Telemedicine: A practice-based approach to technology. *Human Relations, 63* (4), 501–524.

Giddens, A. (1984). *The constitution of society: Outline of the theory of structuration*. Berkeley and Los Angeles: University of California Press.

Giroux, H. & Taylor, J. R. (2002). The justification of knowledge: Tracking the translations of quality. *Management Learning, 33*, 497–517.

Goffman, E. (1959). *The presentation of self in everyday life*. Garden City, NY: Doubleday.

Goffman, E. (1969). *Strategic interaction*. Philadelphia, PA: University of Pennsylvania Press.

Goffman, E. (1974). *Frame analysis: An essay on the organization of experience*. Boston: Northeastern University Press.

Goffman, E. (1981). *Forms of talk*. Philadelphia, PA: University of Pennsylvania Press.

Goody, J. (1999). *L'Orient en Occident* [The East in the West]. Paris: Seuil.

Gouldner, A. W. (1954). *Patterns of industrial bureaucracy*. New York: The Free Press.

Grant, D. C., Hardy, C., Oswick, C., & Putnam, L. (2004). *The Sage handbook of organizational discourse*. Thousand Oaks, CA: Sage.

Grant, D. C., Keenoy, T., & Oswick, C. (1998). Organizational discourse: Of diversity, dichotomy and multi-disciplinarity. In D. Grant, T. Keenoy, & C. Oswick (Eds.), *Discourse and organization* (pp. 1–13). London: Sage.

Güney, S. (2004). *Organizational identity and sensemaking in collaborative development of technology: An ethnographic case study of "building the box."* Unpublished doctoral dissertation, The University of Texas at Austin.

Güney, S. (2006). Making sense of a conflict as the (missing) link between collaborators. In F. Cooren, J. R. Taylor, & E. J. Van Every (Eds.), *Communication as organizing: Empirical and theoretical explorations in the dynamic of text and conversation.* (pp. 19–35). Mahwah, NJ: Lawrence Erlbaum.

Guo, J. (1995). The interactional basis of the Mandarin *néng* "can." In J. Bybee & S. Fleischman (Eds.), *Modality in grammar and discourse* (pp. 205–38). Amsterdam & Philadelphia: John Benjamins.

Haley, J. (1976). *Problem-solving therapy.* New York: Harper & Row.

Halliday, M. A. K. (Ed.) (2002). Language structure and language function. *Collected Works of M. A. K. Halliday. Volume 1: On grammar* (pp. 173–95). London, New York: Continuum. (First published 1970 in J. Lyons (Ed.), *New horizons in linguistics* (pp. 140–65). Harmondsworth, UK: Penguin.)

Halliday, M. A. K. & Hasan, R. (1989). *Language, context, and text: aspects of language in a social-semiotic perspective.* Oxford, UK: Oxford University Press.

Halliday, M. A. K. & Webster, J. J. (Eds.) (2006) *On language and linguistics.* New York: Continuum.

Hammer, M. (1996). *Beyond reengineering: How the process-centered organization is changing our work and our lives.* New York: Harper.

Hammer, M. & Champy, J. (1993). *Reengineering the corporation: A manifesto for business revolution.* New York: Harper.

Hardy, C., Palmer, I., & Phillips, N. (2000). Discourse as strategic resource, *Human Relations, 53,* 1227–48.

Heritage, J. (1984). *Garfinkel and ethnomethodology.* Oxford, UK: Polity Press.

Hoppenbrouwers, S. (2003). *Freezing language: Conceptualisation processes across ICT-supported organisations.* Unpublished doctoral dissertation, Catholic University of Nijmegen, the Netherlands.

Hutchins, E. (1995). *Cognition in the wild.* Cambridge, MA: MIT Press.

Jacques, R. (1996). *Manufacturing the employee: Management knowledge from the 19th to 21st centuries.* Thousand Oaks, CA: Sage.

Jian, G., Schmisseur, A. M., & Fairhurst, G. T. (2008). Organizational communication and discourse: The progeny of Proteus. *Discourse and Communication, 2* (3), 299–320.

Joas, H. (1985). *G. H. Mead: A contemporary re-examination of his thought.* Cambridge, MA: MIT Press.

Kalai, E. (2009). The complexity of computing Nash equilibrium. *Communications of the ACM, 52* (2), 89.

Katambwe, J. M. (2004). *La nature du lien organisationnel: Une étude de cas selon une approche discursive* [The nature of the organizational bond: A case study taking a discursive approach]. Unpublished doctoral dissertation, Université de Montréal.

Katambwe, J. M. & Taylor, J. R. (2006). Modes of organizational integration. In F. Cooren, J. R. Taylor, & E. J. Van Every (Eds.), *Communication as organizing: Empirical and theoretical explorations in the dynamic of text and conversation* (pp. 55–77). Mahwah, NJ: Lawrence Erlbaum.

Kirsch, D. & Neff, G. (2008). The materiality of failure: What artifacts say about the process of disorganization. *Paper presented to the conference on What is an organization? Materiality, agency and discourse, Université de Montréal, May 21–2.*

Krippendorff, K. (2008). Organizations as networks of conversations and stakeholders. *Paper presented to the conference on What is an organization? Materiality, agency and discourse, Université de Montréal, May 21–2.*

Kuhn, T. (2008). A communicative theory of the firm: Developing an alternative perspective on intra-organizational power and stakeholder relationships. *Organization Studies, 29,* 1227–54.

Labov, W. & Fanshel, D. (1977). *Therapeutic discourse: Psychotherapy as conversation.* New York: Academic Press.

Latour, B. (1986). The powers of association. In J. Law (Ed.), *Power, action and belief—A new sociology of knowledge* (pp. 264–80). London: Routledge & Kegan Paul.

Latour, B. (1987). *Science in action.* Cambridge, MA: Harvard University Press.

Latour, B. (1994). On technical mediation—philosophy, sociology, genealogy. *Common Knowledge, 3* (2), 29–64.

Latour, B. (forthcoming). What's organizing: A meditation on the bust of Emilio Bootme in praise of Jim Taylor. In D. Robichaud & F. Cooren, eds., *Organization and organizing: Materiality, agency and discourse.*

Lave, J. & Wenger, E. (1991). *Situated learning: Legitimate peripheral participation.* Cambridge, UK: Cambridge University Press.

Lawrence, P. R. & Lorsch, J. W. (1969). *Organization and environment: Managing differentiation and integration.* Homewood, IL: Irwin.

Leiter, K. (1980). *A primer on ethnomethodology.* New York, Oxford, UK: Oxford University Press.

Levina, N. & Orlikowski, W. J. (2009). Understanding shifting power relations within and across organizations: A critical genre analysis. *The Academy of Management Journal, 52* (4), 672–703.

Linde, C. (1988). Who's in charge here? Cooperative Work and authority negotiation in police helicopter missions. *Proceedings of the conference on Computer-supported cooperative work, September 26–8,* (pp. 52–64). Portland, Oregon.

Lindley, D. (2007). *Uncertainty: Einstein, Heisenberg, Bohr, and the struggle for the soul of science.* New York: Anchor Books (Random House).

Llewelyn, N. (2008). Organization in actual episodes of work: Harvey Sacks and organization studies. *Organization Studies, 29* (5), 763–91.

Lowe, A. (2004). Postsocial relations: Toward a performative view of accounting knowledge. *Accounting, Auditing and Accountability Journal, 17* (4), 604–28.

Lowe, A. & Jones, A. (2004). Emergent strategy and the measurement of performance: The formulation of performance indicators at the microlevel. *Organization Studies, 25* (8), 1313–37.

Lyons, J. (1977). *Semantics.* Cambridge, UK: Cambridge University Press.

Manning, P. K. (2008). Goffman on Organizations. *Organization Studies, 29* (5), 677–99.

March, J. G. & Simon, H. A. (1958). *Organizations*. New York: John Wiley.

Marcus, G. (1999). The uses of complicity in the changing mise-en-scene of anthropological fieldwork. *Representations*, 59 (Summer: special issue: *The fate of "culture"*), 85–108.

Massey, D. (2005). *For space*. London & Thousand Oaks, CA: Sage.

Mattesich, R. (1995). Conditional-narrative accounting methodology: Incorporating value judgments and means-end relations of an applied science. *Accounting, Organizations and Society*, 20, 259–84.

Maturana, H. (1997). *La objetividad: Un argumento para obligar* [Objectivity: A compelling argument]. Santiago, Chile: Dolmen.

Maturana, H. R. & Varela, F. J. (1987). *The tree of knowledge: The biological roots of understanding*. Boston: Shambhala.

Maturana, H. R. & Varela, F. J. (1994). *De máquinas y seres vivos. Autopoiesis: la organización de lo vivo* [Of machines and living beings: Autopoiesis, the organization of life]. Santiago, Chile: Editorial Universitaria.

Mayo, E. (1933). *The social problems of an industrial civilization*. New York: Macmillan.

McPhee, R. D. & Tompkins, P.K. (Eds.) (1985). *Organizational communication: Traditional themes and new directions*. Beverly Hills, CA: Sage.

Mead, G. H. (1967). *Mind, self and society*. Chicago: University of Chicago Press. (Original work published 1934.)

Merton, R. K. (1957). *Social theory and social structure*. New York: The Free Press.

Meunier, D. & Vasquez, C. (2008). On shadowing the hybrid character of action: A communicational approach. *Communication Methods and Measures*, 2 (3), 167–92.

Mooney, J. D. & Riley, A. C. (1931). *Onward industry!* New York: Harper.

Morgan, G. (1988). Accounting as reality construction: Towards a new epistemology for accounting practice. *Accounting, Organizations and Society*, 13 (5), 477–85.

Morgan, G. (1986, 2006). *Images of organization* (Rev. ed.). Thousand Oaks, CA: Sage. (Original work published 1986.)

Nicotera, A. (forthcoming). Ontologizing organizational entities: Musings on communicative constitution. In D. Robichaud & F. Cooren (Eds.), *Organization and organizing: Materiality, agency and discourse*.

Oswick, C., Hardy, C., Keenoy, T., Bevergungen, A., Ellis, N., Sabelis, I., & Ybema, S. (2007). Discourse, practice, policy and organizing: Some opening comments. *International Journal of Sociology and Social Policy*, 27 (11/12), 429–32.

Palmer, F. R. (1986). *Mood and modality*. Cambridge, UK: Cambridge University Press.

Peirce, C. S. (1940). *Pragmatism as a principle and method of right thinking: The 1903 Harvard lectures on pragmatism* (P. A. Turrisi, Ed.). Albany, NY: State University of New York Press.

Peirce, C. S. (1955). *Philosophical writings of Peirce; selected and edited by J. Buchler*. New York: Dover. (Original work published 1940, London: Routledge & Kegan Paul.)

Phillips, N., Lawrence, T. B., & Hardy, C. (2004). Discourse and institutions. *Academy of Management Review*, 29 (4), 635–52.

Pickering, A. (1995). *The mangle of practice.* Chicago: University of Chicago Press.

Piette, I. (forthcoming). Restructuring identity through sectoral narratives. In D. Robichaud & F. Cooren (Eds.), *Organization and organizing: Materiality, agency and discourse.*

Putnam, L. L. (forthcoming). Dialectics, contradictions, and the question of agency. In D. Robichaud & F. Cooren (Eds.), *Organization and organizing: Materiality, agency and discourse.*

Putnam, L. L. & Pacanowsky, M. E. (Eds.) (1983). *Communication and organizations.* Beverly Hills, CA: Sage.

Putnam, L. L. & Fairhurst, G. T. (2001). Discourse analysis in organizations. In F. M. Jablin & L. L. Putnam (Eds.), *The new handbook of organizational communication* (pp. 78–136). Thousand Oaks, CA: Sage.

Putnam, L. L. & Krone, K. J. (2006). *Organizational communication* (5 Vols.). Thousand Oaks, CA: Sage.

Putnam, L. L. & Casali, A. M. (2009). Introduction: A Brazilian story on the development of organizational communication, *Management Communication Quarterly*, 22 (4), 642–7.

Rawls, A. W. (2008). Harold Garfinkel, ethnomethodology and workplace studies. *Organization Studies*, 29 (5), 701–32.

Redding, W. C. (1985). Stumbling toward identity: The emergence of organizational communication as a field of study. In R. D. McPhee & P. K. Tompkins (Eds.), *Organizational communication: Traditional themes and new directions* (pp. 15–54). Beverly Hills, CA: Sage.

Ricoeur, P. (1991). *From text to action: Essays in hermeneutics, II* (K. Blamey & J. B. Thompson, Trans.). Evanston, IL: Northwestern University. (Originally published as *Du texte à l'action: Essais d'hermeneutique.* Paris: Seuil, 1986).

Robichaud, D. (2006). Steps toward a relational view of agency. In F. Cooren, J. R. Taylor, & E. J. Van Every (Eds.), *Communication as organizing: Empirical and theoretical explorations in the dynamic of text and conversation* (pp. 101–14). Mahwah, NJ: Lawrence Erlbaum.

Robichaud, D. & Cooren, F. (forthcoming). *Organization and organizing: Materiality, agency and discourse.*

Robichaud, D., Giroux, H., & Taylor, J. R. (2004). The metaconversation: The recursive property of language as a key to organizing. *The Academy of Management Review*, 29 (4), 617–34.

Roethlisberger, F. G. & Dickson, W. J. (1939). *Management and the worker.* Cambridge, MA: Harvard University Press.

Sachs, P. (1995). Transforming work: Collaboration, learning and design. *Communications of the ACM*, 38 (9), 36–44.

Sacks, H. (1992). *Lectures on conversation* (Gail Jefferson, Ed.) (2 Vols.). Oxford, UK: Blackwell.

Schank, R. & Abelson, R. (1977). *Scripts, goals, plans and understanding.* Hillsdale, NJ: Lawrence Erlbaum.

Schatzki, T. R. (1996). *Social practices: A Wittgensteinian approach to human activity and the social.* Cambridge, UK: Cambridge University Press.

Schatzki, T. R., Knorr-Cetina, K., & Von Savigny, E. (Eds.) (2001). *The practice turn in contemporary theory.* London & New York: Routledge.

Schegloff, E. A. (1992). To Searle on conversations. In J. R. Searle et al., *Searle on conversation* (pp. 113–28). Amsterdam & Philadelphia: John Benjamins.

Schutz, A. (1970). *On phenomenology and social relations.* Chicago: University of Chicago Press.

Searle, J. R. (1969). *Speech acts.* Cambridge, UK: Cambridge University Press.

Searle, J. R. (1989). How performatives work. *Linguistics and Philosophy, 12,* 535–58.

Sebeok, T. A. & Umiker-Sebeok, J. (1983). "You know my method": A juxtaposition of Charles S. Peirce and Sherlock Holmes. In U. Eco & T. A. Sebeok (eds.), *The sign of three: Dupin, Holmes, Peirce* (pp. 11–54). Bloomington & Indianapolis IN: Indiana University Press.

Selznick, P. (1949). *TVA and the grass roots.* Berkeley: University of California Press.

Sergi, V. (forthcoming). Constituting the temporary organization: Documents in the context of projects. In D. Robichaud & F. Cooren (Eds.), *Organization and organizing: Materiality, agency and discourse.*

Shannon, C. E. (1948). A mathematical theory of communication. *Bell System Technical Journal, 27,* 379–428, 623–56.

Shannon, C. E. & Weaver, W. (1949). *The mathematical theory of communication.* Urbana, IL: University of Illinois Press.

Simmel, G. (1950). *The sociology of Georg Simmel* (K. H. Wolff, Trans.). New York: The Free Press. (Original work published 1908.)

Simmel, G. (1955). Conflict and the web of group affiliations (K. H. Wolff & R. Bendix Trans.). New York: The Free Press.

Smith, D. E. (2001). Texts and the ontology of organizations and institutions. *Studies in Culture, Organizations, and Societies, 6,* 159–98.

Smith, R. C. (1993). Images of organizational communication: Root metaphors of the organization-communication relation. *Paper presented to the International Communication Association Annual Conference,* Washington DC, May.

Star, S. L. & Griesemer, J. (1989). Institutional ecology, "translations" and coherence: Amateurs and professionals in Berkeley's Museum of Vertebrate Zoology, 1907–1939. *Social Studies of Science, 19,* 387–420.

Suchman, L. (1987). *Plans and situated action: The problem of human/machine interaction.* New York: Cambridge University Press.

Suchman, L. (1995). Making work visible. *Communications of the ACM, 38* (9), 56-64.

Suchman, L. (1996). Constituting shared workspaces. In Y. Engeström & D. Middleton (Eds.), *Cognition and communication at work* (pp. 35–60). Cambridge, UK: Cambridge University Press.

Taylor, F. W. (1911). *The principles of scientific management.* New York: Harper.

Taylor, J. R. (1993). *Rethinking the theory of organizational communication.* Norwood, NJ: Ablex.

Taylor, J. R. (2001). Toward a theory of imbrication and organizational communication. *The American Journal of Semiotics, 17* (2), 269–98.

Taylor, J. R. (2004). Dialogue as the search for sustainable organizational co-orientation. In R. Anderson, L. A. Baxter, & K. N. Cissna (Eds.), *Dialogue: theorizing differences in communication studies* (pp. 125–40). Thousand Oaks, CA: Sage.

Taylor, J. R. (2005). Engaging organization through worldview. In S. May & D. K. Mumby (Eds.), *Engaging organizational communication: Theory and research* (pp. 197–221). Thousand Oaks, CA: Sage.

Taylor, J. R. (2008). Communication and discourse: Is the bridge language? Response to Jian et al. *Discourse and Communication*, 2 (3), 347–52.

Taylor, J. R. (2009). Co-orientation theory. In S. W. Littlejohn & K. A. Foss (Eds.), *Encyclopedia of communication theory*, Vol. 1 (pp. 203–204), Vol. II (pp. 709–713). Thousand Oaks, CA: Sage Publications.

Taylor, J. R. (forthcoming). Organizational communication at the crossroads. In D. Robichaud & F. Cooren (Eds.), *Organization and organizing: Materiality, agency and discourse.*

Taylor, J. R. & Gurd, G. (1996). Contrasting perspectives on non-positivist communication research. In L. Thayer (Ed.), *Organization—communication: emerging perspectives III* (pp. 32–73). Norwood, NJ: Ablex.

Taylor, J. R. & Cooren, F. (1997). What makes communication "organizational"? How the many voices of the organization become the *one* voice of an organization. *Journal of Pragmatics*, 27, 409–38.

Taylor, J. R. & Van Every, E. (2000). *The emergent organization: Communication as its site and surface.* Mahwah, NJ: Lawrence Erlbaum Associates.

Taylor, J. R. & Giroux, H. (2005). The role of language in self-organizing systems. In G. Barnett & R. Houston (Eds.), *Advances in self-organizing systems* (pp. 127–63). New York: Hampton Press.

Taylor, J. R. & Robichaud, D. (2007). Management as metaconversation: The search for closure. In F. Cooren (Ed.), *Interacting and organizing: Analyses of a management meeting* (pp. 5–30). Mahwah, NJ: Lawrence Erlbaum Associates.

Taylor, J. R. & Virgili, S. (2008). Why ERPs disappoint: The importance of getting the organizational text right. In B. Grabot, A. Mayère, & I. Bazzet (Eds.), *A socio-technical insight on ERP systems and organizational change* (pp. 59–84). London: Springer-Verlag.

Taylor, J. R., Gurd, G., & Bardini, T. (1997). The worldviews of cooperative work. In G. Bowker, L. Gasser, S. L. Star, & W. Turner (Eds.), *Social science research, technical systems and cooperative work* (pp. 379–413). Mahwah, NJ: Lawrence Erlbaum Associates.

Taylor, J. R., Cooren, F., Giroux, N., & Robichaud, D. (1996). The communicational basis of organization: Between the conversation and the text. *Communication Theory*, 6 (1), 1–39.

Taylor, J. R., Flanagin, A. J., Cheney, G., & Seibold, D. R. (2001). Organizational communication research: Key moments, central concerns, and future challenges. In *Communication Yearbook 24* (pp. 99–137). Thousand Oaks, CA: Sage.

Thatchenkery, T. J. (2001). Mining for meaning: Reading organizations using hermeneutic philosophy. In R. Westwood & S. Linstead (Eds.), *The language of organization* (pp. 112–31). London: Sage.

Thayer, L. O. (1986). Introduction to the series. *Organization—communication: Emerging perspectives* (pp. IX–XV). Norwood, NJ: Ablex.

Thibault, P. J. (1997). *Re-reading Saussure: The dynamics of signs in social life.* London: Routledge.

Tompkins, P. K. & Redding, W. C. (1988). Organizational communication—past and present tenses. In G. M. Goldhaber & G. A. Barnett (Eds.), *Handbook of organizational communication* (pp. 5–34). Norwood, NJ: Ablex.

Van Dijk, T. A. (2007). Discourse and communication: A new journal to bridge two fields. *Discourse and Communication,* (1), 5–7.

Van Maanen, J. (1988). *Tales of the field: On writing ethnography.* Chicago: University of Chicago Press.

Varey, R. (2006). Accounts in interactions: Implications of accounting practices for management. In F. Cooren, J. R. Taylor, & E. J. Van Every (Eds.), *Communication as organizing: Empirical and theoretical explorations in the dynamic of text and conversation* (pp. 181–96). Mahwah, NJ: Lawrence Erlbaum.

Vasquez, C. (forthcoming). Spacing organization (or how to be here and there at the same time). In D. Robichaud & F. Cooren (Eds.), *Organization and organizing: Materiality, agency and discourse.* London & New York: Routledge.

Vasquez, C. (2008). *Espacer l'organisation: Trajectoires d'un projet de diffusion de la science et de la technologie au Chili* [Spacing organization: Trajectories of a Chilean science and technology diffusion project]. Unpublished doctoral dissertation, Université de Montréal.

Virgili, S. (2005). *La construction mutuelle de la technologie et de l'organisation en phase de développement: Une perspective communicationnelle appliquée à l'étude d'un ERP* [The mutual construction of technology and organization during a development phase: A communicational perspective applied to the study of an ERP]. Unpublished doctoral dissertation, Université de Nice Sophia Antipolis.

Vollmer, H. (2007). How to do more with numbers: Elementary stakes, framing, keying, and the three-dimensional character of numerical signs, *Accounting, Organizations and Society, 32,* 577–600.

Von Neumann, J. & Morgenstern, O. (1947). *Theory of games and economic behavior.* Princeton, NJ: Princeton University Press. (Original work published 1944.)

Watzlawick, P., Beavin, J., & Jackson, D. (1967). *The pragmatics of communication.* New York: W.W. Norton.

Weber, M. (1922). *Economy and society: An outline of interpretive sociology* (3 Vols.) (G. Roth & C. Wittich, Trans.). New York: Bedminister Press.

Weick, K. E. (1979). *Social psychology of organizing* (rev. version of 1969 ed.). New York: Random House.

Weick, K. E. (1985). Sources of order in underorganized systems: Themes in recent organizational theory. In Y. S. Lincoln (Ed.), *Organizational theory and inquiry* (pp. 106–36). Beverly Hills, CA: Sage.

Weick, K. E. (1995). *Sensemaking in organizations.* Thousand Oaks, CA: Sage.

Weick, K. E. (2009). Enacting an environment: The infrastructure of organizing. In K. E. Weick (Ed.), *Making sense of the organization: The impermanent organization* (pp. 193–205). Chichester, UK: John Wiley and Sons. (Original work published 2003.)

Weick, K. E. & Roberts, K. H. (1993). Collective mind in organizations: heedful interrelating on flight decks. *Administrative Science Quarterly, 38,* 357–81.

Weick, K. E. & Sutcliffe, K. M. (2001). *Managing the unexpected: Assuring high performance in an age of complexity.* San Francisco: Jossey-Boss.

Wenger, E. (1998). *Communities of practice: Learning, meaning and identity.* New York: Cambridge University Press.

Westwood, R. & Linstead, S. (2001). *The language of organization.* London: Sage.

Wiener, N. (1948). *Cybernetics: Or control and communication in the animal and the machine.* Cambridge, MA: MIT Press.

Williamson, O. E. (1975). *Markets and hierarchies: Analysis and antitrust implications.* New York: The Free Press.

Wittgenstein, L. (1958). *Philosophical investigations* (G. E. M. Anscombe, Trans.). Oxford, UK: Oxford University Press.

Wood, D. (1992). *The power of maps.* New York & London: Guilford.

Author Index

Subject Index

Communication and Organizational Knowledge

Contemporary Issues for Theory and Practice

Edited by Heather E. Canary and Robert D. McPhee

Communication and Organizational Knowledge provides an overview of communication-centered theory and research regarding organizational knowledge and learning. It brings together scholarly work from multiple disciplines to address emerging knowledge issues facing today's organizations. Chapters provide important insights regarding the communication of organizational knowledge, characteristics of knowledge processes, and resources for effectiveness. Taking an intensively communication-centered perspective, contributors to this volume question assumptions about organizational knowledge that often go unexamined when adopting information-centered or technology-centered perspectives. Each chapter offers implications for practice to bridge the gap between theory and practice.

This volume will serve as an important resource for scholars and practitioners studying or working in organizational knowledge management, concepts of knowledge as interactive or social, and organizational learning. It also provides a unique forum in which scholars may consider new directions for future research and theorizing.

ISBN 13 hbk 978–0–415–80403–5
ISBN 13 pbk 978–0–415–80404–2

For ordering and further information please visit:
www.routledge.com

Building Theories of Organization

The Constitutive Role of Communication

Edited by Linda L. Putnam
and Anne M. Nicotera

Building Theories of Organization explores the concept of communication as it applies to organizational theory. Bringing together multiple voices, it focuses on communication's role in the constitution of organization. Editors Linda L. Putnam and Anne M. Nicotera have assembled an all-star cast of contributors, each providing a distinctive voice and perspective.

The contents of this volume compare and contrast approaches to the notion that communication constitutes organization. Chapters also examine the ways that those processes produce patterns that endure over time and that constitute the organization as a whole. This collection bridges different disciplines and serves a vital role in developing dimensions, characteristics, and relationships among concepts that address how communication constitutes organization. It will appeal to scholars and researchers working in organizational communication, organizational studies, management, sociology, social collectives, and organizational psychology and behavior.

ISBN 13 hbk 978–0–8058–4709–3
ISBN 13 pbk 978–0–8058–4710–9

For ordering and further information please visit:
www.routledge.com

The Emergent Organization

Communication As Its Site and Surface

By James R. Taylor and
Elizabeth J. Van Every

Today's organizations face a wide variety of challenges, including such contradictions as maintaining unity of action while becoming increasingly diverse. Even the definition of organization is changing and evolving. In this monograph, the authors apply their academic and professional experience to address the notion of "organization," setting forth communication as the essential modality for the constitution of organization – explaining how an organization can at the same time be both local and global, and how these properties which give organization continuity over time and across geographically dispersed situations also come to be manifested in the day-to-day of human interpersonal exchange.

As a radical rethinking of the traditional discourse approaches in communication theory, this book develops a conceptual framework based on the idea that "organization" emerges in the mix of conversational and textual communicative activities that together construct organizational identity. Applying concepts from the philosophy of language, linguistics, semiotics, system design, sociology and management theory, the authors put forth a convincing argument demonstrating the materiality of language and its constructive role in organization and society.

ISBN 13 hbk 978–0–8058–2193–2
ISBN 13 pbk 978–0–8058–2194–9

For ordering and further information please visit:
www.routledge.com

Destructive Organizational Communication
Processes, Consequences, and Constructive Ways of Organizing

Edited by Pamela Lutgen-Sandvik and Beverly Davenport Sypher

Destructive Organizational Communication brings together highly respected communication and management scholars to examine the destructive communicative processes in organizations. Going beyond descriptions of various types of organizational communication, this volume explores how we might live and work together in a way that organizes our endeavors more humanely. Each problem-focused chapter examines a specific aspect of destructive organizational communication, reviews existing theory and research about that communicative form, and outlines its consequences and associated harms.

Contributors explore such key issues as workplace bullying, incivility, sexual harassment, and the destructive potential of teams and communication technologies. The volume's central focus is on social interactions and meaning systems that organize in destructive ways—ways that constitute abusive, oppressive, harmful, or exploitative organizational environments

The insights provided herein make a valuable contribution toward understanding harmful communication processes in the workplace. This book is an excellent resource for scholars studying destructive organizational communication, managers dealing with hostile workplaces, organizational members trying to understand their current experiences, and instructors of graduate and upper-level undergraduate classes in organizational studies.

ISBN 13 hbk 978–0–415–98993–0
ISBN 13 pbk 978–0–415–98994–7
For ordering and further information please visit:
www.routledge.com